The Bible on Forgiveness

Princeton Theological Monograph Series

K. C. Hanson, Charles M. Collier, and D. Christopher Spinks,
Series Editors

Recent volumes in the series:

William A. Toomans and Michael Lyons, editors
Transforming Visions:
Transformations of Text, Tradition, and Theology in Ezekiel

Lowell K. Handy, editor
Psalm 29 through Time and Tradition

Thomas J. King
The Realignment of the Priestly Literature

Hemchand Gossai
Power and Marginality in the Abraham Narrative, 2nd edition

Matthew J. Marohl
Faithfulness and the Purpose of Hebrews

Christopher W. Skinner
John and Thomas—Gospels in Conflict?

Scott A. Ellington
Risking Truth

Stanley D. Walters, editor
Go Figure! Figuration in Biblical Interpretation

J. Harold Ellens and John T. Greene, editors
Probing the Frontiers of Biblical Studies

The Bible on Forgiveness

Donald E. Gowan

PICKWICK *Publications* · Eugene, Oregon

THE BIBLE ON FORGIVENESS

Princeton Theological Monograph Series 133

Pickwick Publications
An Imprint of Wipf and Stock Publishers
199 W. 8th Ave., Suite 3
Eugene, OR 97401

www.wipfandstock.com

ISBN 13: 978-1-60608-856-2

Cataloging-in-Publication data:

Gowan, Donald E.

The Bible on forgiveness / Donald E. Gowan

Princeton Theological Monograph Series 133

xvi + 220 p. ; 23 cm. Includes bibliographical references.

ISBN 13: 978-1-60608-856-2

1. Forgiveness—Biblical teaching. 2. Forgiveness—Religious aspects. I. Title. II. Series.

BS680.F64 G65 2010

Manufactured in the U.S.A.

To the members of the Adult Bible Class
Parkwood United Presbyterian Church
Allison Park, Pennsylvania

Contents

"I Believe in the Forgiveness of Sins"

> Is there not in the Christian faith yet something other than for-
> giveness of sins? It should be noticed that the Apostles' Creed,
> speaking of Christian life in the present time, mentions only the
> forgiveness of sins. Luther and Calvin did the same, they who
> essentially put forth one truth alone: the forgiveness of sins,
> which they used then to call justification by faith. Were they
> right in thus narrowing down all Christianity, all the Christian
> life and faith to one single point? I think the answer should be:
> Yes, the Creed and the Reformers were right. For the forgive-
> ness of sins is the basis, the sum, the criterion, of all that may be
> called Christian life or faith. (Barth 1960, 132–33)

KARL BARTH'S STATEMENT MAY SEEM A BIT EXTRAVAGANT, BUT THERE
can be no doubt that forgiveness is a central element in the Christian
faith. Indeed, two of the essential documents of Christianity, the
Apostles' Creed and the Lord's Prayer, put a major emphasis on forgiveness. In the Prayer, between the two clauses that speak of the sustenance
of life itself ("give us this day our daily bread"; "deliver us from evil")
lie three clauses concerning sin and forgiveness: "forgive us our debts
as we forgive our debtors, and lead us not into temptation." Christians
are thus reminded frequently in worship of the need for and possibility
of forgiveness of their sins, and the prayer also reminds them that their
character must reflect that of God as they forgive others.

Forgiving others is a part of the Christian message that certainly is
not being neglected in contemporary society. When the John Templeton
Foundation established a series of symposia, in 1997, on "the scientific
foundations of effective living," the first of them dealt with forgiveness
(Worthington 1998). As a result of the conference more than one hundred research proposals were submitted to the foundation. The book

Exploring Forgiveness includes a twenty-two-page bibliography of books and articles, accompanied by something of an apology for incompleteness (Enright & North 1998). A glance at the available titles of books concerning this way of dealing with interpersonal relations suggests that it is a "growth industry." Much of the literature is of the popular, "self-help" kind. Note some of the "how-to" titles:

- How to Forgive When You Don't Know How
- How to Forgive When It's Hard to Forget
- How to Forgive Your Children
- How to Forgive Yourself and Others
- How to Forgive Your Ex-husband (and get on with your life)

We can also learn about:

- Caring Enough Not to Forgive
- Forgiving Your Parents
- Forgiving the Unforgiveable
- The Twelve Steps of Forgiveness

At the scholarly level, most of the writing being done at present comes from psychologists and pastoral counselors, with contributions from philosophers and theologians. The subject has not attracted the attention of many Biblical scholars. One will search in vain for a book in English that surveys the Bible's teachings on forgiveness, so in spite of the apparent surfeit of books on the subject, it seems that a book focused on Scripture may be useful.

The book will focus closely on the message of Scripture and will not attempt to engage in discussion with the philosophers and psychologists except incidentally. They all attempt to define what forgiveness really is, and since this book offers an interpretation of what forgiveness means in the Bible, it seems appropriate to offer some discussion of that here. Definitions vary considerably, depending on the specific interests of the author. We might call some of them limited, as compared with others. Jeffrie Murphy, focusing on interpersonal forgiveness, calls it "the overcoming on moral grounds, of what I will call the *vindictive passions*—the passions of anger, resentment, and even hatred that are often occasioned when one has been deeply wronged by another"

(2003, 16). Note that this, like others, focuses on the forgiver and not on the one forgiven. Frequently, the word means essentially the cancellation of punishment, with the focus now on the one forgiven. In theology, a traditional term is "remission of sins," explained by one author who claims that this is its only meaning in Scripture, as "removal or annulment of some obstacle or barrier to reconciliation" (Taylor 1952, 3). Note that all three definitions are negative, referring to the removal of something.

For many authors these definitions are not adequate, either for interpersonal or for divine forgiveness. It will be helpful, at the beginning, to consider two lists that have been offered, of what forgiveness is not. For Joram Haber, forgiveness is not, 1. deciding the act was not morally wrong; 2. changing one's judgment of the offender, despite the offense; 3. remitting punishment; 4. overcoming resentment (1991, 12–16). Later in his book, he added condonation, pardon, and mercy (59–65). His list is similar to the one provided by Solomon Schimmel, who distinguishes between forgiveness and: forgetting, condoning, excusing, justifying, pardoning, exonerating, atoning, mercy, and reconciliation (2002, 42–43). What then is left? He found two aspects: internal—a change of feelings and attitude, and interpersonal—forgiveness as a *step toward* returning a relationship to what it had been before the offense (43). This is a move toward what many consider to be a more adequate understanding of all that forgiveness involves. Haber's definition is similar: Forgiveness requires a personal relationship, and the forgiver undergoes a change of attitude.

Carl Bråkenhielm describes the effects of being forgiven in both negative and positive terms. The negative side is freedom from something: bitterness and hatred, guilt, a wrongful lifestyle, and punishment. The positive effect is gaining access to something: the reestablishment of personal relationships, or mutual affirmation of worth and dignity (1993, 27–30).

Amid this variety the reader will note considerable overlap, but also some direct contradictions. I do not intend to offer an evaluation of the definitions. They have been offered as part of an introduction just to suggest the extent of interest in the subject, its breadth, and its difficulty, so debate over the proper definition can be bracketed, and we shall move quickly to a preliminary outline of the way the Bible speaks of forgiveness. Most of what it has to say concerns forgiveness of sinful human beings by God. Given the intense interest in human forgiveness in the contemporary literature, readers may find that disappointing, but they may as well know what lies ahead. The Old Testament authors understood sins committed against other people also to be sins against God. While the damage to human relationships might be dealt with variously, they focused on the disrupted relationship with God, realizing that it could be restored only if God would forgive. The New Testament message is influenced by an understanding of sin as more than a series of human acts, but as a power influencing those acts, against which human effort was futile, so once again, hope for overcoming sin and its effects was based on faith that God had taken the initiative. The emphasis in both Testaments is thus on the forgiving God, and in the New Testament it becomes clear that human forgiveness becomes possible because God has forgiven, and is essential because the lives of God's people must reflect God's character. One verse in Colossians sums it up: "Bear with one another and, if anyone has a complaint against another, forgive each other; just as the Lord has forgiven you, so you also must forgive" (Col 3:13).

In my book *Eschatology in the Old Testament* I considered the various promises it records by asking about the human needs to which they responded (Gowan 1987, 2000, 60–65). This led me to a brief description of eschatological forgiveness in those terms, and I have found that it has been a useful way to think about all the forgiveness passages in the Bible as I wrote this book. Three needs are evident, and they can be described variously.

1. Physical distress, understood as punishment for sin, leading to the need for pardon. That a sinful act can lead to physical distress of some sort for the guilty person (today, e.g., a prison sentence, or damage to one's health), is obvious, although the exceptions cannot be overlooked. For most of the Old Testament authors retribution was a major part of their thinking: sin leads to suffering for the sinner and repentance will lead to divine forgiveness (see Lev 26:14–45; 1 Kgs 8:33:33–36, 46–51). This theology was most often appealed to in order to explain national disasters, and it seemed to work fairly well at that level, for there were plenty of disasters and enough evidence of sin to appeal to. The exceptions were not overlooked, however, and questions were raised about

suffering that does not call for repentance and forgiveness (as in Job, Habakkuk, and some of the psalms).

2. The sense of defilement and the need for personal change, called cleansing. Contemporary literature on guilt and forgiveness shows little interest in the feeling of defilement as a result of sin and the association of forgiveness with cleansing. The symbolism is prominent in the Bible, however, and it has continued to be a part of Christian language, so must be more than traditional; must reflect actual experience. In Israel, *ritual* uncleanness was not considered to be normally the result of sinful behavior. It could be acquired inadvertently, was often inevitable, and could even be the result of a righteous act, such as burying the dead. Its removal thus did not call for forgiveness, but for rituals that sometimes involved washing. "Unclean" and "clean" were also used in an ethical sense, however, for they seemed to correspond to feelings produced by guilt and a sense of innocence, so the ideas appear in strongly moral contexts. Jeremiah spoke of the stain of the people's guilt, of defiling themselves by going after the Baals (Jer 2:22–23). Psalm 51 uses cleansing language prominently in its appeals for forgiveness:

> Wash me thoroughly from my iniquity,
> and cleanse me from my sin!
> Wash me, and I shall be whiter than snow.
> Create in me a clean heart, O God. (vv. 2, 7b, 10a)

The promises of forgiveness in the future, in Jeremiah and Ezekiel, also speak of cleansing:

> I will cleanse them from all the guilt of their sin against me, and
> I will forgive all the guilt of their sin and rebellion against me.
> (Jer 33:8)

> I will save them from all the apostasies into which they have
> fallen, and will cleanse them. (Ezek 37:23; cf. 36:25, 33)

John's baptism with water was for repentance for the forgiveness of sins (Mark 1:4), and Christian baptism was "that your sins may be forgiven" (Acts 2:38), so the cleansing power of water came to be used symbolically in a regular way in the church, with reference to forgiveness. Cleansing language was used in various ways: "But you were washed, you were sanctified, you were justified in the name of the Lord

Jesus Christ and in the spirit of our God" (1 Cor 6:11). "He saved us . . . through the water of rebirth and renewal by the Holy Spirit" (Titus 3:5). ". . . forgetful of the cleansing of past sins" (2 Pet 1:9). "He who is faithful and just will forgive us our sins and cleanse us from all unrighteous-ness" (1 John 1:7, cf. v. 9).

Note also the evidently instinctive association of guilt with stain on Pilate's part, when he washed his hands, saying, "I am innocent of this man's blood" (Matt 27:24).

3. Relationships—the need to overcome estrangement. Although con-temporary discussions of forgiveness will deal with questions of forgiv-ing the unrepentant or the deceased, when reestablishment of a broken relationship is not possible, most of the attention in the literature is devoted to overcoming estrangement. In the Bible, restoring relation-ships is also the focus of much that is said about both divine and hu-man forgiveness. In the Old Testament, the imagery that is often used to denote estrangement between God and people is that of distance. After the initial disobedience of Adam and Eve, they were expelled from the garden where God might be found walking in the evening. Indeed, God's question, "Where are you?" which really means, "Why are you hiding?" (Note Adam's answer: Gen 3:9–10) shows that the man and woman had already distanced themselves from him. That this may be in part a mourning question from God is suggested by his laments over Israel's similar behavior in Hos 11:2 and Isa 65:1–2, 12b. The most common word for repentance is thus, not surprisingly, *šuv*, "turn, return," which literally can refer to closing the gap between two parties, but when used of repentance means turning back to God by changing the direction of one's life. The same verb can also be used of turning away from God.

The Sinai covenant was meant to establish an intimate relationship between God and Israel (Exod 19:4–6), but it could be broken by Israel's disobedience, so the question of whether it could be mended by divine forgiveness was a major one for the writers of the Old Testament. Hosea was told to name his son "Lo-ammi [not my people], for you are not my people and I am not your God" (Hos 1:9). The promises of forgiveness in the future, in Jeremiah and Ezekiel, thus contained the reassurance that forgiveness would once again make possible: "I will be their God, and they shall be my people" (Jer 31:33–34; Ezek 36:25–28).

The individual Israelite might also be conscious that sin had led God to turn away from him, so the psalmist, having asked for cleansing, wrote, "Do not cast me away from your presence, and do not take your holy spirit from me" (Ps 51:11). The New Testament focuses entirely on the individual, rather than national relationship with God, and speaks of reconciliation with God as a result of forgiveness (e.g., Rom 5:10; Eph 2:11–22). Human forgiveness also focuses largely on reconciliation (e.g., Matt 5:23–24; 18:15–17; Col 3:12–15).

Having written about forgiveness in these terms in the 1980s, later, I found in George Caird's *New Testament Theology* a discussion of sin in the New Testament that corresponded in several ways to what I had found concerning forgiveness in the Old Testament (1994, 87–90). He wrote that what sin means is most clearly reflected in the language of redemption used by the New Testament writers: *justification* implies a guilt to be cancelled; *consecration* is needed because there is a stain to be erased; *reconciliation* dispels an enmity; and *redemption* abolishes a servitude. He never put them all under the umbrella of forgiveness; one of my arguments will be that it is appropriate to do so. We will find that justification is peculiarly Pauline, so its use as we survey the whole Bible is limited; and will see (as Caird noted) that the sense of being slaves to sin so that redemption is needed is a New Testament idea, for it appears only once in the Old Testament (Ps 130:8). It will be useful to keep his four metaphors in mind, as they come directly from his work with the biblical material, unlike some of the other studies noted above.

The abundance of literature on forgiveness that is being produced is another reminder of how much pain there is in the world. This is pain that is produced by our own actions; none of it is unexplained for it is the result of sin, on the victim and on the offender. Books like those listed above are filled with story after story of terrible harm that people have done to one another, leading up to accounts of the place forgiveness did or did not play in the efforts to redeem something from those terrible experiences. It is not one of the obvious ways of dealing with evil, but the other options have done us little good over the centuries, and so not only those who believe in a forgiving God, but also those with completely secular outlooks appeal to that mysterious possibility—forgiveness. There is wide agreement that only one who has experienced forgiveness can truly be forgiving, for this is not something that can be taught; it must happen. Christians and Jews then insist that for them the certainty that forgiveness is possible comes from the experience of first being estranged from God, then of finding that God has made things right.

Karl Barth was not the only author who has identified Christianity with forgiveness in a unique way. H. R. Mackintosh, who wrote a helpful book on the subject, said, "The certainty of forgiveness in Christ is, if not the sum, at least the secret of Christian religion" (1934, 6). If forgiveness is that important, then surely we ought to know as much as possible of what the Bible says about it, and this book contains an attempt to contribute something to that search. With the Old Testament, we shall find that very soon we have touched on the mystery of divine forgiveness. The writers of the Old Testament had to record a great many sins, and they were clearly convinced that these were not only offenses against their fellow human beings, but also offenses against God himself. So it was that they testified to their belief that the only solution must begin with the just God, who is the judge of sin but who by forgiving enables the story to continue. We begin our study, then, with the long and tension-filled story of God and Israel, struggling with the question, what kind of relationship can there be between a just God and a sinful people?

PART ONE

The Old Testament

I, I am He who blots out your transgressions for my own sake,
and I will not remember your sins.

—Isaiah 43:25

God Forgives Us

Sin, Judgment, and Mercy in Genesis and Exodus 1–31

THE WRITERS OF THE OLD TESTAMENT BELIEVED IN A GOD WHO IS judge of all the earth, with righteousness and justice the foundation of his throne (e.g., Pss 96:10, 13; 97:2; 98:9). From Genesis on they recorded a history of human injustice and unrighteousness, however, so it might have been a history solely of divine judgment. It is not, because they also believed in a God who is "merciful and gracious, slow to anger, and abounding in steadfast love and faithfulness, keeping steadfast love for the thousandth generation, forgiving iniquity and transgression and sin" (Exod 34:6–7). Although they believed in the universal sovereignty of God, they spoke of divine forgiveness only with reference to God's relationship with Israel. Prophets did look forward to the conversion of the nations in the last days (e.g., Isa 2:2–4; 19:18–25; Zech 8:20–23; 14:16–19), but they did not use terms referring to repentance and forgiveness. Forgiveness and the covenant relationship between God and Israel were thus intimately related. The two covenants in Genesis were covenants of divine promise and did not depend on human responsibility for their continuance (Gen 9:1–17; 17:1–14; Freedman 1964). This probably accounts for the fact that although many sins are recorded in that book, divine forgiveness is not a significant theme, as will be noted later in this section. On the other hand, the relationship God established with Israel in the Sinai covenant required obedience to the standards he gave them: "Now therefore, if you obey my voice and keep my covenant . . ." (Exod 19:5), so at that point disobedience became a major issue, and divine forgiveness the good news that enabled the relationship to continue.

The story of that relationship begins with a crisis. The making of the golden calf (Exodus 32) raised an immediate question whether the people God had chosen and rescued from slavery in Egypt could live up to his standards. The message of forgiveness meant God's character could and would maintain the relationship even when Israel's character did not. When another crisis arose, however, the rise of the empire-building nations, Assyria and Babylonia, which brought the kingdoms of Israel and Judah to an end, the prophets explained the disaster in moral terms. It happened, they said, because of the people's refusal—indeed, inability—to repent, leading now to God's refusal to forgive. Beyond the disaster, however, they foresaw a new era, which would be created solely because of God's forgiving nature.

So, after some preliminary remarks about vocabulary and the treatment of sin in Genesis, we shall begin with the accounts of those two great crises, whose authors struggled with the question whether any continuing relationship between the holy God and sinful humanity is possible. Then we shall turn to the rest of what the Old Testament has to say about forgiveness.

The Vocabulary of Forgiveness

The importance of this theme is reflected in the remarkable variety of terms used by the Old Testament authors. A whole book may be devoted to the study of the words (Stamm 1940), but the approach taken in this book enables a brief survey to be adequate. Most of the terms are metaphors, but there is one, *salah*, which is a technical term for "forgive" (sometimes translated "pardon"); it means nothing else. It is used of forgiving sin—"who forgives all your iniquity, who heals all your diseases" (Ps 103:3)—and of forgiving people—"and forgive your people who have sinned against you" (2 Chr 6:39). The second-most frequently used word, *nasa'*, literally means "lift up, bear, carry," and it occurs many times in the Old Testament with those meanings, but at times it becomes a metaphor used with sin as its object. It can designate guilt, as when one must "bear his iniquity" (Lev 5:1), but it is used of forgiveness, presumably with an original sense of lifting up guilt from a person: "Consider my affliction and my trouble, and forgive all my sins" (Ps 25:18). It has been suggested that it may also indicate that the one who forgives *bears* the other's sins, but the contexts do not offer clear support for that. The term has lost all of its metaphorical overtones when (like *salah*) it is used of forgiving a person: ". . . just as you have pardoned [*nasa'*] this people, from Egypt even until now" (Num 14:19).

Other terms are always metaphorical, usually taking sin-words as their objects. Three of those sin-words appear regularly. The root *hata'* ("sin") is used both as a verb and as a noun. It has the physical sense of missing the mark, thus of going wrong. The noun usually translated "iniquity" (*'awon*) has a range of meanings, from the sinful act to the resulting guilt to the punishment that ensues. The strongest sin-word is the root *pasa'*, since it carries the sense of rebellion. It appears typically in translation as the verb "transgress" or the noun "transgression." It will be noted in the quotations that follow that these words are often used as synonyms.

Sin may be taken away (*he'avir*) by forgiveness: "Why do you not pardon [*nasa'*] my transgression and take away my iniquity?" (Job 7:21; cf. 2 Sam 12:13; 24:10=1 Chr 21:8; Zech 3:4) It may be covered (*kasah*): "Happy are those whose transgression is forgiven [*nasa'*], whose sin is covered" (Ps 32:1; cf. Neh 4:5; Ps 85:2; Prov 17:9). It may be wiped or blotted out, or swept away (*mahah*): "I, I am He who blots out your transgressions for my own sake, and I will not remember your sins" (Isa 43:25; cf. Neh 4:5; Pss 51:9; 109:14; Isa 44:22; Jer 18:23).

Forgiveness not only removes the sin but changes the sinner, leading to healing (*rapha'*), used metaphorically of personal change as well as physical healing: "Return, O faithless children, I will heal your faithlessness" (Jer 3:22; Isa 6:10; 53:5; 57:18–19; Hos 6:11b—7:1; 14:4). That change could also be called cleansing: "Wash [*kavas*] me thoroughly from my iniquity, and cleanse [*tahar*] me from my sin" (Ps 51:2; cf. Ps 51:7, 10; Jer 33:8; Ezek 36:33). God was also said to change, with reference to memory: "I will forgive [*salah*] their iniquity, and remember their sin no more" (Jer 31:34; Pss 25:7; 32:2; 79:8; Isa 43:25; 64:9; Ezek 33:16).

One other word is sometimes appropriately translated "forgive." It is *kipper*, which is usually rendered by "atone" or "make atonement." Most of the occurrences of the word refer to ritual acts that have been prescribed by God as the first step people can take in an effort to reestablish a healthy relationship with God that has been endangered by some act of theirs. Many of the offerings prescribed in Leviticus thus associate the act of atonement with divine forgiveness, as in Lev 5:13: "Thus the priest shall make atonement on your behalf for whichever of these sins you have committed, and you shall be forgiven [*salah*]." Atonement and forgiveness ordinarily are not identical, but there are several cases where it is appropriate to translate *kipper* as "forgive," as in Ps 65:3: "When deeds of iniquity overwhelm us, you forgive our transgressions" (cf. Deut 21:8 [where NRSV uses "absolve"]; 2 Chr 30:18; Pss 78:38; 79:9; Isa 6:7; 22:14; Jer 18:23; Ezek 16:63). The relationship between sacrifice and forgiveness will be discussed later in the Old Testament section.

From Eden to Sinai

The claim made earlier, that forgiveness begins to be discussed seriously first in connection with the sin of the golden calf, should be justified before we turn to Exodus 32–34. Having identified the principle terms used of forgiveness, when we look for them in Genesis and Exodus 1–31, we find two passages to consider in Genesis and two in the relevant chapters of Exodus. All four texts are unusual. In the dialogue between Abraham and God concerning the fate of Sodom in Gen 18:22–33, Abraham asks whether, if God finds fifty righteous people in the city, "will you then sweep away the place and not forgive [*nasa'*] it? (v. 24). God replies, "I will forgive the whole place for their sakes" (v. 26). So the NRSV and the Revised English Bible (REB) render *nasa'*, but other translations and commentators on Genesis do not take this to be a true forgiveness passage. Other versions translate it as "spare," and since the verb here refers only to remission of punishment, it does not correspond to forgiveness as the Old Testament speaks of it elsewhere (Westermann 1985, 292). One example of forgiveness at the human level appears in Genesis, in the reconciliation scene between Joseph and his brothers (50:17). This is unusual, because the Old Testament does not say much about interpersonal forgiveness. We shall return to the passage in the section called "We Forgive One Another." In Exod 10:17 Pharaoh addresses Moses with a surprising appeal for forgiveness of his sin. One cannot help but wonder whether the author is being deliberately ironic in putting these words into the king's mouth, for this is scarcely to be taken as a sincere act of repentance. There was no forgiveness in Genesis

18–19 or Exodus 10, and the fourth occurrence of *nasa'* also threatens no forgiveness. In Exod 23:21 God promises to send an angel to guide the people from Sinai to the Promised Land, but warns them: "Do not rebel against him, for he will not pardon your transgression: for my name is in him." That verse seems to speak of a covenant relationship in which forgiveness plays no role, so it is not surprising that the sin of the golden calf left Moses very uncertain about whether any future for the people was possible.

Those four passages speak of the possibility of human forgiveness, but only raise the question of whether God is willing to forgive sin. Another way to approach the question is to look at the explicit references to sin in these chapters in order to see how God deals with it. Although the chapters preceding Exodus 32 do not speak positively of divine forgiveness, they do record examples of God's mercy, so the distinction between mercy and forgiveness should be noted here, with reference to some examples. Writers who have offered careful definitions of forgiveness emphasize that it is not to be identified with mercy. Mercy and forgiveness are alike in that neither declares the wrongdoer to be innocent. Sin is identified as sin, and they are also alike in that both qualities lead the one sinned against not to treat the guilty one as that person deserves to be treated. They differ in that mercy can be bestowed only by a stronger party who has the power to inflict punishment, while forgiveness may be offered between equals, or from a weaker party to a stronger. That distinction does not apply where God is concerned, of course. Another distinction is applicable, and the examples that follow will illustrate it. A decision to show mercy may not include overcoming resentment or restoring a harmonious relationship, but forgiveness includes both.

Readers of Genesis 3 have noticed that God, having judged Adam and Eve severely for their disobedience, then eases their misery somewhat. Now that they are ashamed of their nakedness they need clothes, and God provides the clothes for them (Gen 3:21). God also responded mercifully to Cain's complaint about his punishment for murdering his brother, "Anyone who meets me may kill me" (Gen 4:14), putting on him a protective sign so that the killer would not be killed (v. 9). In both cases forgiveness is missing—estrangement continues—but the guilty parties are not punished as severely as they might have been.

The vocabulary of sin first appears in the Cain-story: *hata'* in God's warning, "Sin is lurking at the door" (Gen 4:7), and *'awon* in Cain's complaint, "My punishment is greater than I can bear" (v. 13). The words do not occur often in the succeeding chapters until one reaches the stories concerning the tensions between Jacob and Laban (Genesis 31) and between Joseph and his brothers (Genesis 37–50). In the latter chapters they occur frequently, but God is not said to be directly involved in dealing with the sins alluded to, although Joseph does say that to commit adultery with Potiphar's wife would be a sin against God (Gen 39:9). God does deal with evil (*ra'* or *ra'ah*) and wickedness (*raša'*) with strict justice in the stories of the flood and of the destruction of Sodom and Gomorrah; sorting out for salvation the few righteous people, the families of Noah and of Lot, and destroying all the rest (Genesis 6–8, 19). This brief summary of a large amount of material has been offered only to emphasize by contrast the intense concern with sin and forgiveness that appears in Exodus 32–34.

Two Crises: A. The Golden Calf

God had told Moses, "Israel is my firstborn son" (Exod 4:22), and had insisted of the Pharaoh, "Let my people go" (Exod 5:1; 7:16; 8:1, 20; 9:1, 13; 10:3). After rescuing the Hebrews from slavery in Egypt he had brought them to Mount Sinai, and there entered into a unique and intimate relationship with them (Exod 19:4–6). The Sinai covenant included more than God's offer of special blessings for the people he had chosen; it required obedience on their part to the standards of living that would mark them as the people of God, and it required faithfulness to God's insistence that he alone was to be acknowledged as their God (Exod 20:1–6). Throughout most of Exodus, the people had played a passive role; Moses had acted on their behalf, but at Sinai they did enthusiastically affirm, "Everything that the Lord has spoken we will do" (Exod 19:8). Then Moses spent forty days on the mountain and the people took the initiative for the first time: "Come, make gods for us, who shall go for us" (Exod 32:1). Aaron did not resist, but made a golden calf, then declared of it, "These are your gods, O Israel, who brought you up out of the land of Egypt" (v. 4). Within forty days Israel had broken the first two commandments. The account in chs. 32–34 thus wrestles with the question whether a relationship that requires obedience can be maintained in the face of fundamental disobedience. The passage is filled with tensions—literary and theological—for it struggles with a major theological issue: how God can be both just and merciful. It reaches a resolution with God's own self-definition as one whose nature it is to forgive. In many respects this is the most important forgiveness passage in the Bible, for it speaks of the worst of sins—in effect denying one's relationship with God. It struggles at length with the possibilities of restoring a broken relationship, and finally declares that the only possibility is to be found in the character of God himself.

This is the first passage in Scripture to deal with forgiveness at any length. In our survey of Genesis and Exodus 1–31, we found only a little material that contributed to the study of this theme, but now the vocabulary of forgiveness appears with great prominence. It is a difficult passage to work with, for the continuity from one section to another is not at all clear. Efforts at source critical analysis have not succeeded in resolving the problems, so most recent commentators do their best to offer a coherent reading of the text as it stands. The discontinuities remain a puzzle, however. For example, why is Aaron's sin emphasized, but he is not punished for it? What does the slaughter carried out by the Levites actually accomplish, when immediately afterwards Moses attempts to atone for the people's sins (32:25–30)? Why does the description of the tent interrupt the narrative in 33:7–11? The impression left by these chapters is that the author responsible for their final form had access to a group of old traditions concerning the wilderness period, associated with the sin of the golden calf, which he combined as best he could. It may be that the incident concerning the Levites and the description of the tent of meeting were not originally connected with the golden calf incident, but the author thought they fit best in this context. At any rate, for our purpose—a study of forgiveness—most of those problems can be bracketed. We shall assume that the author was not a mere collector of traditions and that these materials were used because they contributed something to the intended message. There is more than one important theme here, but we shall simplify the reading of the complex passage by asking only about the ways forgiveness figures in it.

As the story of the golden calf is told, it becomes clear that the fundamental sin against God, which raises the question whether the covenant can possibly endure, is violation of God's exclusive claim upon Israel, as expressed in the first two commandments. So, a whole cluster of words about sin appears for the first time, for now that God has established the covenant this choice of another god, unlike anything before, defines the nature of sin.

God refuses to acknowledge the idolaters as his people any longer:

> The LORD said to Moses, "Go down at once! Your people, whom you brought up out of the land of Egypt, have acted perversely; they have been quick to turn aside from the way that I commanded them; they have cast for themselves an image of a calf, and have worshiped it and sacrificed to it, and said, 'These are your gods, O Israel, who brought you up out of the land of Egypt!'" The LORD said to Moses, "I have seen this people, how stiff-necked they are. Now let me alone, so that my wrath may burn hot against them and I may consume them; and of you I will make a great nation." (Exod 32:7–10)

In v. 7 he tells Moses that they are "your people" and in v. 9 calls them "this people." They have "acted perversely" (v. 7). The verb *šaḥat* is also used in the introduction to the story of the flood: "all flesh had corrupted its ways" (Gen 6:12), and God proposes here to do what he had done earlier; wipe out the sinners and start over. The root seems to describe something like rot, which destroys the things corrupted, so "act perversely" may be a mild translation (see also Deut 4:16, 35; 9:12; 31:29; Judg 2:19; Zeph 3:7). God continues by calling the violation of the commandments "turning aside" (*sur*), a verb used elsewhere of idolatry (e.g., Deut 11:16; 28:14; Judg 2:17). He adds to the indictment by using another term for sinfulness, "stiff-necked," a term that is repeated in 33:3, 5; 34:9 (also Deut 9:6, 13). Combination of the two words (*qᵉšeh-'oreph*) also appears elsewhere, often translated "stubborn," but this is an insidious kind of stubbornness. In Neh 9:16–17 and v. 29, it is refusal to obey God and in Deut 31:27 it is associated with rebelliousness (see also Deut 10:16; Judg 2:19; 2 Kgs 17:14; Jer 7:26; 17:23; 19:15). The seriousness of Israel's sin is thus emphasized in three ways as God reveals to Moses what has happened while he was on the mountain. As the story continues, the author has another term for their behavior, translated "running wild" in the NRSV. The word *para'* literally means "break loose," and parallels elsewhere show that it can mean to cast off restraint or get out of control (2 Chr 28:19; Prov 29:18). Then the common words for sin begin to appear: *hata'* in 32:21, 30, 31, 32, 33, 34; 34:7, 9, *'awon* in 34:7, 9, and *paša'* in 34:7. The choice of words thus makes it clear how critical the situation is, and emphasizes what a turning point will be reached when for the first time God's forgiving nature is revealed.

Moses' first prayer already hints at the radical nature of the revelation what will eventually come, for he does not ask God to forgive. God had declared the covenant to be broken, and had announced his intention to wipe out the sinful people and to start over with Moses (Exod 32:7–10). Moses does not ask for forgiveness; he asks God only to change his mind concerning the destruction of the people (v. 12).

> But Moses implored the LORD his God, and said, "O LORD, why does your wrath burn hot against your people, whom you brought out of the land of Egypt with great power and with a mighty hand? Why should the Egyptians say, 'It was with evil intent that he brought them out to kill them in the mountains, and to consume them from the face of the earth'? Turn from your fierce wrath; change your mind and do not bring disaster on your people. Remember Abraham, Isaac, and Israel, your servants, how you swore to them by your own self, saying to them, 'I will multiply your descendants like the stars of heaven, and all this land that I have promised I will give to your descendants, and they shall inherit it forever.'" (vv. 11–13)

His three arguments make no reference to compassion or mercy. He reminds God first of the effort expended to bring the people out of slavery (v. 11), then questions whether God would want the Egyptians to think all that had been done with evil intent (v. 12), and finally does appeal to something involving God's own character. God had sworn by his own self to Abraham, Isaac and Israel that he would multiply their descendents and give them a land (v. 13). Actually God had no intention of violating his oath, for in starting over with Moses he would have been continuing the line of Abraham. But he lets Moses persuade him. "And the LORD changed his mind about the disaster that he planned to bring on his people" (v. 14).

In the past, translators made an unfortunate choice, rendering *hinnahem* here and elsewhere with "repent." The English word always suggests turning away from sin, so interpreters have then had to explain the special meaning of God's "repentance," since it never means God turns away from sin. In fact, the word means God changes his mind, as the NRSV has translated it, almost always in favor of mercy rather than judgment.

What has been accomplished, so far? God allows the idolaters to live—only that. There is nothing resembling forgiveness as we shall find it in Scripture; neither remission of punishment (as we shall soon see) nor restoration of the covenant relationship. As Moses descends the mountain and sees for himself what the people are doing, he breaks the tablets, and that reflects the situation accurately. The covenant has been broken.

The sections that follow in ch. 32 raise many questions for the reader, but if we take this to be a story of forgiveness (and there are other ways to read it) we find three human efforts to deal with sin— Moses' expedients—before he finally appeals for forgiveness. It does not come easily, and we begin to feel the author ascribing tension to God himself, and not only to Moses. First, Moses destroyed the calf, burned it (was it a wooden figure covered with gold?), ground it to powder, and mixed that with water, which he forced the people to drink (v. 20). Was this intended to be trial by ordeal (as in Num 5:11–31), so that the guilty parties would be sickened? We are not told, and are not told that it had any effect. Next Moses set out to divide righteous from wicked with the cry, "Who is on the Lord's side" (v. 26)? This led the Levites to massacre about three thousand people, for which Moses praised them. This disturbing story probably did not originally belong with the golden calf tradition, for it accomplishes nothing. The sinners are not all dead after all, for in the next verse, Moses attempts to do something more about them. We might look at the first two human expedients this way: First, he got rid of the object that was the result of their sinful desire and that would have been a continuing source of temptation, but that was not enough. It did not touch the desire. Then he tried a sadly familiar way of dealing with wickedness—kill the wicked, but who would be left if all the wicked were killed? The author does not offer any interpretation of these two efforts, but since as told they seem to have been futile we may be justified in understanding them in this way.

Moses' third expedient involves just a single word, *kipper*; "perhaps I can make atonement for your sin" (v. 30). How he thought he might do that is not explained, for it does not accomplish anything, either. A good many scholars do think that the ensuing prayer, "if not, blot me out of the book that you have written" (v. 32), is Moses' request to be a substitute victim, suffering vicariously for his people's sins. That seems unlikely, however, as the most straightforward reading of the text would have him simply insist that he wishes to die with his people. Could the act of atonement then simply be his intercessory prayer? Atonement is not spoken of that way elsewhere, so we might read Moses' "perhaps" as an indication that he does not know what he might be able to do (v. 30).

Here, the idea of divine forgiveness appears for the first time.

> On the next day Moses said to the people, "You have sinned a great sin. But now I will go up to the LORD; perhaps I can make atonement for your sin." So Moses returned to the LORD and said, "Alas, this people has sinned a great sin; they have made for themselves gods of gold. But now, if you will only forgive their sin—but if not, blot me out of the book that you have written." But the LORD said to Moses, "Whoever has sinned against me I will blot out of my book. But now go, lead the people to the place about which I have spoken to you; see, my angel shall go in front of you. Nevertheless, when the day comes for punishment, I will punish them for their sin." (vv. 30–34)

In vv. 30–34 "sin" appears eight times, and "forgive" (*nasa'*) once, in an "if-clause" that has no apodosis (v. 32). Moses cannot predict what the result of forgiveness might be. Having proposed it, he can think only of the present situation—a people worthy of death—and he will not accept God's earlier offer to start over with him. "Let me die with them" (v. 32). God's response, "Whoever has sinned against me I will blot out of my book," might be taken as a refusal to consider forgiveness, but this would introduce more tension into the narrative than seems necessary. It seems best to understand it as a refusal to blot out Moses, who had not sinned.

No progress has been made with respect to the broken covenant. God will not destroy the people and will remain faithful to his promise to Abraham (v. 34) but, "Nevertheless, when the day comes for punishment, I will punish them for their sins." When the author wrote that sentence, how much of Israel's subsequent history may he have had in mind? Then, punishment is mentioned immediately, in v. 35, a plague which is the result of the calf, emphasizing that Moses' efforts have so far made no progress toward forgiveness.

If our subject had been the presence of God, the discussion of chapter 33 would occupy considerable space. Much of the chapter can be dealt with briefly as we trace the theme of forgiveness, however. That the punishment referred to in 32:35 did nothing to restore the covenant relationship is made clear by the theme of the distancing of God that appears in 33:1–6.

> The LORD said to Moses, "Go, leave this place, you and the people whom you have brought up out of the land of Egypt, and go to the land of which I swore to Abraham, Isaac, and Jacob, saying, 'To your descendants I will give it.' I will send an angel before you, and I will drive out the Canaanites, the Amorites, the Hittites, the Perizzites, the Hivites, and the Jebusites. Go up to a land flowing with milk and honey; but I will not go up among you, or I would consume you on the way, for you are a stiff-necked people." When the people heard these harsh words, they mourned, and no one put on ornaments. For the LORD had said to Moses, 'Say to the Israelites, 'You are a stiff-necked people; if for a single moment I should go up among you, I would consume you. So now take off your ornaments, and I will decide what to do to you.'" Therefore the Israelites stripped themselves of their ornaments, from Mount Horeb onward. (33:1–6)

God repeats his intention to fulfill the promise to Abraham, in vv. 1–3 (recall 32:34), but these are a stiff-necked people, and the presence of the holy God in their midst would lead to that annihilation that he had decided against. How this is to be understood with respect to the earlier reference to an angel in 23:20–21 is never explained and we will not pause to struggle with it except to recall that the angel in 23:21 does not forgive. What is important for our purposes is the people's reaction to this protective distancing of God. It may be protective, but they realize it means the covenant relationship is no longer in effect.

Many scholars take the mourning of the people in 33:4, accompanied by removal of their ornaments, to be a reference to true repentance on their part, which opens the way for forgiveness. That would make the story fit the familiar pattern—repentance first, followed by forgiveness—but the choice of words here offers little support for it. The usual verb for "repent," *shuv*, does not appear. The verb translated "mourn" (*'aval*) usually refers to lamentation at the time of a death (Gen 37:34 and many other texts). Three times it is used of the reactions of righteous men to the state of their people (Ezra 10:6; Neh 1:4;

Dan 10:2). Figuratively, nature also mourns (e.g., Isa 24:4). Mourning is nothing to be commended or desired, as repentance is, for it can be overcome by joy (e.g., Neh 8:9; Isa 60:20; 61:2). There is one occurrence of the verb that might support introducing the idea of repentance here; in a text that has many parallels to Exodus 32–34; i.e. Num 14:39–40. That passage deals with the people's refusal to attempt to enter Canaan, leading God to declare that only their children, not they, may eventually enter the land. This leads to mourning and perhaps repentance, since they change their minds and say they will go, admitting that they have sinned. God does not accept this as legitimate repentance, however, and does not change his mind. The author's choice of the verb in 33:4 thus does not suggest anything more than regret, and if the people's actions had represented repentance, surely Moses' prayer in 33:12–16 would have appealed to that. He can appeal to nothing but his own status, however, so the evidence in these chapters all points to a message about forgiveness without repentance.

Moses' isolation from his people is emphasized by the insertion of the description of the tent of meeting in 33:7–11. When he was not on the mountain he still had access to God in a tent that stood outside the camp, not in the center, as the tabernacle later did. Everything focuses on Moses who, in the strange conversation that follows in vv. 12–23, is not even sure of his own status before God.

> Moses said to the LORD, "See, you have said to me, 'Bring up this people'; but you have not let me know whom you will send with me. Yet you have said, 'I know you by name, and you have also found favor in my sight.' Now if I have found favor in your sight, show me your ways, so that I may know you and find favor in your sight. Consider too that this nation is your people." He said, "My presence will go with you, and I will give you rest." And he said to him, "If your presence will not go, do not carry us up from here. For how shall it be known that I have found favor in your sight, I and your people, unless you go with us? In this way, we shall be distinct, I and your people, from every people on the face of the earth." (33:12–16)

He asks reassurance from God, but as an intercessor for the people, who have no status: "Consider too that this nation is your people" (v. 13; not acknowledged by God). As he asks for God's presence with them, ignoring the potential destruction God had warned of in v. 5, Moses twice says, "I and your people" (v. 16). God's response is an assurance only to

Moses, however. Throughout chs. 32–33 no progress seems to have been made toward restoration of the covenant, until God announces that he will appear to Moses with a new proclamation of his name, YHWH. "I will make all my goodness pass before you, and will proclaim before you the name, 'The LORD'; and I will be gracious to whom I will be gracious, and will show mercy on whom I will show mercy" (v. 19). Grace and mercy; this is a new subject. Without further explanation, God then set about to announce the establishment of a new covenant, but 33:19 has introduced the only possible basis for it.

Without any explanation except the promise that God would make his goodness pass before Moses, and proclaim his name, God now instructs him to prepare for a restoration of the covenant by cutting two new stone tablets and once again ascending the mountain (34:1–4). Having done so, Moses then received a formal introduction to the Lord, unlike those recorded in Exod 3:14–22 and 6:2–8, except for the proclamation of the divine name. Before, God had told Moses what he was going to do; now he tells Moses who he is, with a striking series of words elaborating on the graciousness and mercy he had spoken of in 33:19. They will become the basis for Israel's hope throughout all the distress that they will suffer in the future.

> The LORD, the LORD,
> a God merciful and gracious,
> slow to anger,
> and abounding in steadfast love and faithfulness,
> keeping steadfast love for the thousandth generation,
> forgiving iniquity and transgression and sin,
> yet by no means clearing the guilty,
> but visiting the iniquity of the parents
> upon the children
> and the children's children,
> to the third and fourth generation. (34:6–7)

The first two words, "merciful and gracious" (better: "compassionate and gracious") appear together eleven times in the Old Testament as unique designations of the character of God (Exod 34:6; 2 Chr 30:9; Neh 9:17, 31; Pss 86:15; 103:8; 111:4; 112:4; 145:8; Joel 4:2; Jonah 4:2). They are forms of the common roots *rhm* and *hnn*, but are distinctive forms (*rahum* and *hannun*) that are used only of God (Ps 112:4 is a possible exception). The Old Testament authors had to compare God with human beings; they had no other option, but their choice of special forms of words is a reminder that no aspect of God's character can be exactly identified with those human virtues.

Forms of the root *rhm* are translated "compassion/compassionate, mercy/merciful, pity." We have seen that mercy may be extended to a person with whom one does not have a close relationship, but *rhm* often has an intensely personal sense, so compassion is the more appropriate translation in many places, including this verse, since relationship is the issue. It is often noted that the form *rehem* means "womb," so that may justify carrying over the sense of "mother-love" to other forms of the word. "Can a woman forget her nursing child, or show no compassion (*merahem*) for the child of her womb (*beten*)?" (Isa 49:15; mother-love also in 1 Kgs 3:26) The word is used to compare God's compassion for those who fear him with that of a father for his children in Ps 103:13. In Isa 54: 7–8 God's promise to restore Israel from exile is described as a reconciliation of husband and wife, and the basis for that restored relation is compassion (and steadfast love, as in Exod 34:6–7). The root appears with reference to a fourth family relationship in the account of Joseph's reconciliation with his brothers (Gen 43:30), more evidence of the strongly emotional overtones of the word.

The appearance of this word at the beginning of God's self-definition thus insists that as mothers and fathers hurt by their wayward children, husbands hurt by their unfaithful wives, and brothers who have been betrayed, find *something* in themselves to make it possible to work toward a restored relationship, that something, multiplied many times, is present, and in fact originates, in God (Simian-Yofre 2004, 452).

The multiplication is carried out here by the remarkable series of words that follow. Gracious (*hannun*) is the second of the special forms used only of God. Other forms of the root *hnn* are widely used of human relationships where good will is involved. The favorable ways that Potiphar treated Joseph, and Saul treated David at the beginning of those relationships are denoted by *hnn* (Gen 39:4–6; 1 Sam 16;:20–22). The concern that Boaz showed for Ruth is described as finding favor in his sight. In these cases, note that the gracious one holds a favorable opinion of the other, but this is hardly true of God's opinion of Israel in this context. Often, the appeal to God for gracious treatment comes from those in distress (for whom God would normally be concerned;

e.g., Pss 4:1; 6:2; 9:13), but there are other uses of the word to denote undeserved favor (2 Sam 12:22; 2 Kgs 13:22; Pss 25:16–18; 41:4).

"Slow to anger" might seem out-of-keeping with God's earlier intention to wipe out the entire community, so this assurance that God is also patient is essential. The wrath of God seems to play such a large role in the Old Testament that it may be significant to note that words for anger have not often occurred in Genesis and Exodus. The references in Gen 18:30, 32 and Exod 4:14 are not of great significance, and this makes the next appearance of anger, in Exod 22:24, of considerable importance.

"You shall not wrong or oppress a resident alien, for you were aliens in the land of Egypt. You shall not abuse any widow or orphan. If you do abuse them, when they cry out to me, I will surely heed their cry; my wrath will burn, and I will kill you with the sword, and your wives shall become widows and your children orphans" (Exod 22:21–24).

It is in the Covenant Code, and is directly associated with the Old Testament's classic definition of righteous behavior—care for the widows, orphans, and aliens. Wronging or oppressing one of them will lead to the one dire threat to be found in the motive clauses associated with Old Testament law. This suggests that Israel thought of the wrath of God as the inevitable negative result of the rupture of their relationship with the source of all that is good. But God is slow to anger. There may be time. Ezekiel developed the theme of God's patience at length in 20:5–31, retelling Israel's history from Egypt to the Promised Land as a history of their continual rebellion, which ought to have led God to pour out his wrath long ago, but God had remained patient for a long time, until the present, when judgment had finally fallen upon them.

"Steadfast love" (ḥesed) appears twice, associated first with "faithfulness" ('emeth), and then emphasized by saying it is for thousands (probably of generations). Book-length studies have been devoted to ḥesed (Glueck 1967; Sakenfeld 1978); here it (with 'emeth) might be seen as the guarantee that compassion and graciousness can be completely depended on forever.

Because these words describe the true nature of God, then forgiveness is possible. The root there is nasa', the verb Moses had tentatively used in 32:32, and the extent of the promise now contained in that word is revealed by the use of all three of the major sin-words: iniquity and transgression and sin. When chs. 32–34 are read as a story of sin and forgiveness, this line becomes the climax. Forgiveness, that is the possibility of renewing a broken relationship, is possible because of God's compassion—he is personally moved by the moral worthlessness of those people he had chosen; because of his graciousness—he will treat them as deserving, even though they are not; because of his patience—he will restrain as long as possible the natural consequences of wickedness; and because he is utterly dependable in acting in accordance with his true nature.

Yet—the whole story has not yet been told. Does God contradict himself with the words that follow? "Yet by no means clearing the guilty, but visiting the iniquity of the parents upon the children and upon the children's children, to the third and fourth generation." Here we seem to encounter the conflict, or paradox even, between justice and mercy, but there may be a way to understand how all of this does fit together. Walter Brueggemann (1994, 947) has claimed, "It is inadmissible to resolve the tension programmatically. Israel has discerned that there is in the very core existence of Yahweh a profound and durable incongruity." These three chapters have certainly pointed toward tensions within God himself, where forgiveness is concerned, but these verses may not be completely paradoxical if we find in the three chapters a definition of what the Old Testament author understood forgiveness to be, and not to be. Here, God insists that forgiveness does not eliminate the just treatment of sin. It is not remission of punishment, as some definitions have it, but is the re-establishment of a broken relationship, while suffering as a consequence of sin does take place. Note that the psalmist finds no paradox in writing "You were a forgiving God to them, but an avenger of their wrongdoings" (Ps 99:8). This certainly fits many of our experiences of forgiveness at the human level. Iniquity has inevitable results, we are told here, but God's mercy means it need not cut off any possibility of a better future.

The reference to the third and fourth generation is not to be taken as suggesting a God who holds a grudge for a long time. It refers instead to a realistic understanding of the effects of sin (Freedman 1955). The Old Testament authors knew well that the good one person does brings blessings to the whole family, or tribe, or nation, whether deserved or not, and the evil one person does likewise brings suffering. Some families today may have five generations alive at the same time, but in ancient Israel it is not likely that there would be more than four, and often there were probably only three. The reference to third and fourth generations thus is best taken to remind one that the whole family will suffer the effects of any one member's sin, and that in fact is how it is. While iniquity is visited upon the present, however, the Lord's steadfast love extends to the thousandth generation. Note the importance of the development of thought between these verses and the similar words in the Decalogue, which do not yet speak of forgiveness: "I the LORD your God am a jealous God, punishing children for the iniquity of parents, to the third and the fourth generation of those who reject me, but showing steadfast love to the thousandth generation of those who love me and keep my commandments." In Exod 20:5–6 God's steadfast love is offered only to those who love him and keep his commandments.

Moses responded to this amazing new revelation in the only appropriate ways. First, he "bowed his head toward the earth, and worshiped" (34:8). He then proceeded with some uncertainty, for despite God's revelation of himself as one who forgives sin, he has not said explicitly what he intends to do with these people. So Moses began with the explicit reassurance he had received, "If now I have found favor in your sight . . ," then returned to the question of God's presence, which had been left so uncertain in ch. 33, "let the Lord go with us." There has been no repentance of the people to which he could appeal—"although this is a stiff-necked people"—but God has spoken for the first time of forgiveness, so Moses requests a future for his people based on that. He uses a different verb, *salah*, but I see nothing in the context or in the uses of *salah* and *nasa'* elsewhere that would suggest any difference in meaning (see Num 14:19). Then he added a new term, inheritance (root *nhl*), which reinforces our definition of forgiveness as referring to covenant relationship. In early Israel, before social changes disrupted the system, the families' ownership of their property was inalienable. An "owner" could not dispose of his land, for in effect he simply held it in trust for his descendants, as his ancestors had held it in trust for him. So, on the numerous occasions when Israel is spoken of as Yahweh's inheritance (or heritage, or possession; e.g., Deut 4:20; 1 Kgs 8:53; Ps 33:12; Mic 7:18), the point is that the relationship is permanent, inalienable. Moses has thus made a dramatic request as his hope for what forgiveness may mean. This is the first time "inheritance" has been used with respect to the covenant relationship. So, the comments of several scholars on the meaning of *salah* are surely correct. It does not mean canceling sins or eliminating punishment, but renewing the covenant relationship.

That is what happens; it is Yahweh's direct response to Moses' request. There is no more negotiation, but instead the promise of a new covenant, put in amazingly extravagant terms. "He said: 'I hereby make a covenant. Before all your people I will perform marvels, such as have not been performed in all the earth or in any nation; and all the people among whom you live shall see the work of the LORD; for it is an awesome thing that I will do with you'" (34:10). Here is forgiveness without evidence of repentance. On this disputed matter of whether there can be forgiveness without repentance, note the way Psalm 78 comments on the wilderness period. Repentance is described in vv. 34–35, but as the psalmist recalls the wilderness tradition he concludes it was not sincere: "But they flattered him with their mouths; they lied to him with their tongues. Their heart was not steadfast toward him; they were not true to his covenant (vv. 36–37). Then he adds, "Yet he, being compassionate, forgave their iniquity, and did not destroy them; often he restrained his anger, and did not stir up all his wrath. He remembered that they were but flesh, a wind that passes and does not come again" (vv. 38–39). What follows in Exodus 34, however, is not a covenant relationship without responsibility. It has been pointed out that 34:11–26 reinstates the covenant with specific reference to the sin of ch. 32, for it primarily elaborates the strictures of the first and second commandments. This is the "cultic decalogue." Actually, it may be earlier than much of the material around it, as scholars generally agree, perhaps earlier than Exod 20:1–17. The historical relationship between the two decalogues is not completely clear, but the problem of origins need not affect our use of the material. No matter what the earlier history may have been, what is important for the study of forgiveness is the way the final author of Exodus used it—assuming he saw in it a message concerning the possibility of an ongoing relationship between a sinful people and the Holy One.

Now, how did the author know all this? We weren't there, so cannot give an honest answer, only opinions, which are worth little, but the question comes up because it is involved with the question of the truth of what these words say about God, and that matters much. So, others offer answers: Moses wrote it; or it is the communal testimony of Israel; or it is merely a late work of fiction. We cannot conclusively prove or disprove any of those, so I move away from the frustrating question of origins in order to look for another kind of evidence for truth, and I find that in the effect those words have had on individual lives and on the history of the communities that have believed them. We shall turn, shortly, to the uses made in the Old Testament of these very words, but a general comment may provide a helpful context for them.

We shall ask what difference it made to Israelites that they believed in a God like this. What might they have naturally deduced about God from the world they lived in? Israel experienced far more defeats than victories, and they were taught to blame their defeats on their own sinfulness—God being the judge of them. Issues between people were frequently settled violently. We shall see that the Old Testament says little about human relationships being maintained by forgiveness. It is apparently not a natural part of the human personality. This means that in passages such as Exod 34:6–7 and parallels they did not speak of a God who reflected the world they lived in—not an echo of the natural world or of society or of human personality. They dared to speak of compassion, which allowed for forgiveness, and something had happened in history that led them to insist that this is what God is like.

The Confirmation: Numbers 14

Soon Moses needed to know how steadfast was the steadfast love God had announced at Sinai. The people had moved from the mountain to the border of the Promised Land when a new, potentially fatal crisis developed. Numbers 13 tells of the mission of twelve spies who were sent to reconnoiter the land, and of their frightening report of fortified cities and giant inhabitants. Only Joshua and Caleb attempted to assure the people that with God's help they would be able to conquer the land (Num 13:30; 14:6–9), but they were not believed. The words of "the whole congregation" are keys to the development of the story.

"Would that we had died in the land of Egypt! Or would that we had died in this wilderness! Why is the LORD bringing us into this land to fall by the sword? Our wives and our little ones will become booty; would it not be better for us to go back to Egypt?" So they said to one another, "Let us choose a captain, and go back to Egypt" (Num 14:2b–4).

They blame God for leading them to their deaths. They wish they had already died in Egypt or in the wilderness. And they propose to choose a new leader who will take them back to Egypt. It has been claimed that this rebellion is even worse than the case of the golden calf, since they now plan to reverse the saving act of the exodus.

God's reaction, Moses' intervention, and the result of his prayer contain remarkable parallels to Exodus 32–34. "And the Lord said to Moses, 'How long will this people despise me? And how long will they refuse to believe in me, in spite of all the signs that I have done among them? I will strike them with pestilence and disinherit them, and I will make of you a nation greater and mightier than they'" (vv. 11–12). This time God uses personal terms for what the people are doing. They despise him (*n's*) and refuse to believe in him (*'mn*; v. 11). So he intends to strike them with pestilence (which had happened before, e.g., Exod 32:35), and disinherit them—a new word, which would mean the end of the covenant relationship. As in Exodus 32, God proposed to start over with Moses.

Moses' intervention (vv. 13–19) parallels his prayer in Exod 32:11–13 at first, as he develops the earlier argument concerning God's reputation among the Egyptians, but what is important for our purposes is his quotation of God's own words in Exod 34:6–7. These words will be partially quoted numerous times in the Old Testament, and this also is partial. There is no obvious explanation for what Moses omits—the first two attributes, compassion and mercy, the pairing of faithfulness with steadfast love, the reference to sin along with iniquity and transgression, the reference to the thousandth generation, and the reference to children's children.

> And now, therefore, let the power of the Lord be great in the
> way that you promised when you spoke, saying,
> "The Lord is slow to anger,
> and abounding in steadfast love,
> forgiving iniquity and transgression,
> but by no means clearing the guilty,
> visiting the iniquity of the parents upon the children
> to the third and the fourth generation."
> Forgive the iniquity of this people according to the greatness of
> your steadfast love, just as you have pardoned this people, from
> Egypt even until now. (vv. 17–19)

What puzzles interpreters most about the omissions is the resulting relative emphasis on judgment, when Moses is pleading for forgiveness. In his appeal (v. 19) he uses the two words for forgiveness that had appeared in Exodus 34; first *salah* (cf. 34:9), then *nasa'* (cf. 34:7; also in 14:18). It is God's steadfast love that he holds up as the primary basis for his appeal, reminding God that now he is known to be a forgiving God—"just as you have pardoned this people, from Egypt even until now"—even though we know of only one previous case of forgiveness.

The Lord responded directly this time: "I do forgive (*salah*), just as you have asked" (v. 20), but then immediately turned to a lengthy speech of judgment (vv. 21–35). The people had said they wished they had died in the wilderness; they will do so, the whole generation except for Joshua and Caleb. But God's promise to Abraham will still be fulfilled; the covenant has not been abrogated, for the second generation, those younger than twenty, will inherit the land.

Those harsh words led to mourning, once again, as in Exod 33:4, but it is too late for repentance (note that repentance seldom appears in Genesis through Kings), and their effort to invade Canaan after all is a failure (14:39–45).

All this leads interpreters to debate what is really meant by the Lord's word, "I do forgive, just as you asked." There are several who find nothing in the passage that they can call forgiveness. For example, Walter Brueggemann concluded, "In this text there is not an ounce of room for steadfast love outside of adherence to Yahweh's commanding authority" (1997, 307). Jacob Milgrom uses what we called earlier a limited definition of forgiveness, exoneration of sin, so he will not translate *salah* and *nasa'* as "forgive." He wrote, "Moses asks for reconciliation not forgiveness, for the assurance that Israel will be brought to the land and not that the sin of the Exodus generation will be exonerated" (1990, 396). His words are helpful, for they reveal what is involved in some judgments about the passage. But, whose definition should we use? After defining at some length what forgiveness means in Numbers 14, Michael Widmer concluded, "In sum, we can say that Moses never asked for forgiveness, at least not in the sense a modern reader would most readily understand the term" (2004, 318). Earlier, he indicated what that understanding would be: "annulment of guilt and sin," "elimination of punishment" (316). But the meaning of *nasa'* and *salah* in this passage is clearly different. We have already begun to find evidence, and more will be forthcoming, that forgiveness in Scripture ought not to be defined by "the modern reader," in the narrow sense of annulment of punishment. Katharine Sakenfeld's conclusion about the passage corresponds with what we shall find elsewhere: "Forgiveness is understood basically as preservation of the community, and this preservation need not be precluded or even cheapened by punishment of the community while the relationship is being continued" (1975, 327).

If we recall the three aspects of forgiveness described in the introduction to the book it is evident that personal renewal-cleansing has not appeared in any sense in Exodus and Numbers. Relief from personal distress appears, but not as freedom from all punishment. In both stories punishment is mitigated. The rebellious people lived on; most of them lived out their natural life spans, but they suffered for their sins and were not permitted to enter the Promised Land. As the scholars noted above have said, the third aspect, relationship—specifically the continuance of the covenant—is the primary meaning ascribed to forgiveness by the authors of these stories. So, in spite of the negative readings of Numbers 14 offered by some interpreters, it seems justified to call the passage a confirmation of God's words in Exod 34:6–7. In the midst of another potentially fatal crisis, Moses needed to find out whether they could be depended on for all time (although "visiting the iniquity" was part of it), and God's response indicated that they could be.

We have begun to make some progress toward understanding what forgiveness means in the Old Testament. Having just encountered some common definitions—exoneration of sin, annulment of punishment, or removal of guilt—we recognize that these are not very helpful for understanding Exodus 32–34 or Numbers 14. The author's primary interest is in the qualities in God that enable him to maintain a beneficent relationship even with people who continually offend him. Continually—that is the issue. When will repentance, actually turning away from sin, appear in this literature, and how can it be possible? Can forgiveness accomplish more than continuance of an uneasy relationship? Old Testament authors will struggle with these questions, but they show us that they did depend on the truth of God's self-definition when they were in need, because of their sin or because of distress of any kind. Exodus 34:6–7 is partially quoted in a variety of settings; in prayers confessing Israel's sins (Neh 9:17, 31; Ps 78:38), in hymns of praise (Pss 103:8; 111:4; 145:8), in laments (Pss 77:7–9; 86:3, 5, 15; Lam 3:32), in admonitions to turn to God (2 Chr 30:9; Joel 2:18), and in narratives (2 Kgs 13:23; Jonah 4:2). The emphasis in all of these is on God's graciousness. Only in Deut 7:9–10; Jer 32:18; and Nah 1:3 are there allusions to Exodus 34 that include references to not clearing the guilty.

Except for the psalms, which may be early, the citations of Exodus 34 all seem to be exilic or post-exilic. Those were times when critical theological questions had arisen, as the next major section will show, and the character of God was appealed to as the basis for hope for a better future. The experience of the fall of Jerusalem might have led to the conclusion that Yahweh was weak and unable to help, or unreliable or vindictive. But they used these words to counter what might have been the natural reaction. The dates of these texts have suggested to many scholars that Exod 34:6–7 is a later insertion into earlier material concerning Sinai. That is not a matter of great importance for our study, since this is not an attempt to write a history of the development of belief in forgiveness. The aim of this book is rather to bring together all aspects of thought about forgiveness in order to see what the biblical authors concluded about the place of forgiveness in the relationship between God and human beings, and eventually to consider forgiveness between human beings.

The trouble Israel experienced led them to acknowledge their failures, in confessions of sin, and to refer back to Sinai to find a basis for hope. In Ezra's long prayer of confession, he recalled God's mighty acts and set against them Israel's failure to obey, but cited Exod 34: 6–7 in order to account for the continuance of the covenant relationship, which Israel had so often broken: "But you are a God ready to forgive, gracious and merciful, slow to anger and abounding in steadfast love, and you did not forsake them . . . Nevertheless, in your great mercies you did not make an end of them or forsake them, for you are a gracious and merciful God" (Neh 9:17, 31). Another rather full quotation appears in Joel 2:13, in a passage that is usually taken as a call to repentance.

> Return to the LORD, your God,
> for he is gracious and merciful,
> slow to anger, and abounding in steadfast love,
> and relents from punishing.

The crisis is a plague of locusts, and the prophet calls upon the people to fast and appeal to the Lord for help. He says nothing about sinfulness, however, so his call, which is usually translated "return," i.e., repent, may possibly mean just "turn to the Lord" (for help). At any rate, he does not include the reference to forgiveness in Exod 34:6–7, but instead adds words that allude to Exod 32:12–13, "relents from punishing." The author of Jonah used the identical words, but in a highly ironic way. Instead of being a basis for hope, they have been the cause of Jonah's dilemma. He had been ordered to announce God's judgment of Nineveh, which did not come true because of their repentance. He expressed his anger at having thus become a false prophet, saying he had tried to resist proclaiming judgment because he knew that God is merciful." That is why I fled to Tarshish at the beginning; for I knew that you are a gracious God and merciful, slow to anger, and abounding in steadfast love, and ready to relent from punishing" (Jonah 4:3). Note that this citation also does not mention forgiveness, perhaps because there was nothing like re-establishing a covenant relationship with the Assyrians.

Individual failure led the author of Psalm 86 to allude to elements of Exod 34: 6–7 as the basis for confidence that God would help. "But you, O Lord, are a God merciful and gracious, slow to anger and abounding in steadfast love and faithfulness" (v. 15). The conviction that those verses ought to be true led to the anguished cry of Ps 77:7–9:

> Will the Lord spurn forever, and never again be favorable?
> Has his steadfast love ceased forever?
> Are his promises at an end for all time?
> Has God forgotten to be gracious?
> Has he in anger shut up his compassion?

But Ps 103:8–14 introduces praise of the forgiving nature of God with a citation of the familiar words, "The Lord is merciful and gracious, slow to anger and abounding in steadfast love," and Ps 145:8 uses them as part of the praise of God's mighty works (cf. Ps 111:4). Finally, without anything like a direct quotation, the hymn to the forgiving God in Micah 7:18–20 is clearly reminiscent of Exod 34:6–7, although that is partly hidden in the NRSV, which translates *hesed* as "clemency" in v. 18 and "loyalty" in v. 20.

> Who is a God like you, pardoning iniquity
>   and passing over the transgression
>   of the remnant of your possession?
> He does not retain his anger forever,
>   because he delights in clemency.

> He will again have compassion upon us;
>> he will tread our iniquities under foot.
> You will cast all our sins into the depths of the sea.
> You will show faithfulness to Jacob
>> and unswerving loyalty to Abraham,
> as you have sworn to our ancestors
>> from days of old.

More will be said about some of these texts later, in the section called, "In the Meantime."

A possibly premature thought: Does what these Old Testament authors say about divine forgiveness have some relationship with what Paul says of justification, which is entirely the result of God's righteousness and in no sense deserved by us? "While we were yet sinners . . ." (Rom 5:8). We shall have to consider this later; but note that, like Genesis through Kings, Paul says very little about repentance.

Two Crises: B. The Exile

"The end has come upon my people Israel" (Amos 8:2). Early in the twentieth century James Cameron Todd wrote, in an introduction to the Old Testament, "The Old Testament is the epos of the Fall of Jerusalem. From the first verse of Genesis to the last of Malachi there rings through it the note of the Capture, the Sack, and the Destruction of the City by the Babylonian Army in 586 B.C." (1904, 1). There may be exceptional passages (consider the Song of Solomon), but it is certainly true that failure, what has brought about failure, and the question whether anything can reverse its results dominates much of the thinking of author after author in the Old Testament. We shall encounter in the section after this the anguish of individuals for whom life had gone wrong, but for the time being will continue to focus on the people Israel, chosen to live in covenant relationship with God, but with the fall of Samaria in 722 and of Jerusalem in 587, having evidently lost all that the covenant promised.

A few blamed God for it. "The LORD has destroyed without mercy all the dwellings of Jacob" (Lam 2:2). Ezekiel quoted the exiles as saying, "The parents have eaten sour grapes, and the children's teeth are set on edge" (Ezek 18:2). That is, why should *we* suffer for our ancestors' sins? The psalmist could find no acceptable explanation for the end of the Davidic dynasty: "But now you have spurned and rejected him; you are full of wrath against your anointed. You have renounced the covenant with your servant" (Ps 89:38–39a). Most of the authors of the Old Testament blamed Israel for it, however. In the early prophetic books the theme of forgiveness, when it appears at all, is a negative theme. Unlike Exodus and Numbers, where God forgives an unrepentant people in order to keep the covenant relationship in effect, the prophets spoke of inescapable punishment for the sins of Israel in the most devastating way—the threat of exile from the Promised Land.

Different circumstances called for a different theology. The author or authors of Exodus and Numbers offered a theological explanation of success in spite of human inadequacy. The people had survived the wilderness experience, had succeeded in establishing themselves in Canaan, and had achieved some security thanks to David. The stories of the golden calf and of rebellion in the wilderness insisted, contrary to normal human attitudes, that this was not something they deserved, but was the result of God's gracious willingness to forgive, in spite of their perennial unfaithfulness. The prophets, however, faced a major turning point in the history of the ancient Near East, one that would lead to a fatal crisis for Israel. They also offered a theological explanation of that new event. It would not be simply because Assyria and Babylonia had better armies. It would lead to the annulment of God's promises, and they believed that had to be God's doing. So, they spoke of deserved judgment, not of undeserved forgiveness. The judgment did come, but one of the most remarkable things about the Old Testament is the reappearance of forgiveness in the later messages of the prophets, and the evidence in history that forgiveness had in fact been granted.

In the mid-eighth century, prophets began to appear, announcing the impending end of the relationship between God and Israel. Assyria had begun its empire-building activities, which would lead to the fall of Samaria in 722 B.C., and the end of the Northern Kingdom. The message of the eighth and seventh century prophets was essentially, "There will be no forgiveness. You have been tried and found guilty, and the sentence will soon be executed." When they refer to the Exodus and Sinai traditions they claim that the grace of God, which had borne with an unworthy people in the past, had now been withdrawn.

> You only have I known of all the families of the earth;

therefore I will punish you for all your iniquities.
(Amos 3:2)

"Name her Lo-ruhamah, for I will no longer have pity on the house
of Israel or forgive them" (Hos 1:6). If the prophets knew the tradition of
Moses the intercessor, they found that they could not accomplish what
Moses had done. Amos tried and failed (Amos 7:1–9, and see below),
and God ordered Jeremiah not to attempt to intercede, for it was too
late (Jer 7:16; 14:11–12). In the late seventh and early sixth centuries,
when Babylon brought Judah's national existence to an end with the
destruction of Jerusalem, Zephaniah, Jeremiah, and Ezekiel offered the
same interpretation of that disaster.

Before turning to the prophets' analysis of their history, it will be
instructive to look at the interpretation offered by the Deuteronomistic
Historian in Joshua, Judges, Samuel, and Kings. This great work was
evidently completed not many years after the fall of Jerusalem (2 Kgs
25:27–30), and it makes the case that the divine promise had come to
nothing because of Israel's failures. The themes of repentance and forgiveness do not often appear in this long work, but their occurrences are
significant, and provide some background for our consideration of the
messages of the prophets.

The History records God's fulfillment of his promise to Abraham,
from the occupation of the land in Joshua and Judges to David's suc-
cesses in 1 and 2 Samuel, but beginning with the later years of David's
reign the story takes a downward turn, telling how the Northern and
Southern Kingdoms came to an end, and leading to such extreme expressions as, "Indeed, Jerusalem and Judah so angered the LORD that he
expelled them from his presence" (2 Kgs 24:20; cf. 23:27; 24:3). There is
a somewhat hopeful conclusion, with the account of king Jehoiachin's
release from house arrest in Babylon (2 Kgs 25:27–30), but there has
been debate over the question whether the Historian had any hope for
restoration of the covenant relationship. (Hoffman 1995)

For our purposes, the few occurrences of references to forgiveness
are significant. Except for 1 Kings 8, which will be the most important
passage, forgiveness is mentioned only four times, and repentance
only three times in all these pages. We shall consider a case of human
forgiveness later, Abigail's request of David (1 Sam 25:28). An unusual
prayer for divine forgiveness occurs in 2 Kgs 5:18, where Naaman the
Syrian, who has converted to Yahwism, asks God to forgive him if he

continues to bow before the Syrian god Rimmon as part of his official duties when he returns to Syria. The author simply reports this without comment as to whether God might grant such a request. The other two references are negative, and their location seems significant; at the beginning, when Joshua tells the Israelites gathered at Shechem, "You cannot serve the LORD, for he is a holy God. He is a jealous God; he will not forgive your transgressions or your sins" (Josh 24:19), and at the end, when the author begins to recount the fall of Jerusalem and claims the sins of king Manasseh were so exorbitant that "the LORD was not willing to pardon" (2 Kgs 24:4).

Repentance occurs only in an if-clause that introduces a speech of Samuel, "If you are returning to the LORD with all your heart, then put away the foreign gods . . ." (1 Sam 7:3), in a prophetic warning, which Israel and Judah did not heed, "Turn from your evil ways . . ." (2 Kgs 17:13), and in a commendation of king Josiah, "Before him there was no king like him who turned to the LORD with all his heart, with all his soul, and with all his might . . ." (2 Kgs 23:25).

For the historian, the Exodus-message of free pardon was of no help, for that had not happened in the story he had to recount. He believed in a forgiving God, but he was able to account for the disasters that had befallen his people with a theology that understood repentance to be a prerequisite for forgiveness. That theology is made clear in one passage that contains elements of hope, the prayer of Solomon at the dedication of the Jerusalem Temple, in 1 Kgs 8:22–53.

The long prayer asks God to "hear in heaven" and to intervene in order to make right seven needs that may occur in the future. The second, third, and seventh speak explicitly of sin, repentance, and forgiveness. The second and third speak of defeat in battle and of drought, which are believed to be the result of sin (vv. 33–36). The hope is that prayer in or addressed toward the Temple, and (in v. 35) turning (*šuv*) from their sin, will lead God to forgive. The seventh (vv. 46–53) contemplates exile as punishment for sin, but unlike the prophetic promises of restoration that we shall soon encounter, it expresses only a modest hope for forgiveness. It speaks again of repentance (vv. 47–48), and asks for forgiveness (v. 50) so that the exiles' captors may have compassion on them—and that is all.

> . . . if they repent with all their heart and soul in the land of
> their enemies, who took them captive, and pray to you toward

> their land, which you gave to their ancestors, the city that you
> have chosen, and the house that I have built for your name; then
> hear in heaven your dwelling place their prayer and their plea,
> maintain their cause and forgive your people who have sinned
> against you, and all their transgression that they have commit-
> ted against you; and grant them compassion in the sight of their
> captors, so that they may have compassion on them (for they are
> your people and heritage, which you brought out of Egypt, from
> the midst of the iron-smelter). (1 Kgs 8:48–51)

The Historian does appeal to the Exodus tradition in the hope that the
relationship with God may be restored, but does not think of forgiveness as undoing all the effects of sin, for he does not speak of a hope for
return to the land. He has added something we did not find in Exodus
and Numbers, namely personal change—"if they repent with all their
heart and soul"—but here also the ongoing effects of sin even on a forgiven people cannot be denied.

Amos

The Historian agreed with the explanation that the prophets, from Amos
to Ezekiel, had offered concerning disasters that had befallen Israel. It
was Israel's fault, divine punishment for persistent failure to obey the
provisions of the covenant. Amos first introduced the sorrowful theme
that would reappear in the messages of the prophets that followed
him. Its essence was: "You have not repented and you do not repent.
Therefore . . ." Valiant efforts have been made by very able scholars to
find a different message—an appeal for repentance so that judgment
might be avoided, but they must admit such a message is implicit, for
the prophets do not exactly say that. G. A. F. Knight commented, "It is
remarkable that men should read the prophets and suppose that their
call to Israel was: 'Repent, come back to God, and he will forgive you all
your sins'" (1959, 230), and recent studies have clearly shown that their
message was, with very few exceptions, that judgment was inevitable. A.
Vanlier Hunter, who produced a detailed study of the few exhortations
that do appear in the eighth and seventh century prophets, concluded,
"Normally, one would expect repentance to be efficacious and to help
determine the future, which lies at least partly open and is subject to
the interplay of divine and human decision. But another aspect of the

terribly radical stance of the classical prophets is that the immediate future is in their view no longer open but subject only to the decision of Yahweh" (1982, 278).

In the earliest of the prophetic books, however, there appears an apparent point of contact between Amos and Moses: Both offered prayers of intercession, asking forgiveness for Israel. The accounts of Amos's visions in 7:1–9; 8: 1–3 lead to a quite different result from Moses' prayers, for the forgiveness promised there appears to be only temporary, if it should even be called forgiveness. The first two of his visions depicted destruction, by a locust plague, then by cosmic fire. The last two called Amos' attention to objects, the names of which were used by God as word plays denoting his rejection of Israel (Gowan 1996, 406–7, 414). There is a downward progression, from Amos's plea, "forgive," then "cease," to which God responds, "It shall not be," to God's response in 8:2, "The end has come." The book provides no setting for the visions, nor any explanation for separating the fourth from the others by the account of Amos's meeting with Amaziah, in 7:10–17, so the conclusions we can draw from this account of attempted intercession are limited. That Amos understood the locust plague to be punishment for Israel's sins is indicated by his appeal to God to forgive (*salah* never means anything else), but he, like Moses, cannot claim Israel deserves forgiveness. "He is so small" is the only motive offered, and God is known for his concern for the weak. As in Exodus 32, we are told the Lord changed his mind (*nhm*, NRSV "relented"), but his response, "It shall not be," left Israel's actual status uncertain. This may be why Amos's second appeal was simply, "Cease!" The Lord once again relented, but for reasons we cannot guess the accounts of the third and fourth visions contain no reference to an effort on Amos's part to intercede. So far, forgiveness is not a part of Amos's message.

He speaks of failure to repent in 4:6–12, recounting a series of disasters that had beset Israel that, as Amos saw it, should have led them to ask, "What have we done to deserve this?" as people usually do. So, the refrain, "yet you did not return (*shuv*) to me" recurs five times, and the conclusion of the passage, "Prepare to meet your God, O Israel!" is not to be taken as good news. Thus we find in Amos no repentance and no forgiveness. The graciousness of God is offered only to those who "seek good and not evil," only as a possibility—"it may be," and at best only to the remnant of Joseph (5:14–15).

Hosea and Isaiah 1–39 contain a few references to repentance and forgiveness. The authorship of most of those passages has been much debated, because of the widespread assumption that promissory texts must be exilic or postexilic. Their origin and date need not be a critical matter for our consideration of the prophets' understanding of forgiveness, however, for no matter whether they come from the eighth century or later, they all presuppose exile. Hence there is no eighth or seventh century evidence in the prophetic books for a hope that divine forgiveness will avert the judgment Israel deserves. We shall simply consider the texts as part of the prophetic hope for eventual forgiveness of a people who have suffered the appropriate punishment for their sins, and can do so briefly, since the message is expressed most effectively from Jeremiah on.

Hosea

There are elements of hope in Hosea, but they are mingled with words of judgment that are as thoroughgoing as those found in Amos. Hosea makes extensive use of the Exodus tradition, and the first chapter reminds us in several ways of Exodus 32–34. The prophet's second child was to be named Lo-ruhama, usually translated "Not pitied," but *ruhamah* reminds us of *rahum*, that first attribute of God in Exod 34:7, "compassionate." Hosea now reverses it: No compassion, "for I will no longer have pity [or compassion] on the house of Israel or forgive [*nasa'*] them" (Hos 1:6). Hosea thus goes beyond Amos in making an outright denial of forgiveness. The complete reversal of what Moses had accomplished is confirmed by the name of Hosea's third child: Lo-ammi, "for you are not my people and I am not your God" (1:9). We are reminded of Exod 32:7–10, in which God refused to call Israel his people.

After these terrible words Hosea seems to contradict himself, in 1:10–11 (and see v. 7). There is evidence throughout the book that the work of this northern prophet was edited for the benefit of Judean readers (note the list of Judean kings in 1:1), and one likely explanation of the promises in the book is that they are the work of later redactors. If so, their work was not completely out of touch with Hosea's view of judgment, for he spoke of it as being inflicted for a disciplinary, corrective purpose. So, in chapter 2 he reversed the Exodus story, taking Israel back into the wilderness in order to restore the original relationship.

The closest he comes to speaking of forgiveness is in his use of *rapha'* "heal." It appears in a negative sense in 7:1, what God would have done if they had made it possible, but it is a promise for the future in 14:4: "I will heal their disloyalty [a word derived from *shuv*]; I will love them freely, for my anger has turned from them." We shall see from its occurrences elsewhere that "heal" is one of the synonyms for forgiveness, and that makes this verse of some importance, for it is the first one we have encountered that speaks of forgiveness as changing those who receive it. That will become an important theme as we continue working through the prophetic books.

The promise is preceded by a call for repentance in 14:1–2: "Return, O Israel to the LORD your God, for you have stumbled because of your iniquity. Take words with you and return to the LORD; say to him, Take away [*nasa'*] all guilt; accept that which is good, and we will offer the fruit of our lips." It immediately follows a terrible threat against Samaria (13:16), which did in fact come true, so if the promises in chapter 14 do come from Hosea they must represent a futile hope on his part. They are like the insights of later prophets, however, who looked beyond the time of judgment to a time of thoroughgoing forgiveness. The root *shuv*, which occurs several times in chapter 14 is one of Hosea's favorite terms, and in its various forms it can be used as a summary of the message of the book. Israel has turned to Baal, thus turned away from Yahweh (7:16). They refuse to return to Yahweh (7:10; 11:5b). Even though they claim to do so (2:7) their deeds do not permit it (5:4; 6:11–7:1). As a result, God will turn away from them (5:15), will requite (a form of *shuv*) them for their deeds (4:9; 12:2, 14), and will *take back* the grain, wine, wool, and flax (2:4), and they will return to Egypt (8:13; 9:3; 11:5). But there are also appeals to return to Yahweh (12:6; 14:1–2), and God turns back to them. In "I will not again destroy Ephraim" (11:9) it is *shuv* that is translated "again." God's anger will turn from them and he will heal their turning away (NRSV, disloyalty; 14:4), so Israel will finally be able to return to Yahweh (3:5), and be returned to their homes (11:11).

Isaiah 1–39

The sixth chapter of Isaiah contains the most appalling statement in Scripture about the inescapability of judgment. After the prophet had responded to the vision of the Lord who asked, "Whom shall I send?"

with "Here I am. Send me," he learned that his mission was to make sure that there would be no repentance, thus no reprieve:

> Make the mind of this people dull
>> and stop their ears,
>> and shut their eyes,
> so that they may not look with their eyes,
>> and listen with their ears,
> and comprehend with their minds,
>> and turn and be healed. (Isa 6:10)

As in Isaiah's contemporary, Hosea, "heal" is used of forgiveness, but it is not to happen. It is no wonder that Isaiah reacted with "How long, O LORD?" but God's response to that was completely negative. Note that in the same context Isaiah did receive God's assurance of personal forgiveness, which made it possible for him to respond to the call: "Now that this has touched your lips, your guilt has departed [*sur*] and your sin is blotted out [*kipper*]" (v. 7b). The verb *kipper*, which usually means to make atonement, is probably used because the altar is involved in the vision. Here there appears a sense of forgiveness that has not been a part of any of the texts discussed thus far. Isaiah's awareness of guilt (his people's and his own) is expressed in terms of uncleanness, so forgiveness must involve a personal change, an aspect that will become more important as we move chronologically through the prophetic books. Note that although the verbs of cleansing that will be used of forgiveness elsewhere do not appear, the NRSV alludes to Isaiah's feeling of uncleanness by choosing "blotted out" for *kipper*.

Although Isaiah's book is characterized by assurances that Jerusalem will not fall to the Assyrians, there is no question that Judah stands under God's judgment and forgiveness cannot be offered. "Surely this iniquity will not be forgiven [*kipper*] you until you die, says the LORD God of hosts" (22:14). Isaiah, like Amos and Hosea, recognized that the basis for judgment was refusal to repent: "The people did not turn to him who struck them, or seek the LORD of hosts" (9:13). "In returning and rest you shall be saved, in quietness and in trust shall be your strength. But you refused . . ." (30:15). The prophet even seems to appeal for no forgiveness in 2:9.

One passage, Isa 1:16–20, is often appealed to as evidence that prophets sometimes did call for repentance with a promise that judgment could be averted if the people changed.

Wash yourselves; make yourselves clean;
remove the evil of your doings from before my eyes;
cease to do evil, learn to do good;
seek justice, rescue the oppressed,
defend the orphan, plead for the widow.
Come now, let us argue it out, says the LORD:
though your sins are like scarlet, they shall become like snow;
though they are red like crimson, they shall become like wool.
If you are willing and obedient, you shall eat the good of the land;
but if you refuse and rebel, you shall be devoured by the sword;
for the mouth of the LORD has spoken.

Taken with the rest of the message of Isaiah's book, however, it seems more likely that it simply spells out God's basic requirement that might have saved them, but, as the rest of the book indicates, has not done so. At any rate, when this book does speak positively of repentance and forgiveness it is with reference to "that day," the uncertain time in the future, beyond the judgment, when God will make things right, the prophetic eschatology that will take on special importance in Jeremiah and the prophets that succeeded him. For example, what seems to be a present tense appeal: "Turn back to him whom you have deeply betrayed, O people of Israel," immediately becomes a reference to another time: "For on that day all of you shall throw away your idols of silver and idols of gold, which your hands have sinfully made for you" (31:6). A few other passages speak of repentance in the future: "Zion shall be redeemed by justice, and those in her who repent by righteousness" (1:27; cf. vv. 25–26). Isaiah's cryptic use of *shuv* in his son's symbolic name, Shear-jashub, "a remnant shall return" (to God?; from exile?; or both?) reappears in another promise for the future, "A remnant will return, the remnant of Jacob, to the mighty God" (10:21).

Forgiveness "in that day" is cleansing, in Isa 4:4: "The LORD has washed away [*rahats*] the filth of the daughters of Zion and cleansed [*dawah*] the bloodstains of Jerusalem from its midst by a spirit of judgment and by a spirit of burning." This may be compared with 1:25, which speaks of purging the effects of sin as the first step toward forgiveness: "I will turn my hand against you; I will smelt away your dross with lye and remove all your alloy"; and see the promise that follows in vv. 26–27. This imagery provided another way to speak of change within those who will be forgiven.

A rather cryptic oracle of promise appears in Isa 33:17–24. It speaks of a time when there will be a king once again in a new Jerusalem, which will surprisingly be graced with broad rivers and streams. All that is important for our purposes in this passage, however, is the conclusion: "And no inhabitant will say, 'I am sick'; the people who live there will be forgiven [*nasa'*] their iniquity" (33:24). Sickness is evidently considered to be a punishment for sin, a common point of view that we shall consider with care in connection with some of the Psalms, and later, in the New Testament. For the time being, the verse serves only as an indication that when the prophets spoke of an ideal future, forgiveness was a necessary part of it.

One of the most remarkable passages in the Old Testament speaks of forgiveness for Egypt (Isa 19:18–25; see Gowan 1998, 218 n. 118) The prophet here expressed a hope not exactly paralleled anywhere else, that the day will come when the Lord will say, "Blessed be Egypt my people, and Assyria the work of my hands, and Israel my heritage" (v. 25). Egypt's future history is described in vv. 19–22 as a parallel to Israel's early history. The altar in the center of the land and the pillar at its border reminds us of Josh 8:70 and 4:20. The savior whom the Lord will send when the Egyptians cry to him because of oppressors reminds us of the period of the Judges (e.g., Judg 3:9), and the pattern of striking and healing (v. 22) may allude to the pattern spelled out in Judges 2. But since "heal" is one of the synonyms for forgiveness we include this passage in our group of texts concerning eschatological forgiveness, even though nothing is said here of Egypt's sin.

Micah

The fourth book ascribed to an eighth century prophet, Micah, contains nothing about forgiveness except for the chapter that concludes the book. Whether Micah himself was the creator of the poem need not concern us, for it is different from either the words of judgment or the eschatological promises that have appeared in the other eighth century books. It is the lament of an individual, with numerous parallels to the Psalms of lament. At one point the poet confesses his sinfulness and admits he is worthy of punishment (7:8), but then makes the remarkable move of using "justice" terminology to speak of his conviction that God will take his side, even though he is undeserving.

"I must bear the indignation of the LORD, because I have sinned against him, until he takes my side [*yarib ribi* "pleads my case"] and executes judgment for me [*we 'asah mishpati*]. He will bring me out to the light; I shall see his vindication [*tsidqatho* "righteousness"]."

The chapter then concludes with a hymn of praise to the forgiving God, not quoting Exod 34:6–7, but using many of the same terms (7:18–20). It is more typical of the language and thought we shall consider in the part of this book called "In the Meantime," and will appropriately be recalled there. That it could be made the conclusion of a prophetic book that contains the terrible message, "Zion shall be plowed as a field" (3:12) is a reminder that even in the worst of times there were faithful individuals who continued to trust in the God who had revealed his true character at Sinai.

Jeremiah

Inescapable judgment will continue to be announced by Jeremiah and Ezekiel, but those prophets lived through the fall of Jerusalem in 587 B.C., and the presence in their books of powerful promises addressed to the people who had experienced and survived judgment makes a major contribution to the Old Testament message concerning forgiveness. They move from an insistence that God refuses to forgive in the present to a vision of a future beyond the time of judgment when forgiveness will be the first of many blessings.

The book of Jeremiah offers special challenges to the interpreter because of the presence in it of three distinct types of literature: poetic oracles comparable to those of the earlier prophets, prose speeches that are remarkably similar to the diction and thought of Deuteronomy and 1 and 2 Kings, and extended narratives concerning incidents in the life of the prophet. For our purposes it will not be necessary to rehearse the complex discussions of the relation of these types to the life of Jeremiah himself. An issue is created for us, however, by the fact that the oracles and the prose speeches ("sermons") do not use repentance and forgiveness in the same way in accounting for the end of Israel's existence as a nation. The question is usually put this way: Did Jeremiah at some point in his career call for repentance with the promise that it could avert disaster (Gowan 1998, 106)? I am inclined to agree with those who attribute the prose materials to reinterpretation of Jeremiah's message for the benefit of the exiles in Babylonia, with much more influence of Deuteronomistic theology than probably existed in Jeremiah's original words. Since the effort to reconstruct the career of Jeremiah can never lead to certain conclusions, and it is not crucial for our purposes to know what one person in the past believed, we can find a more helpful way to proceed than to discuss authorship. There is no question that the book contains two views of repentance. What is important for us is not who held those views but the fact that they existed in Judah in the late seventh and early sixth centuries.

The prose materials contain the same understanding of repentance and forgiveness that we found in the History. God had sent prophets to call his people to repentance, but they had not responded, so divine judgment was fully justified. Jeremiah's words in Jer 25: 4–7 and 35:15 are close echoes of 2 Kgs 17:13–18:

"I have sent to you all my servants the prophets, sending them persistently, saying, 'Turn [*šuv*] now every one of you from your evil way, and amend your doings, and do not go after other gods to serve them, and then you shall live in the land that I gave to you and to your ancestors.' But you did not incline your ear or obey me" (Jer 35:15).

This is not a message that we have found in the canonical prophets who preceded Jeremiah, but there may well have been other prophets who did preach this way, as the Historian claimed. Jeremiah's biographer puts the same open possibility into the prophet's speech in 26:3 and 36:3, 7: "It may be that when the house of Judah hears of all the disasters that I intend to do to them, all of them may turn [*šuv* from their evil ways, so that I may forgive [*salaḥ*] their iniquity and their sin" (36:3).

Two hypothetical situations are proposed in another prose passage, which contains an appeal to repent associated with a promise (Jer 18:5–11). The initial one assures the house of Israel that, even when God has decided to destroy a nation, turning from evil will lead God to change his mind. Here is the typical use of *hinnahem*, with God as subject, that we found in Exod 32:14; the move from justice to mercy. But this passage takes the unusual course of adding the opposite possibility; God will change his mind away from the intention to bless a nation when it persists in doing evil. (The verb is used in this way also in Gen 6:6, 7; 1 Sam 15:11, 29, 35.) These passages attribute to Jeremiah a familiar understanding of forgiveness. God desires repentance and is ready to forgive the sinner—in this case the sinful nation—who turns away from sin and toward righteousness. Israel had every opportunity to change its ways, down to the very last days of its national existence, when Jeremiah spoke.

This was certainly a more acceptable message than the one we found in the eighth century prophets and will find in the poetry of Jeremiah and the sermons of Ezekiel: that it is too late. There is no other way to interpret the oracles.

> See if you can find one person who acts justly and seeks truth—
> so that I may pardon [*salaḥ*] Jerusalem. (Jer 5:1)
> They have refused to turn back [*šuv*]. (5:3)
> Their apostasies [*mešuvoth*, "turnings-away"] are great. (5:6)
> How can I pardon [*salaḥ*] you? Your children have forsaken me,
> and have sworn by those who are no gods. (5:7)

Judah's failure to repent is lamented again in 8:4–6; 15:7; and 23:14. Jeremiah seems to have reached the extreme conclusion, for an Israelite, that his people did not have the ability to repent:

> Can Ethiopians change their skin or leopards their spots?
> Then also you can do good who are accustomed to do evil.
> (13:23)

> The heart is devious above all else;
> It is perverse—Who can understand it? (17:9; cf. 6:10)

So, for the immediate future, there is no hope.

Interpreters who claim that Jeremiah did preach repentance early in his career and turned to this desperate message only later appeal to Jer 3:6–4:4, a lengthy passage concerning "return" that speaks of a new future in 3:12–14, 22; 4:1–2. It is important to observe, however, that this passage makes a clear distinction between Judah and Israel, the Northern Kingdom that had come to an end a hundred years earlier.

> Then the LORD said to me: Faithless Israel has shown herself
> less guilty than false Judah. Go, proclaim these words toward
> the north, and say:
> Return, faithless Israel, says the LORD.
> I will not look on you in anger,
> for I am merciful, says the LORD;
> I will not be angry forever. (3:11–12)

Jeremiah was concerned not just about Judah, but also about the remnant of the Northern Kingdom, those who had already suffered the judgment. This passage expresses some hope for them, but not for Judah. The prose section, 3:6–11 (here prose and poetry seem to express the same point of view), claims Judah has been worse than Israel and remains unrepentant, and the oracle that introduces this passage, 3:1–5, uses the law concerning a divorced wife in Deut 24: 1–4 to rule out amnesty for the Southern Kingdom. The divorced wife who had married another man and been divorced by him was prohibited from returning to the first husband. Jeremiah draws an analogy; Judah had abandoned the Lord for many lovers, "and would you return to me? says the LORD" (3:1).

This discussion of the two Kingdoms points toward the positive place of forgiveness in the message of the prophets. Even for the Northern Kingdom there remains hope. Judgment does not mean the complete failure of God's work to create a faithful people. "Return, O faithless children, I will heal [rapha'] your faithlessness" (3:22). For Judah, it would be those who experienced the fullest course of judgment, the exiles in Babylonia, who would be offered the message of eventual forgiveness. Again, there is discussion about attributing all or any of the promises to Jeremiah, but authorship need not concern us. The book contains a vitally important message about forgiveness in the future, and it does not matter theologically who originated it. The eschatological passages in the prophetic books challenge the apparent completeness and finality of the disasters that reached their climax with the fall of Jerusalem in 587 B.C. Amos had said of Israel, "The end has come," and Jeremiah's words against Judah were no less grim. What basis could there be for hope, when the prophetic analysis of their people's failures was so thoroughgoing? The answer is surely to be found in their belief that Yahweh's will could not be completely thwarted by anything people might do. So, they claimed there will certainly come a new divine initiative, to make right all that had gone wrong. It would begin with restoration to the Promised Land, for loss of the land had been the surest sign that the covenant relationship was no longer in effect. Prophetic eschatology would offer a comprehensive picture of God's eventual transformation of all that he had made, in order to bring an end to evil, but it would be inappropriate to outline all of that here (Gowan 1987). Forgiveness will play an essential part in that transformation, and we shall see that the prophets' understanding of the nature of eschatological forgiveness supplements and confirms the true nature of the relationship between God and human beings already suggested by Exodus 32–34.

It may seem at first that the most surprising aspect of prophetic eschatology is that the promises are unconditional. The pattern of repentance followed by forgiveness that we have found elsewhere is missing, but that is understandable. Appeals for repentance have not worked—"The heart is devious above all else; it is perverse—who can understand it? (Jer 17:9)—so if anything is to go right it will be God who does it. Each of the promissory texts that we find in Jeremiah thus begins with God's initiative. Jeremiah's promises dealt with an issue left unresolved in Exodus 34 and in the promises contained in earlier prophetic books. Most Old Testament authors had a relatively optimistic view of human potential. People could obey God if only they were determined to do so. Deuteronomy 30 can thus appeal to Israel to repent, assuming that is possible, as we shall see in the next section. Moses, however, had asked forgiveness of a stiff-necked people (Exod 34:9). Jeremiah certainly would have agreed with that judgment of them, and with God's own judgment, recorded in the epilogue to the story of the Flood: "the inclination of the human heart is evil from youth" (Gen 8:21). God's compassion had enabled the relationship with that stiff-necked people to continue for a long time, but as the prophets foresaw the end of the nations Israel and Judah, they did not attribute the disaster to the power of Assyrian and Babylonian armies, as we would do, but they concluded that a relationship so consistently violated by one party could not be continued forever. Forgiveness had mitigated punishment and had kept the covenant in effect, but something more was needed if the relationship between God and humans could be what God intended; so Jeremiah concluded.

A few texts in his book thus represent a major turning point in Israel's thinking about forgiveness. In the introduction to this book, three aspects of forgiveness in the Old Testament were listed, and one of them appears with prominence now—cleansing; i.e. change of the human personality in order to make obedient living possible. Jeremiah and Ezekiel will speak of God's intention to change the heart (the seat of the "rational will," i.e. the ability to reason and decide what to do), now dominated by the evil inclination, with sin inscribed on it. Jeremiah does not always associate that transformation explicitly with forgiveness, but the two are certainly closely related, and we shall have to think about how they are related after examining each of the texts.

The letter to the exiles recorded in Jeremiah 29 does not speak explicitly of repentance and forgiveness, but forgiveness is implicit, for in it the prophet promises a restoration of the relationship between God and people (vv. 10–14). There are no conditions; in seventy years, they are told, God will bring them back to Jerusalem (29:10). Actually, it will be their children who will go back; the number seventy, the hoped-for life span (Ps 90:10), emphasized that. God has plans for their welfare, for a future with hope. Then, when they search for him with all their heart he will let them find him. How it might be possible for them to do that is not said, but Jeremiah elsewhere will say that God will first change the heart. It is not likely, then, that this text puts the initiative on the people.

In chapter 24, the exiles who had gone to Babylonia in 597 and the people left in Jerusalem are compared with baskets of good and of inedible figs. What God says of the "good figs" leads us into the most distinctive part of the prophetic message. "Like these good figs, so I will regard as good the exiles from Judah" (v. 5). The verb translated "regard" (*nkr* hifil) could mean to acknowledge them for what they really are: good (as in Deut 21:17; Isa 61:9; 63:16), but that would be a remarkable thought to find in Jeremiah. In Dan 11:39 the verb is used of those who acknowledge the legitimacy of the arch-tyrant, who is certainly not legitimate, according to the author. Proverbs 34:19 says that God does not regard the rich more than the poor, and these two references suggest that the verb can refer to how one is treated, rather than one's own qualities. That is what Jer 24:6 goes on to say: "I will set my eyes on them for good," followed by the promise of restoration to the land, then a new promise, the gift of the ability to be God's people. "I will give them a heart to know that I am the LORD; and they shall be my people and I will be their God, for they shall return to me with their whole heart" (v. 7). The day is coming, Jeremiah says, when the heart, which he has identified as the source of all that has gone wrong, will be changed, so that knowledge of God, that term frequently used to denote the relationship God desires, will become possible. Immediately the covenant formulary follows: "they shall be my people and I will be their God." Several commentators have remarked on what a revolutionary passage this is, in the context of Jeremiah's repeated and thoroughgoing message of judgment. The future will be different, it will begin with the exiles in Babylonia, it will require remaking the human will, and it will be entirely the result of God's initiative. Then, "they shall return to me with their whole heart." The order of the sentence is certainly correct: first, God's work, then human response is possible. It is true that *ki* "for" is ambiguous. It might mean "if they return with their whole heart," as Drinkard claims (Craigie, et al. 1991, 360), thus making repentance a condition for God's blessing, but this is doubtful, given what Jeremiah has said about the heart (note the "evil heart" in 3:17; 7:24; 11:8; 18:12, in addition to the texts cited above). This "return" is the result, not the cause (Fretheim 2002, 351; McKane 1986, 609).

It seems remarkable that these two promises, and the one that will follow, do not speak of sin and the need to overcome its effects, so there is no explicit reference to forgiveness. They are entirely forward-looking, and the need to overcome the effects of the past is only alluded to by the references to a gift in the future of a new heart. Eventually we shall see, however, that there is a series of parallels that link these texts and make each one relevant to the promise of forgiveness.

The promise is repeated in Jer 32:36–44. After reiterating to Jeremiah his decision to judge Jerusalem for the sins of its people (vv. 27–35), God speaks of the future in familiar terms. There will be restoration from exile (v. 37), the covenant will be re-established (vv. 38, 40), and "I will give them one heart and one way, that they may fear me for all time, for their own good and the good of their children after them" (v. 39). Then, they will not "turn from me," using *shuv* of apostasy rather than repentance (v. 40). Fear of God, rather than knowledge of God is the result of the new heart here, but the terms are related. The fear of the Lord is the beginning of wisdom, after all (Job 28:28; Ps 111:10; Prov 1:7; 9:10), and as the term is used in Scripture it means something like "reverent obedience" (cf. Deut 10:12). Although the sins of past and present have just been recapitulated in the preceding paragraph, this paragraph does not say what God will do about them except implicitly, with reference to one heart and one way. Once again, the change will be entirely God's work, in no way dependent on what humans might be capable of.

The promises continue in Jeremiah 33, with some new terminology and with a promise of forgiveness. Jerusalem is still the focus of God's concern. Twice the word "heal" (*rapha'*) is used, of the city and of the populace. "I am going to bring it recovery and healing; I will heal them and reveal to them abundance of prosperity and security" (v. 6). Here, it probably refers to all the good that God intends to do, rather than specifically forgiveness, although that is included, as v. 8 reveals. "I will cleanse them from all the guilt of their sin against me, and I will forgive all the guilt of their sin and rebellion against me." Rebuilding takes the place of return from exile (v. 7), and the sins that have led to the desolation of Jerusalem now are central to the passage. The three most common words for sin that we have observed elsewhere appear five times in a single verse. Forgiveness is emphasized by the use of two verbs, *tahar* "cleanse" and *salah* "forgive." The new heart is not mentioned in this text. Could it be that the cleansing and forgiveness are equivalent to the gift of a new heart? That goes beyond what one can say with certainty about these verses, but fear of the Lord is once again the result (v. 9), and the next passage we deal with, Jer 31:31–34, plus Ezekiel's references to cleansing provide some support for the idea.

Familiar terminology appears in Jer 31:31–34, formulated in a new way.

> The days are surely coming, says the LORD, when I will make a new covenant with the house of Israel and with the house of Judah. It will not be like the covenant that I made with their ancestors when I took them by the hand to bring them out of the land of Egypt—a covenant that they broke, though I was their husband, says the LORD. But this is the covenant that I will make with the house of Israel after those days, says the LORD: I will put my law within them, and I will write it on their heart; and I will be their God, and they shall be my people. No longer shall they teach one another, or say to each other, "Know the LORD," for they shall all know me, from the least of them to the greatest, says the LORD; for I will forgive their iniquity, and remember their sin no more.

Restoration to the land does not appear in this paragraph, but is promised in vv. 21–30 and 38–40. The first unique element is to denote the covenant that God will restore as "new." The Sinai covenant had been broken, as all the prophets had insisted, and the possibility of re-establishing it was very unlikely given Jeremiah's analysis of human potential. So there must be something new about it, and once again the heart appears. "I will put my law within them, and I will write it on their hearts," then the covenant formulary can be proclaimed (v. 33). As in 24:7, the result will be knowledge of God, described now in a most extravagant way (v. 34). No more teaching or exhortation will be needed, for it will have been accomplished. And, the climax of the passage is, "for I will forgive their iniquity, and remember their sin no more." Here, as in 33:6–9, the need to deal with the past is prominent, so the promise of forgiveness appears, but how comprehensive is the gift of forgiveness, as Jeremiah speaks of it in these two texts? Is it the first step, preliminary to and making possible the gift of a new heart, or is writing the law on the heart a *part* of the act of forgiveness? How powerful is *kî* "for" at the beginning of this clause? Does it determine everything that precedes it? This does not seem to be a question that can be answered with any certainty, based on the Jeremiah texts, but they do raise it, and what we shall find elsewhere in both Testaments will indicate that it is not an insignificant question.

One passage remains, only two verses (50:19–20), beginning with the familiar promise of return to the land and continuing with a rather astonishing prediction of forgiveness. "In those days and at that time, says the LORD, the iniquity of Israel shall be sought, and there shall be none; and the sins of Judah, and none shall be found; for I will pardon [*salah*] the remnant that I have spared." Does this speak of an eschatological forgiveness that will leave Israel and Judah unable to sin? Some of the New Testament authors will struggle with that idea. Commentators generally conclude that it speaks of God erasing the past so that the future is in no way determined by former sins, rather than making sin impossible in the future. For no obvious reason, only two of the hopes for Israel's future are expressed here, but they represent the essentials, as Israel saw it: physical—a place to live, and spiritual—the ability to live rightly.

Ezekiel

This prophet experienced the judgment that had been foretold. He survived the fall of Jerusalem to the Babylonian army in 597 B.C. and the forced march to Babylonia with the first group of exiles. The sufferings this involved (although he never spoke of them) may partly explain the severity of much of his language. It is not surprising that this younger contemporary of Jeremiah proclaimed a message that was similar in many ways, but Ezekiel's methods and parts of his message were highly original. Both prophets were certain that Jerusalem would be destroyed, and that everything Judeans had depended on for their national existence would be lost. Both spoke of internal change as an essential part of the new future God had authorized them to proclaim. Ezekiel, however, had the new commission to begin the reconstruction—better, the new creation—of the people of God among the exiles, those who had gone through the judgment. It was an unpromising group with which to begin. God himself defined them as people of "a hard forehead and a stubborn heart" (3:7; cf. 2:3–7), and that also partly accounts for Ezekiel's special methods, for it was not easy to get a hearing. His lengthy efforts to persuade the exiles that they were not going to return home and that Jerusalem would certainly be destroyed need not concern us at this point, except for one text that tends to sum up the work of all his predecessors, with respect to forgiveness.

His allegory of Jerusalem as a corroded pot mixes metaphors rather confusingly, but at the end he introduces a term that was part of his priestly heritage, cleansing (24:13). "Because I would have cleansed [*tahar*] you and you were not cleansed from your filthiness [*tem'ah*] you shall not be cleansed any more till I have satisfied my fury upon you" (RSV).

These are the same terms that Ezekiel uses when he promises forgiveness in 36:25, 33; 37:23. Cleansing (*tahar* or *kavas*) literally referred to the ritual acts carried out by priests, with *tem'ah* "uncleanness" its object, but uncleanness frequently came to be used metaphorically of sin. Isaiah speaks of his "unclean lips" (Isa 6:5), uncleanness is associated with transgression and sin in Lev 16:16, and Ezekiel frequently speaks of idolatry as uncleanness (or defilement; e.g., 14:11; 20:7, 18, 31; 22:3–4). So, verbs of cleansing will sometimes be used with sin as their object (Lev 16:30; Ps 51:2, 7, 10; Prov 20:9; Jer 33:8), and this is Ezekiel's chosen metaphor.

Because clean and unclean were frequently ritual terms without moral content it should be helpful at this point to clarify two distinct uses of the terms, as they have been defined by recent studies (Klawans 2000, 15, 27). Ritual uncleanness comes from contact with various natural substances, is contagious but temporary, and can be removed by bathing and sometimes waiting for a fixed period of time. No guilt is associated with it; it happens to everyone. Moral uncleanness is the result of sinful acts, specifically idolatry, murder, and forbidden sexual acts. It is permanent; no ritual act can remove it. Although the same terms are used of both kinds of cleanness and uncleanness, the two states are quite different. To be morally clean is associated with righteousness (Job 4:17; 17:9) and freedom from sin (Prov 20:9; cf. Gen 35:2: Lev 16:30; Josh 22:17; Ps 51:2; Jer 13:27; 33:8; Ezek 36:33; 37:23), so it is a quality of one's character and behavior.

It was possible to speak of cleansing oneself, i.e. of true repentance (Gen 35:2; Lev 16:30; Josh 22:17; Isa 1:16), but some denied that possibility (Job 4:17; Prov 20:9; Ps 73:13). In Psalm 51, which we shall consider in the next section, cleansing is the chosen metaphor for forgiveness, as it is in Ezekiel (note that the two terms are equated in Jer 33:8). In both sources it seems that forgiveness, understood as cleansing, involves a change of one's character. As ritual cleansing restored one to a normal state, so forgiveness restored to one the ability to obey, to lead a righteous life. But according to Ezek 24:13, God's efforts to cleanse had been successfully resisted, so for now, there will not be another offer of forgiveness.

Jerusalem fell to the Babylonians again, in 587, and much of the city was destroyed. When the news reached the exiles of 597 (33:21), all seemed to be lost. Their saying, "Our bones are dried up, and our hope is lost, we are cut off completely" (37:11), was confirmed by Ezekiel's vision of the valley of dry bones. Indeed, Israel was dead, and the surprising question that came to the prophet was "Can these bones live" (37:3)? Does God intend to raise the dead? Answer: "I am going to open your graves, and bring you up from your graves, O my people; and I will bring you back to the land of Israel" (v. 12). Ezekiel's work thus became radically different from that of the prophets who preceded him, for it was his task to contribute to the birth of a new people. As a result, his book contains two kinds of messages concerning forgiveness: eschatological promises, and challenges to repent. The promises are clearly in continuity with those of Jeremiah, but calls for repentance are something new, possible because God was already at work to do a new thing.

Ezekiel's original ways of speaking of forgiveness have led to various interpretations of the texts that concern us, so it may be helpful to gather and compare the various terms that occur in the book. The most common words for "forgive," *salah* and *nasa'*, do not appear. There is one occurrence of *kipper*, in 16:63, where "forgive" seems to be the appropriate translation. "Cleanse" (*tahar*) is an important term for Ezekiel, whose priestly background is evident when he speaks of ritual cleansing elsewhere (e.g., 22:26; 39:12, 14, 16; 43:20–23; 44:23, 26; 45:18). But the term is used in a moral sense in 35:25, "I will sprinkle clean water upon you, and you shall be clean from all your uncleannesses, and from all your idols I will cleanse you." That this cleansing is forgiveness is more explicit in 36:33, "On the day that I cleanse you from all your iniquities . . ." In 36:29 God promises to "save" Israel from all their uncleannesses, and in 37:23 "save" is used in parallel with "cleanse." The familiar Christian idea of being saved from sin seldom occurs in the Old Testament, but it does appear twice in Ezekiel. It has often been noted that Ezekiel does not speak of God in the terms of Exod 34:6–7, leading to frequent comments about the harshness of the God he speaks for. There is just one occurrence of "mercy" (*raham*) in a forgiveness text. "Now I will restore the fortunes of Jacob, and have mercy on the whole house of Israel; and I will be jealous for my holy name" (39:25). God's memory is also referred to with the sense of forgiveness: "None of the sins that they have committed shall be remembered against them" (33:16; cf. the positive use of remember in 16:60).

Ezekiel 36 contains a quite comprehensive picture of the transformative work God intends to do in the future. Even more strongly than his predecessors, Ezekiel emphasizes that the only basis for a new future is to be found in the character of God: "It is not for your sake, O house of Israel, that I am about to act, but for the sake of my holy name, which you have profaned among the nations to which you came" (36:22).

"I will sprinkle clean water upon you, and you shall be clean from all your uncleannesses, and from all your idols I will cleanse you. A new heart I will give you, and a new spirit I will put within you; and I will remove from your body the heart of stone and give you a heart of flesh. I will put my spirit within you, and make you follow my statutes and be careful to observe my ordinances" (vv. 25–27).

Israel has nothing to offer but defilement, but God's holiness will be manifested when he brings them back to their land (v. 24), cleanses them (especially from idolatry; vv. 25, 33), gives them a new heart and a new spirit (v. 26), which makes obedience possible (v. 27), restores the covenant relationship (v. 28), and renews the fertility of the land (vv. 29–30, 34–36). The reaction to all these blessings will be, "Then you shall remember your evil ways and your dealings that were not good;

and you shall loathe yourselves for your iniquities and your abominable deeds" (v. 31).

Ezekiel's distinctive language leads to many questions that cannot be ignored. We shall focus on 36:22–36 because of its comprehensiveness, calling attention where appropriate to the other forgiveness promises (16:59–63; 20:40–44; 37:21–28; 39:25–29). What was largely implicit in the promises of the other prophetic books—that there is no basis for restoration in human behavior—is made emphatically explicit in Ezekiel. "It is not for your sake, O house of Israel, that I am about to act" (36:22). What "for your sake" (*lᵉmaʿan*) means is made explicit in 20:44: "when I deal with you for my name's sake, not according to your evil ways, or corrupt deeds." God's motive, expressed in 36:23 and elsewhere, to sanctify his great name, has been judged quite harshly by many commentators. Not to dwell on it at length here, we may let Daniel Block speak for others:

"The modern reader may find Yahweh's apparent heartlessness at this point disturbing, if not offensive. Yahweh looks like a stuffy egotistical monarch, upset that his subjects have not given him the honor he demands. His response hardly enhances his image. Absent is any compassion toward a bleeding nation, any mercy, or any hint of forgiveness. Absent also is any reference to the covenant promises" (1998, 352).

Keith Carley has expressed another opinion, with which this writer is inclined to agree: "It should be remembered that he [Yahweh] is portrayed as a God who showed compassion to a repulsive outcast and lavished his attentions on an undeserving Israel . . . Also, when the prophet speaks of Yahweh acting 'for the sake of his name' he was alluding not to divine self-interest, but to the necessity of Yahweh vindicating his character as a God of compassion and forgiveness, as well as of uncompromising wrath against the impenitent" (1975, 59).

Is there in fact no hint of forgiveness here, as Block claims? Obviously, it depends on one's definition. I find here the remission of punishment, the re-establishment of the covenant relationship, and personal transformation—the three aspects of forgiveness as it appears in Scripture. The problem is the sensitivity of "the modern reader" to Ezekiel's language, as Block admits, but more can be said about *lemaʿan*, which may show that Ezekiel does not make God appear to be as uncaring as the translation "not for your sake" suggests. It can mean "with reference to" and "on account of," as well as "for the sake of." The last translation suggests "for God's benefit," not Israel's, and this is supported by God's reference to concern for his name and sanctifying his name in vv. 21 and 23. But the Psalmists ask God to help them for the sake of his loving kindness (6:4; 44:26; 109:21) or his righteousness (143:11; cf. Isa 43:21), i.e., "on account of" or in accordance with God's character (note the inclusion of forgiveness in Isa 43:25). The term in Ezek 36:22, 32 may thus also include a reference to Israel's character—"not on your account"—character which stands in a striking contrast to that revealed in God's holy name. The positive side of the contrast, which Ezekiel emphasizes so strongly, is the insistence that God remains faithful to "his own intrinsic nature," (Eichrodt 1970, 496) and that God has the power to carry out the sweeping promises contained in this part of his book. As the oracle in 37:1–14 concludes: "I the LORD have spoken and I have done it, says the LORD" (RSV).

In the day to come God, entirely for his own reasons, will revoke the punishment of exile, the first step in forgiveness. "I will take you from the nations, and gather you from all the countries, and bring you into your own land" (36:24, 26a, 29b–30, 33–38; cf. 11:17; 20:42; 37:21, 25; 39:23). Then comes the promise of internal change, the necessary transformation of human character that will make obedience possible:

"I will sprinkle clean water upon you, and you shall be clean from all your uncleannesses, and from all your idols I will cleanse you. A new heart I will give you, and a new spirit I will put within you; and I will remove from your body the heart of stone and give you a heart of flesh. I will put my spirit within you, and make you follow my statutes and be careful to observe my ordinances" (36:25–27; cf. 11:19–20; 37:23; 39:29).

Jeremiah had spoken of a new covenant to be written on the heart (Jer 31:31–34); Ezekiel elaborates the idea. Recalling that the heart was used in Hebrew to refer to the rational will, we understand Ezekiel's imagery of the heart of stone as a vivid way to speak of the present inability to make right decisions. That is a loss of true humanity, as God intended it, for the new heart will be a heart of flesh. Added to it will be the gift of a new spirit, meaning the ability to act on the right decisions the new heart will make. This takes forgiveness to a new level, for it does not only deal with the past, so that the future need not be dictated by past sins, it also promises to change the sinner so that a new future will truly be possible. And this hope came to two men who lived under the most hopeless circumstances, Jeremiah and Ezekiel. Eichrodt has summarized the meaning of these verses very effectively:

> But forgiveness must on no account be limited to a forensic acquittal from guilt, as if that exhausted its whole meaning. Within the context of ch. 18, such an acquittal was the main point at stake, without which there could be no certainty of a new future. But acquittal did not exclude either the enslaving effects of habitual alienation from God nor the possibility of backsliding. And so the marvellous deepening of fellowship with God as a result of the implanting of the divine nature in man's heart means the revelation of the full extent of God's action of forgiveness, by which the will that decides in faith is assured that it will reach its goal in spite of all human weakness. (1970, 501–2)

The restoration of the broken relationship between God and his people is promised many times, first, in ch. 36, with the covenant formulary, "you shall be my people, and I will be your God" (v. 28b; also 11:20; 16:60, 62; 37:23, 27). Other passages speak of the covenant explicitly (16:60, 62; 37:26). The new relationship is alluded to in other ways, as well: "My dwelling place shall be with them . . . when my sanctuary is among them forevermore" (37:27a, 28b). "I will never again hide my face from them" (39:29a).

The expected human reaction to God's restorative work surprises contemporary readers. It will not be a sense of joy and peace, according to Ezekiel, but shame and self-loathing (36:31–32; 16:61, 63; 20:43). The NRSV seems to contradict that in 39:26, reading, "They shall forget their shame," but the reading they moved to the margin, "They shall bear their shame," is more likely to be original. This does in fact correspond to the actual experience of receiving forgiveness, however, as Calvin noted long ago: "And surely the more any one has tasted of the grace of God, the more ready he is to condemn himself, and as unbelief is proud, so the more any one proceeds in the faith of God's grace, he is thus humbled more and more before him" (1850, 2:184). Contrary to the pattern known so well from the New Testament, then, in these eschatological passages repentance follows forgiveness. Note the relationship that is drawn between repentance and one's former sins in one who has received a right mind by true faith, in the Second Helvetic Confession (Ch. 14):

WHAT IS REPENTANCE? By repentance we understand (1) the recovery of a right mind in sinful man awakened by the Word of the Gospel and the Holy Spirit, and received by true faith, by which the sinner immediately acknowledges his innate corruption and all his sins accused by the Word of God; and (2) grieves for them from his heart, and not only bewails and frankly confesses them before God with a feeling of shame, but also (3) with indignation abominates them; and (4) now zealously considers the amendment of his ways and constantly strives for innocence and virtue in which conscientiously to exercise himself all the rest of his life.

Among the many recent studies of shame in the ancient world, Jacqueline Lapsley's is the most helpful for our present concerns. The details of her study do not need to be rehearsed here. One of her conclusions is worth citing, as a parallel, in quite different language, to the early texts just cited:

But the inversion of conventional thinking about shame goes even further: the very capacity to experience shame constitutes a salvific act by Yahweh—it is a gift from God. This disgrace-shame is a gift from God because it strips the people of their delusions about themselves, their old self disintegrates, paving the way for the people's identity to be shaped in a new way by the self-knowledge that results from the experience of shame. And this new identity, in which the people see themselves as "they really are," i.e., as Yahweh sees them, will ultimately led to the restoration of their relationship with Yahweh. (2000, 145)

Ezekiel's keen insight, which has been validated by experience, is that it is only when one is convinced that forgiveness is possible that one can fully acknowledge one's sinfulness, able to see oneself truthfully and thus gain the fully repentant spirit. He does not use the traditional term *shuv* "turn, return" here, as he will elsewhere, but by "shame" he is surely referring to an inevitable aspect of true repentance.

Having spoken of the eschatological gift of a new heart and new spirit, elsewhere in the book Ezekiel urges his people to *get themselves* a new heart and a new spirit (18:31). Do the texts come from different authors, does Ezekiel contradict himself, or has he changed his mind? One way to read his appeals for repentance, which will be followed here, is to take them as part of his work as a pastor to a defeated people, in the effort to overcome their hopelessness and their cynicism. We have just seen Ezekiel's claim that full awareness of one's sinfulness will only become true after God's restorative work. Chapter 18 begins with one of the exiles' proverbs that shows they were in fact not fully aware of their sinfulness: "The parents have eaten sour grapes, and the children's teeth are set on edge" (18:2). "Why should we suffer for our parents' sins?" they were asking. Ezekiel's response first took the form of a series of cases, citing traditional law and dealing with them as judicial process would do, in order to insist that each generation is judged strictly according to its own behavior (vv. 4–20). Of course, it is not literally true that we do not suffer because of our ancestors' sins or benefit from their righteousness. We do, and note that they exiles actually want that to be true (v. 19), although they claim to be complaining, for that would enable them to avoid accepting responsibility for what has happened. But Ezekiel dwelt on individual responsibility in order to move toward his real point: change is possible, and since that is true one can move beyond one's sins. So, his second set of cases (vv. 21–28) concern individuals who "turn," toward or away from wickedness, with the assurance that the past can be *revoked!* He uses no forgiveness vocabulary, but in another of his highly original ways speaks of the possibility. God's most passionate speech, in the whole book, appears at this point:

"Repent and turn from all your transgressions; otherwise iniquity will be your ruin. Cast away from you all the transgressions that you have committed against me, and get yourselves a new heart and a new spirit! Why will you die, O house of Israel? For I have no pleasure in the death of anyone, says the Lord GOD. Turn, then, and live" (vv. 30b–32).

We might expect that Calvin would have been troubled by "get yourselves a new heart and a new spirit," since the free gift of God in Ezekiel 36 was much more in accord with his theology, but he found truth in this passage as well. He said God instructs us in what is right, what we ought to do, not merely in what we are able to do (1850, 2:261–64).

Much more could be written on ch. 18 and the related passages, and indeed there is a substantial literature on them, but as we trace the significant changes in the understanding of divine forgiveness that appear in the prophetic books it may be enough to recognize that these parts of Ezekiel are addressed to a people who no longer stand under inevitable judgment. Ezekiel began to work with a people for whom the future was open, so we are already looking forward to the next section of this book: "In the Meantime."

Second Isaiah

The anonymous prophet to the second generation of exiles offered promises of divine forgiveness, but the message of Isaiah 40–55 does not begin that way. The initial good news is, You have been punished enough. The penalty is paid (*niṣrah* paid off). Now restoration is at hand. They have not been forgiven, according to the prophet, but have suffered the punishment for their sins in full, and even more: "She has received from the LORD's hand double for all her sins" (40:2). This may be a reference to provisions in the law for both punishment and payment of damages for certain crimes (Exod 22:1, 7, 9; 2 Sam 12:6). But forgiveness is emphatically promised in two other passages. God reintroduces himself in a way that reminds us of Exod 34:6–7, although the vocabulary is different: "I, I am He who blots out your transgressions for my own sake, and I will not remember your sins" (43:25). God wipes out (*mahah*) the record of Israel's guilt, here and in the next passage, 44:21–22. He will not remember their sins, but he will remember *them*: "O Israel, you will not be forgotten by me. I have swept away [*mahah*] your transgressions like a cloud, and your sins like mist; return to me, for I have redeemed you." Notice that the call to return comes after the assurance that past sins no longer bar the way to God, and that return is possible because, "I have redeemed [*ga'al*] you." Here is a new verb to be used with reference to forgiveness. The prophet alludes to God's act of freeing Israel from slavery in Egypt, called redemption elsewhere (e.g., Exod 15:13; Deut 7:8; 2 Sam 7:23; Mic 6:4). It probably has a double meaning here, referring both to the imminent release of the exiles from captivity in Babylonia, and also to release from the burden of sin. At one point the prophet takes up the kind of appeal for change that we found in Ezekiel 18, which makes repentance lead to forgiveness: "Seek the LORD while he may be found, call upon him while he is near; let the wicked forsake their way, and the unrighteous their thoughts; let them return to the LORD, that he may have mercy [*raham*] on them, and to our God, for he will abundantly pardon [*salah*]" (55:6–7).

Isaiah 52:13—53:12 takes a wholly new approach to sin and forgiveness, one that appears nowhere else in the Old Testament. English translations of Isa 52:13–53:12 do not contain the words "forgive" or "pardon," but they speak of sin, iniquity, and transgression, of healing, of making intercession, and even of being made righteous, so we need to try to understand what this unique passage may be saying about our subject. This is another case where much of the scholarly discussion of a passage can be bracketed, for our purposes, since it contributes only a little to our concerns about forgiveness. Indeed, we would like to be able to answer with certainty the most debated question, who is this servant? but we cannot, so will not survey the many theories. Our reflections will in fact deepen the mystery of his identity.

The Servant has done something about the sins of the people who speak in this song, but they do not say explicitly that they have been forgiven. The verb *salah* does not appear, and *nasa'* is not used of forgiveness but of bearing infirmities and sin (vv. 4, 12). That use makes it one of the key words, as we shall see, eventually. We need to be a bit careful, then, in speaking of forgiveness as we draw conclusions about what this mysterious figure has done for these anonymous sinners, but what he accomplished will be our focus, and we will try the unusual approach of looking just at the verses that refer to that accomplishment.

The sins of the unidentified speakers have been punished, but someone else, not they, has suffered for them, someone who in no way deserved to suffer. Once again, it is God who has taken the initiative in making forgiveness possible, but in a most shocking way: punishment will not be remitted, but will be inflicted instead on an innocent person, "my servant," instead of the guilty. "It was the will of the LORD" (53:10), but also the servant's own choice: "He poured himself out to death" (53:12).

"Heal" was an appropriate choice for the first reference to what the Servant had done for the speakers, since it stands in sharp contrast to the extensive references to the pain suffered by the Servant. The word *rapha'*, "heal," appears early in the passage (53:5), and we have found it in texts where it clearly means forgive (Isa 6:10; 57:18–19; Jer 3:22; Hos 6:11b-7:1; 14:4), and in others that are ambiguous—physical healing, forgiveness, or both (Pss 41:5; 103:3; 107:20; 147:3). The speakers confess their sinfulness, and claim they have been healed, made whole (v. 5), made righteous (v. 11). They speak of their infirmities and diseases (v. 4), words that might refer to actual illness or be metaphors for sin. Since the two words are paralleled by transgressions and iniquities

in v. 5, we can at least say that the "diseases" represent either sins or ill-
nesses that they consider to be punishment for sin. The poem thus must
have something to do with forgiveness, but it speaks of it in an almost
completely new way. The speakers' renewal is said to be God's work carried out through the suffering of the Servant (53:6b, 10), which means
he was far more than an intercessor such as Moses and Daniel.

At first, the speakers confess, they had drawn the usual conclusion
about the suffering of the Servant. Sin, it was believed, was regularly
punished by suffering, and they thought the pain experienced by the
Servant, emphasized throughout, must have been deserved. His appearance was "marred beyond human semblance" (52:14). He was a man
of suffering and acquainted with infirmity (53:3), stricken and afflicted
(v. 4), wounded, crushed, bruised (v. 5), oppressed, afflicted (v. 7), and
crushed with pain (v. 10). This must be God's work, they assumed
(53:4, 10), and the Servant must deserve it (53:3b, 4b). But then they
had changed their minds, and drawn a conclusion that we can scarcely
understand. Part of it corresponds to human experience—he suffered
because of the sins of others. This happens daily. Innocent people bear
the sins of others, suffering unjustly. That may be partly what the poem
refers to, but it is not the important part. The speakers claim first, that
the Servant was innocent, not being punished for his own sins (v. 9b).
Why they concluded that we shall think about in a moment. They said,
"The LORD has laid on him the iniquity of us all" (v. 6). "Iniquity," 'awon,
is a word also meaning punishment. He was punished for our sins, and
that is re-emphasized in vv. 11 and 12. So, one aspect of forgiveness,
the remission of punishment, had been really experienced somehow
by these people, and here they credit that not simply to a gracious act
on God's part, but to the willing acceptance of a terrible fate by the
Servant. "He poured out himself to death" (53:12). Claus Westermann,
who says more about forgiveness than most commentators, wrote,
"Thus, the healing gained by the others (v. 5) by his stripes includes as
well the forgiveness of their sins and the removal of their punishment,
that is to say, the suffering" (1969, 263). Then, they claim that because of
his sufferings they had been changed. How that could be, they do not,
probably cannot say. Westermann commented, "All we can say about the
discovery made by the speakers in 53:1–11 amounts to no more than
what they say in v. 6, namely that they themselves had been changed"
(1969, 263). They were changed by being healed, made whole (v. 5), and

this might mean only freedom from suffering, but what shall we make of v. 11b, "The righteous one, my servant, shall make many righteous"? We probably cannot go so far as to say this refers to the kind of personal transformation the author of Psalm 51 hoped for, although that remains possible. Here, to be made righteous may be the juridical sense of the root *ṣadaq*, "to be declared innocent." This, if that is all it means, turns the commonsense idea of justice upside down. As Paul Hanson commented, "This is a daring plunge into the heart and mind of a God who suffers so intensely with the people as to lead to a course of action that breaks all conventions of justice" (1995, 158).

What could have led the prophet to venture so far into the *mind* of God? Let us think again about Westermann's comment that all we can say is that the speakers have been changed. Perhaps the text first tells and then hints at more. First, the song tells us explicitly that their attitude toward the Servant had been changed. They had assumed that he was a guilty person because of his sufferings (v. 4b). Now they no longer believe he was guilty (v. 9b). Westermann concludes they believe this because God has exalted him (v. 12a), but that may not have happened yet, so we need to look for another explanation. If something that had to be taken as a clear vindication of the Servant had already happened, then they would have changed their minds about his innocence, but why would they also conclude that somehow he had been suffering for *their* sins (vv. 4a, 5–6, 11b, 12b)? If we knew anything of the circumstances behind the song, the answer might be clear, but that the Lord had laid their iniquity on him (v. 6b) was by no means an obvious conclusion to be drawn from his vindication. They say even more: "by his bruises we are healed" (v. 3b). Surely this means the change they experienced was more than a change of attitude toward the Servant. They must be referring to a personal transformation of some sort, which we might as well call forgiveness in its fullness. If so, it was the change in *them* that led to a belief God would exalt the Servant, and not the exaltation that led to the change.

They do not try to say how that could have happened, except that it was the will of God (vv. 6, 10) and of the Servant also (v. 12): "he poured out himself to death." None of the precedents for the figure of the Servant that have been sought (e.g., Moses, or the prophets) can account for what is said here. In an earlier work I suggested that the symbolic acts of Jeremiah and Ezekiel may account for part of this (1998,

159–61). Jeremiah was forbidden to marry (16:1–4), Ezekiel was forbidden to mourn the death of his wife (Ezek 24:15–24) because as men of God they had to participate in the judgment that befell their people. Most significant is the reference to Ezekiel bearing the punishment (or iniquity, *'awon*) of Israel and Judah as he lay on his side (Ezek 4:4–6). The terms are not identical to those used in Isa 53:6, 11, 13, but they are very similar. Jeremiah and Ezekiel could not take the place of their people, however, as the Servant is said to do. Prosaic background stories have been created in an effort to account for the song, but having read their reconstructions and then turning again to the song we find that they do not explain it (Watts 1987, 222–33; Whybray 1978). The passage has no parallels earlier or later, until we reach the New Testament, and so we are left with nothing more to help us understand what the prophet meant in speaking of the sinful being transformed through the suffering of an innocent individual.

Christians cannot read the text without thinking about Jesus, but I have approached it here asking only what it could have meant to a Jew in the sixth century B.C. When we come to the New Testament I shall explain the work of Christ with reference to the Servant, but here I do not explain the Servant with reference to Christ. If the sixth century prophet did not formulate this song because he already knew about Jesus (and I assume he did not), then he was complicating—shall we say—the subject of divine forgiveness by speaking of a person who could bring healing and peace and righteousness to others by suffering. This surpasses anything a human being could do—as Moses or a Jeremiah or an Ezekiel. Did the prophet realize that, or was he speaking more than he could understand? About that, of course, we can only speculate.

One might read Exodus 32–34 and the pre-exilic prophets on forgiveness in this way: It was an aspect of the patience of God—delaying the fully just treatment of the rebelliousness of his people as long as possible. With the exile, justice did finally prevail, however, and that is exactly the way Ezekiel re-read his people's history in Ezek 20:1–32. Israel's history, as a people of God, thus presented no paradox of mercy triumphing over justice. In order for God's intentions to create a people of his own not to be finally thwarted, eschatological forgiveness meant the re-creation of individuals, so that obedience, in the future, would transcend the sin-forgiveness issue.

In the meantime, however, there were sinful individuals, throughout Israel's history, who felt a burden of guilt, felt estranged from their God, and longed for release from guilt and reconciliation with the God they felt they had offended. The promise that Yahweh was a forgiving God was taken to be good news for individuals, and it is to the texts that speak of forgiveness in daily life that we shall now turn. These will include a few from the post-exilic prophets, as well as prayers, psalms, and instructions for acts of atonement in the cult.

In the Meantime

The authors we have been reading spoke of the covenant relationship between God and Israel, and we have seen the role that forgiveness played in their thinking as they considered how and whether Israel might continue as the chosen people of God. So, we have followed the fortunes and misfortunes of that community as its intended uniqueness was threatened and rescued. In the meantime, in every generation, however, there were individuals who took their relationship with God with the utmost seriousness. They felt themselves to be estranged from their God because of wrongs they had committed, hoped that the alienation might somehow be overcome, heard the message concerning God's true character, and experienced a true sense of renewal when they turned to God for forgiveness. What those individuals understood of forgiveness in their own lives is revealed for the most part in their prayers, although we shall also need to consider in this section the role played by the sacrificial system in offering assurance that God accepts the repentant sinner. In these parts of the Old Testament, forgiveness is a part of daily life rather than part of the theological systems that attempted to account for Israel's existence as God's chosen people, as we have seen in the previous sections.

We shall find four kinds of statements about forgiveness in the passages that speak of sinful individuals and their relationship to God: a) prayers asking God to forgive, b) references to forgiveness having been granted, c) thanks and praise for God's forgiving character, and d) several negative statements about forgiveness.

Prayers Asking God to Forgive

It will be useful to focus on two Psalms (25 and 51) that use very different terminology to express a fervent hope for God to re-establish the relationship broken by sin, with a note on Daniel's intercessory prayer in Daniel 9. Psalm 25 is called a lament because the psalmist appeals to God to take his side against his enemies, a familiar theme of the laments, but it does not follow the usual form at all closely, and it is distinctive for its use of terms typical of the wisdom literature. It is an acrostic poem, with each verse (with a couple of exceptions) beginning with a successive letter of the alphabet, and this surely accounts for many of its unusual features. Adhering to the acrostic pattern does not permit the author to offer a very straightforward development of themes, but we shall see evidence that he has provided additional structure within that pattern.

If we assume that the author deliberately placed the three references to forgiveness (vv. 7, 11, 18) where he did, an interesting structure appears. The poem contains a single-verse introduction and conclusion (vv. 1 and 21), begins and ends with two units of two lines each asking for help against one's enemies (vv. 2–3 and 19–20), and the body contains three units of four lines each, concluding with prayers for forgiveness (vv. 4–7, 8–11, 15–18). A three-verse unit extols the blessings of the righteous life (vv. 12–14), and v. 22 is an apparent addition to the poem, since it does not follow the acrostic pattern and introduces a new subject.

The psalmist begins with a plea that he not be put to shame because of his enemies, but does not dwell on their wickedness or describe what has shamed or may shame him, as the laments frequently do. His distress leads him to focus instead on his own character and to emphasize the sort of life he hopes to live. He knows he is a sinner, but does not dwell on that either, mentioning it only in his three appeals for forgiveness.

> Do not remember the sins of my youth or my transgressions;
>   according to your steadfast love remember me,
>   for your goodness' sake, O LORD! (v. 7)
> For your name's sake, O LORD,
>   pardon my guilt, for it is great. (v. 11)
> Consider my affliction and my trouble,
>   and forgive all my sins. (v. 18)

Instead, the psalm develops at some length the hope for God to become his great Teacher, whose instruction and guidance will make life good (vv. 12–13). He believes God has the power to transform lives and that is what he asks for himself, in a distinctive way, using vocabulary typical of the wisdom literature. This new, transformed life is called the paths of the Lord (vv. 4, 10), the truth (v. 5), the way of the Lord (vv. 8, 9, 12), the right (v. 9), and the Lord's covenant (v. 14). He believes God can lead him in this way by instruction (*yada‘* hifil; *lamad, yarah*), which sounds very different from the references to a new heart and new spirit in Jeremiah and Ezekiel, but in this context teaching seems not to be a purely intellectual thing. It is a rather unusual way, for an Old Testament author, to express a hope for internal change that will make possible a closer relation with God. The nature of that hope is emphasized in v. 14, where a strongly relational term appears: *sod*, "the friendship of the Lord." Compare its uses at the human level in Job 19:19: "All my intimate friends abhor me, and those whom I loved have turned against me . . ." and in Ps 55:13: "But it is you, my equal, my companion, my familiar friend . . ." Such a close relationship with God is possible, the psalmist affirms, for those who fear God. Note that another relational term occurs in this verse; for this author the covenant is something that God "makes known" to the individual worshipper, using one of the several synonyms for instruction (cf. v. 4).

The psalmist makes an abundant use of covenantal language—that is, specifically the language of Exodus 34:6–7—along with the wisdom vocabulary. It is the character of God as revealed in Exodus that forms the basis for his appeals and his sense of confidence. "Mercy" (*raham*) appears in v. 6 along with "steadfast love" (*hesed*), which reappears in vv. 7 and 10. "Faithfulness" (*'emeth*) is added to *hesed* in v. 10 (as in Exod 34:6), and "gracious" (*hanan*) appears in v. 16. Another echo of Exodus 34: 6–7 is the appeal to God to act for his name's sake (v. 11; and see "for your goodness' sake in v. 7). So, God's self-introduction, which in Exodus defined him as a God who forgives sin, is for this psalmist both the basis for forgiveness and for the life-changing work he calls instruction in the way.

Aside from this use of traditional terminology, he does not make it clear how he associates forgiveness with God's work as Teacher. The structure of the poem does not make it the first step in restoring a relationship, as forgiveness is generally described, since his appeals for forgiveness come at the end of each section. At any rate, our author at least associates forgiveness with the three needs outlined at the beginning of this book. a) It is connected with relief from physical distress in vv. 15–18. The psalmist does not directly say that he considers his troubles to be punishment for sin, but that may be so, since it is such a common idea. b) He acknowledges that his guilt is great (v. 11), so obviously feels some sense of estrangement from God because of sin, but evidently does not feel that his relationship with God is completely broken. He still trusts God (v. 2), and he speaks with some confidence of the possibility of friendship with God (v. 14). c) The appeal for forgiveness appears as the conclusion to two appeals for personal transformation, the teaching that will lead sinners in the way (v. 8). Here is that essential element, if forgiveness is really to make possible a righteous life in the future. For the prophets, it was an eschatological hope, but here and even more obviously in Psalm 51 we see that it was a hope for the immediate future of individual Israelites.

The basis for forgiveness is entirely to be found in the grace of God. All that humans contribute is trust (v. 2) and waiting (vv. 3, 5, 21). Those who keep the Lord's covenant and decrees are those who have been taught by him (v. 19). As for the integrity and uprightness of v. 21, are these human qualities that make one deserving of God's blessings? The verse may be read that way, but uprightness is one of God's qualities in v. 8, so v. 21 more likely is a final reference to the same basis for hope that has prevailed throughout the psalm.

Psalm 51 is known as the great penitential psalm, and that is appropriate, for it has no close parallels. It is unusual in many respects. The psalmist is clearly oppressed by his sense of sinfulness, and sin vocabulary is present in abundance, but the usual forgiveness vocabulary, which we have found elsewhere, is completely missing, except for terms referring to cleansing. He asks God to blot out (*mahah*) his transgressions in v. 1, and to wash (*kavas*) him from his iniquity and cleanse (*tahar*) him from his sin in v. 2. The same two verbs reappear in v. 7. Once again, in v. 9, he asks that his iniquities be blotted out, and in v. 10 he expresses his wish that God create in him a clean heart (*tahor*). Nowhere else is there such a cluster of cleansing terms, used in preference to any other of the words for forgiveness. Commentators on the psalm have generally not made much of this, contenting themselves with saying the psalmist is using cultic language, but more should be said about it.

Ritual uncleanness was a matter that could be dealt with in the cult, and it was not identified as sin. "Clean" and "unclean" were thus terms that were used in two ways, for they were also used metaphorically, in a moral sense. Studies of forgiveness have paid little attention to this, but the words seem likely to represent a psychological condition, a sense of being defiled, unclean, because one is oppressed by a feeling of guilt (Wrider, 1985, 67). At any rate, cleansing language is widely used in the Bible to denote righteousness and forgiveness. A survey should help us to appreciate the contribution of Psalm 51. To be clean is to be righteous: "Who can say, I have made my heart clean; I am pure from sin" (Prov 20:9; cf. Job 11:4; 15:14; 25:4; 33:9; Ps 73:13; Ezek 36:25; John 13:10)? Cleansing is equivalent to forgiveness: "I will cleanse them from all their guilt" (Jer 33:8; cf. Prov 30:12; Ezek 36:25, 33; 37:23; John 15:3; 2 Pet 1:9; 1 John 1:7, 9). Washing (1 Cor 6:11; Titus 3:5), sprinkling (Ezek 36:25; Heb 10:22), and wiping out (Isa 43:25; 44:22) are used the same way. Words that speak of sin as defilement also appear in both Testaments (e.g., Prov 30:12; Jer 2:22, 23; Mark 7:15–23; 1 Cor 8:7; 2 Cor 7:1; James 3:6). The uses of these words by several New Testament authors, who had no interest in ritual cleansing, is surely strong evidence that they recognized that a sense of being defiled accompanies awareness of guilt for at least some people, and acceptance of forgiveness leads them to feel cleansed.

The psalm may be divided as follows:

- Appeals for forgiveness—vv. 1–2

  Have mercy on me, O God,
     according to your steadfast love;
  according to your abundant mercy
     blot out my transgressions.
  Wash me thoroughly from my iniquity,
     and cleanse me from my sin.

- Confession of sin—vv. 3–5

  For I know my transgressions,
     and my sin is ever before me.
  Against you, you alone, have I sinned,
     and done what is evil in your sight,
  so that you are justified in your sentence
     and blameless when you pass judgment.

> Indeed, I was born guilty,
>> a sinner when my mother conceived me.

- Continued appeals, referring to hoped-for results: vv. 6–12

> You desire truth in the inward being;
>> therefore teach me wisdom in my secret heart.
> Purge me with hyssop, and I shall be clean;
>> wash me, and I shall be whiter than snow.
> Let me hear joy and gladness;
>> let the bones that you have crushed rejoice.
> Hide your face from my sins,
>> and blot out all my iniquities.
> Create in me a clean heart, O God,
>> and put a new and right spirit within me.
> Do not cast me away from your presence,
>> and do not take your holy spirit from me.
> Restore to me the joy of your salvation,
>> and sustain in me a willing spirit.

- The expected response to God's graciousness—vv. 13–17

> Then I will teach transgressors your ways,
>> and sinners will return to you.
> Deliver me from bloodshed, O God,
>> O God of my salvation,
>> and my tongue will sing aloud of your deliverance.
> O Lord, open my lips,
>> and my mouth will declare your praise.
> For you have no delight in sacrifice;
>> if I were to give a burnt offering, you would not be pleased.
> The sacrifice acceptable to God is a broken spirit;
>> a broken and contrite heart, O God, you will not despise.

- A probable postscript to the psalm, added by someone who did not wish sacrifice to be negated as strongly as it was in v. 16, appears in vv. 18–19.

The appeal is formulated in two pairs of three terms each. God is reminded of his forgiving nature: mercy (ḥanan), steadfast love (ḥesed), and abundant mercy (raḥam). Then he is asked to blot out, wash, and cleanse the three typical forms of sin: transgression, iniquity, and sin. The psalmist is oppressed by his feelings of guilt—"my sin is ever before me" (v. 3), and he has no excuses to offer (v. 4b). Some have questioned whether "against you alone have I sinned" (v. 4a) means he does not think of sins against people, but this is unlikely. This, and v. 5, are simply passionate expressions of the author's complete sense of unworthiness. Verse 5 has been much discussed as a possible Old Testament reference to original sin, but it seems more likely to be just the author's way of saying, "I have always been a sinner."

This psalmist is more explicit about what forgiveness means to him than the author of Psalm 25 was. He reminds us of that psalm in v. 6, though, when he asks God to teach him wisdom, which he equates with "truth in the inward being." Already, the transformation of his character, which the psalmist desires, is alluded to. "Purge me with hyssop" (v. 7) clearly is cultic language (Num 19:18), and we cannot say that the author is not referring to a ritual that he expects to be performed, but the cleanness and whiteness the author hopes for are the results of divine forgiveness, not a ritual act. Verses 7 and 8 anticipate the results of v. 9: "blot out all my iniquities."

The imagery of cleansing adds to the concept of forgiveness something that is not directly suggested by other terms. It suggests a change of the sinner, so has a much more personal implication than the other terms. Negatively, the removal of defilement puts one back the way one was before sinning—innocent. "Wash me, and I shall be whiter than snow" (v. 7). But the author goes beyond this when in v. 10 he asks, "Create in me a clean heart, O God, and put a new and right spirit within me." We have noted in our study of Jeremiah and Ezekiel that one reasons and makes decisions with the heart. The clean heart would thus surely be one that is capable of making right decisions, and not just one that no longer bears guilt for past wrong choices. This conclusion is strongly supported by the additional request for "a new and right spirit," for, as noted in Ezek 36:27, it is the spirit that enables one to act on the decisions made with the heart. The new and right spirit will thus be the divinely given power to act rightly in the future. The psalmist had already referred to this hope in a less striking way in v. 6: "teach me wisdom in my secret heart."

The author does not speak directly of obedience as the result of being cleansed, as Ezekiel did, but expects to rejoice (vv. 8, 12), and to praise God (vv. 14–15), with the expectation that testimony to God's forgiving grace will convert other sinners (v. 13). The plural of "blood" *dammim* may mean bloodguilt, as in the RSV; or threat of death—bloodshed, as in the NRSV. For him, there is nothing that he can contribute toward gaining forgiveness except "a broken spirit; a broken and contrite heart" (v. 17). He is so convinced of that that he even denies the efficacy of sacrifice (vv. 16–17), something a later author felt the need to modify, in vv. 18–19.

Of the three needs we have been tracing, the remission of punishment appears in an unusual way, the author's desire to be freed from an inner feeling, the sense of being defiled by his guilt. He refers briefly to his desire for a restored relationship with God in v. 11: "Do not cast me away from your presence," but he does want God to hide his face from his sins (v. 9). The desire for forgiveness to include more than freedom from the past but also freedom for a better future, because of personal transformation, is expressed more emphatically here than in any other of the Old Testament prayers.

Daniel's prayer, in Dan 9:4–19, contains an emphatic and repeated statement of the attitude we have found expressed in various ways throughout the texts previously discussed. Forgiveness is God's work alone; there is nothing people can do to deserve it. Daniel reminds us of Moses, for his prayer is a work of intercession on behalf of his perennially sinful people. It differs in that Moses referred to one sin while Daniel speaks of a long history of transgression. Also, Daniel does not stand as the one righteous person; he includes himself throughout the confession (e.g., vv. 5–6; 9–10). He speaks of the righteousness (*tsedaqah*) of God in a remarkable way; both in contrast to the shame of Israel (v. 7) and as a quality in God that might lead to forgiveness (v. 16). This is the "salvific" sense of righteousness that appears also in other texts (e.g., Pss 40:10–12; 143:1–2, 11), a usage remarkable to us, since it adds works of mercy to the acts of justice that the word usually denotes (Gowan, 2001, 137–40).

Throughout the prayer Daniel emphasizes that he has nothing to offer on behalf of himself and his people but the confession of their unworthiness. But his hope is based on the long-standing teaching that God's righteousness is associated with his mercy. "We do not present our supplication before you on the ground of our righteousness, but on the ground of your great mercies. O Lord, hear; O Lord, forgive; O Lord, listen and act and do not delay! For your own sake, O my God, because your city and your people bear your name" (vv. 18b–19)! God's righteous (or just) acts were celebrated for taking the part of the oppressed, the weak for whom he had a special concern (e.g., Pss 9:8–9; 10:17–18; 103:6). Some authors, such as Daniel, dared to think that God's righteousness (justice!) included care for the spiritually weak, i.e. the guilty (Dan 9:16). That move was surely possible only because of God's self-definition in Exod 34:6, which led Daniel to appeal to the only possible basis for forgiveness: "for your own sake" (9:17, 19).

Since this is a prayer for the forgiveness of Israel, and specifically for the restoration of Jerusalem, it differs in several ways from Psalms 25 and 51, appeals for individual forgiveness. Israel's sufferings have been the punishment for sin, fully deserved, and relief from punishment is what Daniel seeks, even though he knows that is not deserved. Relational and transformational aspects of forgiveness thus play no significant roles in the prayer.

Prayers for forgiveness may also be found in 2 Sam 24:10; 2 Kgs 5:18; 2 Chr 30:18–20; Pss 41:4; 79:8–9. In Psalm 79 the writer laments the destruction of Jerusalem—"they have defiled your holy temple; they have laid Jerusalem in ruins" (vv. 1b)—and he blames some of it on previous generations, as the exiles did in Ezekiel 18, but he makes no excuses for the present.

> Do not remember against us the iniquities of our ancestors;
> > let your compassion [*rehem*] come speedily to meet us,
> > for we are brought very low.
> Help us, O God of our salvation
> > for the glory of your name;
> deliver us, and forgive [*kipper*] our sins,
> > for your name's sake. (vv. 8–9)

Here, suffering is punishment for sin and forgiveness is simply relief from punishment.

Hezekiah's prayer in 2 Chr 30:18b–19 sought to ward off potential punishment for violation of ritual regulations. Some of those who ate the Passover in Jerusalem were not ritually clean, so the king prayed for them, "The good Lord pardon [*kipper*] all who set their hearts to seek God, the Lord the God of their ancestors, even though not in accordance with the sanctuary's rules of cleanness." He seems to have claimed that good intentions ought to overrule ritual law, and God agreed. "The Lord heard Hezekiah, and healed [*rapha'*] the people" (v. 20). Since nothing is said of any illness, "heal" seems simply to mean "forgive," as it does elsewhere. That verb is used of both physical healing and forgiveness in Psalm 41. This is one of a few Psalms that makes an explicit connection between sin and sickness (Lindström 1994). The whole psalm speaks of the author's sufferings because of illness, and in v. 4 they are attributed to sin: "O LORD, be gracious to me; heal me, for I have sinned against you."

References to Forgiveness Having Been Granted

Before turning to prayers of thanksgiving, it will be of interest to note one assurance in a narrative that forgiveness has been granted. By his authority as a prophet, Nathan declared to David, after the latter confessed his sin with Bathsheba, "Now the LORD has put away [he'evir] your sin; you shall not die" (2 Sam 12:13). God revoked the punishment David deserved, for adultery and Uzziah's murder, because of his repentance. His sins would not be without consequence, however, for Nathan's next sentence began, "Nevertheless." The story is a striking example of a general truth: sin inevitably leads to suffering even though forgiveness allows life to go on. People frequently question God's justice in taking the life of the innocent child born to Bathsheba and David, but in truth it was not the child who was punished; it was the bereaved parents. It seems appropriate to be reminded of this story immediately after the discussion of Psalm 51, with its hopes of becoming "whiter than snow," for it reminds us that even divine forgiveness does not put everything back as if no sin had ever been committed. It makes possible a new future, but the effects of sin do not all disappear.

In Israel's prayers there are reminders of how God dealt with their failings in the past by forgiveness (Pss 78:38; 85:2; 99:8), and God's willingness to do that is even stated as a general rule in Ps 65:3: "When deeds of iniquity overwhelm us, you forgive our transgressions." Psalm 32 is another prayer of an individual, worth considering because it speaks of forgiveness as relief from punishment in ways we did not find in Psalms 25 or 51. It is another of the church's "penitential psalms," taking the form of an individual psalm of thanksgiving. Typical elements of the genre are references to past distress (vv. 3–4) and to the psalmist's appeal to God for help: "Then I acknowledged my sin to you, and I did not hide my iniquity; I said, 'I will confess my transgressions to the LORD,' and you forgave the guilt of my sin" (v. 5). Usually, at this point the author would declare that God had intervened on his behalf, not found here, but perhaps the introduction in the form of proverbs (vv. 1–2) takes its place (cf. Pss 1:1; 112:1; Prov 3:12; 28:14). Typical also are the expressions of confidence in vv. 6–7, testimony in v. 10, and the invitation to the congregation to join in praising God in v. 11.

For this author, physical distress has been interpreted as the result of sin, and the relief he has experienced is then interpreted as the result of divine forgiveness: "I said, 'I will confess my transgressions to the LORD,' and you forgave the guilt of my sin" (v. 5b). Here is the pattern familiar to most discussions of forgiveness, which, however, we have not always found in the Old Testament: sin results in divine punishment (vv. 3–4), but repentance leads God to lift the punishment (v. 5). Verses 3 and 4 suggest that the distress suffered by the psalmist was illness, and we noticed earlier that forgiveness is sometimes called healing (*rapha'*). The verb is used in the same way in Ps 107:17–19, and the same idea appears without the verb in Isa 38:17. It is thus somewhat curious that the psalm which speaks at length of illness, and attributes it to sin (Psalm 38), does not use the verb *rapha'* and does not explicitly ask for forgiveness. "Make haste to help me, O Lord, my salvation" (v. 22) is the extent of the psalmist's request.

Thanks and Praise for God's Forgiving Nature

Echoes of Exod 34:6–7 appear regularly in these prayers. Psalm 103 extols at length the graciousness of the God who forgives. The psalmist knows he has sinned, but he has also experienced the joyous sensation of feeling assured that God has forgiven him. In language of unparalleled beauty he asks the congregation, and indeed all creation, to join in thanking God for that gracious gift. In the prayers discussed previously we found something of what the authors believed forgiveness is. Now the subject is different: the greatness of the God who forgives.

> Bless the LORD, O my soul,
>> and all that is within me,
>> bless his holy name.
> Bless the LORD, O my soul,
>> and do not forget all his benefits—
> who forgives all your iniquity,
>> who heals all your diseases,
> who redeems your life from the Pit,

> who crowns you with steadfast love and mercy,
>   who satisfies you with good as long as you live!
>   so that your youth is renewed like the eagle's. (vv. 1–5)

Since the psalmist calls upon all creation to join in his expression of praise, this may partly explain why he does not refer as explicitly to his own experiences as the authors of the psalms we have read previously. Much of the psalm speaks in general terms, but the exuberance of his words of praise can leave little doubt that the psalm was inspired by a powerful experience of feeling that God had forgiven him. It may be, then, that vv. 2–5, which could apply to many, are a reflection of what happened to the psalmist: He had been sick and near death; he attributed his illness to sins he knew he had committed, and when he was healed and restored to a vigorous life again he believed it was the result of divine forgiveness. It appears that the experience had such an impact on him that he was inspired to add his own interpretation of God's self-definition as one whose character makes forgiveness possible (v. 8; quoting Exod 34:6a).

> The LORD is merciful and gracious,
>   slow to anger and abounding in steadfast love.
> He will not always accuse,
>   nor will he keep his anger forever.
> He does not deal with us according to our sins,
>   nor repay us according to our iniquities.
> For as the heavens are high above the earth,
>   so great is his steadfast love toward those who fear him;
> as far as the east is from the west,
>   so far he removes our transgressions from us. (vv. 8–12)

He had probably thought that his sufferings were the result of God's anger at his sinfulness, but, "He will not always accuse, nor will he keep his anger forever" (v. 9). Indeed, he thinks he deserved worse than he got, and so he must conclude that, "He does not deal with us according to our sins, nor repay us according to our iniquities" (v. 10). Whereas the author of Psalm 51 thought of forgiveness as cleansing, this writer's imagery alludes to an extravagant sense of freedom from sin: "For as the heavens are high above the earth, so great is his steadfast love toward those who fear him; as far as the east is from the west, so far he removes our transgressions from us" (vv. 11–12).

He then attempts to bring one of the astonishing qualities that God attributed to himself in Exod 34:6 into the human realm, to give us a measure of understanding.

> As a father has compassion for his children,
>> so the LORD has compassion for those who fear him.
> For he knows how we were made;
>> he remembers that we are dust. (vv. 13–14)

The root *rhm*, which in v. 8 the NRSV translates "merciful," reappears as a verb in v. 13 and is translated "has compassion." He has seen evidence in the family of a powerful emotion that leads parents (note: fathers as well as mothers) to take extreme measures to care for their children without regard to what they may deserve. If that is possible for people, how much more may God's "justice" (see v. 6) transcend what we deserve. Then the psalmist dares to suggest that the Lord knows we cannot help sinning, and that also inclines him to be merciful (vv. 14–16). "For he knows how we are made; he remembers that we are dust."

The repeated theme in the psalm is *hesed*, the Lord's steadfast love. It is a part of the quotation from Exod 34:6 (v. 8), but is used three times in the author's own original way. God crowns the one who has been forgiven, healed, and redeemed, the crown perhaps a wreath worn at times of celebration (v. 4). The author knows it is the unique character of God, his steadfast love and mercy, that has made all this possible. Again, it is specifically the *hesed* of God that makes forgiveness possible, in the word's second appearance, and its uniqueness is compared with the distance between heaven and earth (v. 11). Finally, the author contrasts the frailty of human beings with the *hesed* of the Lord, which is "from everlasting to everlasting" (v. 17). The result of his gracious work is that desired relationship with God called the fear of the Lord (v. 17) and the ability to keep his covenant (v. 18), a conclusion we have also found in other psalms.

That such a magnificent expression of rejoicing and confidence in a God who turns life around from disobedience to obedience became part of Israel's collection of psalms must indicate that many found it to be an accurate expression of their own experiences of forgiveness, as it is in fact to this day. Exodus 34:6 was thus far more than a series of impressive words; its use in prayer shows that Israelites personally experienced a God who was what those words indicated him to be.

The tone of Psalm 130 is very different from that of Psalm 103, but in its own way it also praises the God who forgives. It is filled with tensions that are fully relieved only in the final two verses. The psalmist cries out to God from the depths. The familiar complaints of other psalms—illness and enemies—are not mentioned, so "depths" must refer to the distance between himself and God which the author has produced by his disobedience. But from that distance he calls out (obviously for help) to that God whose will he had not cared about. Why should God hear the disobedient, and come near the one who had distanced himself? Answer: There is no hope, unless God forgives sins, and he does!

> If you, O LORD, should mark iniquities,
>   Lord, who could stand?
> But there is forgiveness with you,
>   so that you may be revered. (vv. 3–4)

The human predicament, described in Psalm 51 as "a sinner when my mother conceived me" (v. 5), and in Psalm 103 as "we are dust" (v. 14), reappears: "If you, O LORD, should mark iniquities, Lord, who could stand?" People have nothing to offer that can restore the relationship they have hurt. So it is that the necessary quality for a good relationship with God—the fear of the Lord—is here the result of forgiveness, not a condition for it. "But there is forgiveness with you, so that you may be revered [NRSV; or, feared]" (v. 4). Again, we are struck by what seems to us to be a curious choice of words to designate something strongly positive—fear—and commentators on this psalm suggest that in this reassuring verse there is tension also; fear of the Lord is a response to power that is both alarming and restoring.

Tension continues in vv. 5–6, for the psalmist does not yet rejoice in the certainty of forgiveness, but waits for it, with hope.

> I wait for the LORD, my soul waits,
>   and in his word I hope.
> my soul waits for the Lord
>   more than those who watch for the morning,
>   more than those who watch for the morning.

Some commentators believe the original psalm ended with these verses, since vv. 7–8 turn from the individual to the community, but we have seen the same move in other psalms, and in this case the affirmation of faith in the final verses can naturally be understood as the basis for hope that makes waiting possible for the original author.

> O Israel, hope in the LORD!
>> For with the LORD there is steadfast love,
>> and with him is great power to redeem.
>> It is he who will redeem Israel from all its iniquities.

The verses are of some special interest to us because a unique word has been chosen to designate forgiveness, "redeem" (*padah*). It means to "set free," typically by a payment of some kind, and refers to being set free from various kinds of distress, but only here does the Old Testament speak of redemption from sin. This is a new metaphor, potentially a powerful one, being "set free from sin," but it is not developed, and there is no hint that the author thought of any payment being involved, as later writers on forgiveness have done.

This psalm, like the others, emphasizes our absolute dependence on God for forgiveness, but cites only one of the familiar attributes, *hesed*, "steadfast love" (v. 7), that are used to account for the possibility of forgiveness. The term "redeem" might be taken to mean setting one free from the tendency to sin, as "cleanse" does in Psalm 51, but in this context it may mean only freedom from guilt and the punishment of sin.

In the earlier discussion of the book of Micah the comment was made that 7:18–20 properly belonged in this section, for it is a hymn praising the God who forgives. It does not quote Exod 34:6, but uses the key terms in its own way, adding new ways to speak of forgiveness. The three common words for "sin" appear in v. 17, with "pardon" (*nasa'*) paralleled by "passing over" (*'avad*). The NRSV has chosen "showing clemency" (v. 18) and "unswerving loyalty" (v. 20) to represent forms of the root *hsd*, which we most often encounter in translation as "steadfast love." "Compassion" (v. 19) represents *raham*, elsewhere translated "mercy." "Faithfulness" (*'emeth*) also appears with *hesed* (v. 20) as often elsewhere. These qualities, according to the hymn-writer, enable God to "tread our iniquities under foot" and to "cast all our sins into the depths of the sea" (v. 19). The poem that began in 7:1 with "Woe is me!" ends with the marveling question, "Who is a God like you?" The author has confidence based on what the tradition has taught about God's character, but rather than quoting it produces his own testimony, one of the

Old Testament's most powerful expressions of faith in the God who forgives.

The troubles that beset Israel throughout its existence—struggling to make a living in spite of weather and infertility and disease, in pain because of illness and accidents, oppressed by unjust systems, and subject to the ravages of warfare—might have led them to conclude that God was undependable, harsh, and vindictive. These prayers are thus remarkable evidence for a powerful faith that challenged what daily experience suggested, insisting that God is both just and merciful, whether or not one can understand how he could be both. Other experiences, the sense of being forgiven, restored to a harmonious relationship with God and to a better life because of it, confirmed for them the truth of the sacred tradition. God is who he said he is, at Sinai.

Negative Statements about Forgiveness

There are a few threats that God will not forgive Israelites who fail to keep the covenant, in keeping with the message of the prophets. Moses' speech in Deuteronomy 29 warns those individuals who think, "We are safe even though we go our own stubborn ways," that the Lord will be unwilling to pardon them (v. 20), and cites a series of curses that will befall them as a result. Joshua questioned whether his people could obey: "You cannot serve the LORD, for he is a holy God. He is a jealous God; he will not forgive your transgressions or your sins. If you forsake the LORD and serve foreign gods, then he will turn and do you harm, and consume you after having done you good" (Josh 24:19–20). An unusual passage speaks of God's intention to appoint an angel to lead Israel to the Promised Land, with the warning, "do not rebel against him, for he will not pardon your transgressions; for my name is in him" (Exod 23:21). Note that in order for them to have their proper effect as dire warnings nothing is said about a possibility of repentance.

One passage, outside the prophetic books, declares that God did not forgive, and the guilty party, according to the Historian, was king Manasseh. His sins, which were manifold, are cited in 2 Kgs 24: 3–4 as the final explanation for the fall of Judah to Nebuchadnezzar. The Historian had always claimed the fortunes of Judah depended on the righteousness (or otherwise) of her kings (e.g., 2 Kgs 18:5–7; 21:10–16; 23:26–27), but Josiah, who was praised for his extensive reforming activities, met an untimely death (2 Kgs 23:29), and not long afterward the kingdom came to an end, so it seems the best explanation that was available was to refer back to the sins of Manasseh. One of the remarkable differences between Kings and Chronicles is the latter's account of Manasseh's repentance and restoration to the Lord's favor (2 Chr 33:12–13, 19), which, of course, led to a different explanation of the fall of Judah (2 Chr 36:15–16). God did forgive Manasseh, then, according to the Chronicler, although he does not use any of the typical repentance/forgiveness vocabulary.

Outside the prophetic books these are the only explicit statements about God's refusal to forgive Israel.

We shall soon see that the Old Testament says very little about human forgiveness. There are a few texts that derive from the human refusal to forgive, which we include here because that refusal took the form of prayer to God not to forgive. The three passages are remarkably similar. One may wonder whether they echo a kind of cursing formula, but there is not enough evidence to support making anything of that. In one of Jeremiah's complaints he asked of God,

> Do not forgive (*kipper*) their iniquity (*'awon*),
> do not blot out (*mahah*) their sin from your sight. (Jer 18:23)

Nehemiah's appeal for God's help included, "Do not cover (*kasah*) their guilt (*'awon*), and do not let their sin be blotted out (*mahah*) from your sight" (Neh 4:5).

Psalm 109:14 uses the same combination of words, extending the curse into the past:

> May the iniquity (*'awon*) of his father be remembered before the Lord,
> and do not let the sin of his mother be blotted out (*mahah*).

It would not be safe to conclude from the three examples just cited that Israelites frequently asked God not to forgive others, but it is evident that sometimes they did. We shall soon see that one of the remarkable differences between the Testaments is the absence in the Old of any inclination that Israelites prayed for God to forgive others except in the work of the great mediators such as Moses and Daniel.

Finally, we encounter one who is not a sinner (Job 1:1, 8), but who asks why God has not forgiven him. In his efforts to establish dialogue with God, Job thought of every possible way to account for his sufferings, rejecting as impossible the idea that he was being justly punished for his sins. At one point he asks why God would not just forgive him, in case he had sinned:

> If I sin, what do I do to you, you watcher of humanity?
>> Why have you made me your target?
>> Why have I become a burden to you?
> Why do you not pardon my transgression
>> and take away my iniquity? (Job 7:21–22a)

If forgiveness had been needed, Job believed in a God who should have forgiven. His hypothetical situation thus raised a question about one of Israel's central beliefs.

Sacrifice and Forgiveness

Israel's prayers do not suggest that there was any set procedure for being assured of divine forgiveness except for repentance, confession, and appeal to God's mercy. From Ps 51:16–19 we might conclude that sacrifice could somehow be involved, although the original author downgraded its importance. It is in a way a surprise, then, to find another set of texts concerning forgiveness that prescribe a series of acts that will lead to forgiveness of every unintentional sin, and at least some intentional wrongs. These are the *ḥaṭṭath* and *'ašam* offerings, the so-called sin and guilt offerings (Lev 4:13–6:7; 19:20–22; Num 15:22–29). These ritual texts reveal that the priests in Israel claimed to be able to offer assurance that God had forgiven certain sins, once a sacrifice was offered in the appropriate way. The texts are fraught with problems for the modern interpreter, and no one claims to be able to understand them perfectly. We shall not devote a great deal of space to them, for to do so would get us involved with debates over the difficulties of the texts that would leave us with little that we could add with certainty to our understanding of forgiveness in the Old Testament. It is unfortunate, for it was evidently an important matter for the priests, but their literature explains what to do, and not why and what it meant.

Studies of the role played by ritual in cultures like that of ancient Israel are helpful, but they leave many questions unanswered. The priests of Israel considered themselves to be responsible for the maintenance of a stable and thus healthy society. Their words for it were "clean" and "holy" (cf. Lev 10:10), and their rituals were part of a system to assure normalcy, or to restore it whenever it was disrupted. Gorman's definition sums up their point of view neatly in one sentence: "Rituals are thus means of holding back social confusion, indeterminacy, and chaos because they provide patterns for maintaining order and constructive patterns for restoring that order when it has been lost" (Gorman 1990, 29). Sin, as the priests defined it, "doing any one of all the things which the LORD has commanded not to be done" (Lev 4:27, etc.), would cause a major disruption of normalcy, so in a society of this kind forgiveness was part of the structure of community life, and not a purely personal matter between the sinner and God. Clearly, the priests placed limitations on what ritual could accomplish, however, where sin was concerned, and this led to their restriction of the efficacy of sacrifice, with certain exceptions, to sins committed inadvertently. The wording varies: four cases call them unintentional (Lev 4:23, 23, 27; 5:15), three call them hidden (5:2, 34), and one says the sinner did not know it (5:17). These were mistakes, nothing involving defiance of God's will, and the priests seem to have believed God had given to them a procedure that would set things right in such cases. The procedure was called making atonement. Priests could do this, then God would forgive. Sins committed deliberately, however, were a personal affront to God—they may have reasoned—and such challenges to God's will were matters that only God could deal with (see Num 15:30–31).

All scholars agree: The priest makes atonement; God forgives. Making atonement is an act purely at the human level that removes the contamination brought about by sin and leaves the way clear for God to re-establish a proper relationship with the repentant sinner (Levine 1974, 64–66). "Atonement," as the English word is used to translate *kipper* in the Old Testament, is thus not to be equated with the way the word is used in Christian theology, referring to theories that attempt to explain the saving work of Christ on the cross. Some of those theories do refer back to sacrifice in the Old Testament, but they all use the English word in a much broader sense than it has in translations of the Old Testament. The term *kipper* has been discussed at length, but most of the research that can be found summarized in the wordbooks does not help us. For our purposes, the definition provided at the beginning of the paragraph will suffice, although we may remind ourselves that in a few other contexts the term was actually used with the meaning "forgive" (see Deut 21:8; 2 Chr 30:18; Pss 78:38; 79:9; Isa 27:9; Jer 18:23; Ezek 16:63).

Acts contrary to God's law, even when committed inadvertently, resulted in a burden of guilt that needed to be purged from the community. If and when the person involved realized he had sinned (Lev 4:14, 23, 28; 5:3, 4), there was a public act available to set things right. What was done for a sinful person in the rituals described in these texts? 1) The community, we might say, provided a way for a person feeling guilt, feeling estranged from God, to be assured of forgiveness. But the community would not have said it provided the way; they believed the entire cultic system had been provided by God. 2) The procedure required a gift as an indication of one's sincerity. Sometimes, at least, it was preceded by confession (5:5). In Lev 4:13–35 the gift is called *ḥaṭṭah*, traditionally translated "sin offering" but now often called "purification offering." In Lev 5:6–26 it is called *ʾašam*, "guilt offering," or "reparation offering," as in Jacob Milgrom's full discussion of these terms and the theories attempting to explain them (Milgrom 1991, 226–378). The differences between these two offerings have been the subject of extended debate, and it would not profit us to begin discussing that debate. Properly, the gift should be an animal, since blood usually played the central role in the ritual, but provision was made for the poor, who could not afford one (Lev 5:11–13). This raises one of the many questions about the ritual. If blood was essential for atonement, how could a non-bloody offering be effective? At any rate, the ritual did not suggest that one was buying forgiveness, since the required offering was not graduated according to the severity of the sin (Lev 4:13–5:13). 3) The sinner laid his hand on the head of the animal, identifying it as his gift, then killed it. 4) Normally, the priest sprinkled some of the blood of the animal on the altar and poured out the rest at its base. 5) The fat was burnt on the altar as an offering to God (4:31, 35). 6) These actions by the priest were called "making atonement" for the sinner, or for his sin, or both. 7) The text declares (did the priest declare it at the time?) that the sinner shall be forgiven. Literally, the words may be read either "it [the sin] shall be forgiven for him" or "he shall be forgiven for it," although 4:20 must be "it shall be forgiven for them."

There is one passage that gives us some insight into the reason blood was thought to have the power to clear the way for God to forgive. In Lev 17:10–14 a reason is provided for the restriction that blood is never to be eaten. The reason is two-fold. Blood is equated with life. God is the giver of life, and although he permits animals to be killed for food (Gen 9: 3–6) it must be acknowledged that life belongs to God by pouring out the blood so that it sinks into the earth (Deut 12:23–24). Most of the blood of the sin and guilt offerings was also poured out at the base of the altar. The second part is more relevant to our concern. God says, "I have given it to you for making atonement for your lives on the altar; for, as life, it is the blood that makes atonement" (Lev 17:11). The sentence is difficult and has been translated in various ways, but at least it seems to emphasize two things: It is life that makes atonement and it can do that because God has so determined it (Milgrom 2000, 1479). We must leave it at that for now, and not become distracted by the complex and conflicting attempts to explain the function of blood and the meaning of atonement in the priestly literature, for scholars admit that to gain a full understanding of what sacrifice meant in ancient Israel is beyond us now. At this point in our work we needed to note these texts largely because of the importance played by the blood of Christ in New Testament authors' discussions of forgiveness.

The Day of Atonement (Leviticus 16) should also be important for our work, but once again we are left with more questions than answers, so the details of the ceremony will be omitted here. What ought to be important is that Israel's "iniquities, transgressions and sins" are (symbolically? actually?) put upon the head of one of the goats chosen for the ceremony as Aaron lays his hand on its head and confesses their sins. Then the goat bears their iniquities into the wilderness, to Azazel. Aggravating the matter is our uncertainty about what *'aza'zel* means, and the fact that the removal of sins is distinct from the ceremonies of atonement by the blood of other animals (e.g., 16:16). "Atonement for the assembly" (16:17) is not likely to mean forgiveness at this point in the ceremony, but of the entire ritual it is said, "Atonement shall be made for you, to cleanse you; from all your sins you shall be clean before the LORD" (v. 30). One of the synonyms for forgiveness that we have seen elsewhere (*tahar*) thus assured Israelites that once a year ritual could gain forgiveness for them of all their sins (v. 34). The requirement that they all had to "deny" themselves (or fast) does presumably mean, however, that failure to repent would make all this of no avail.

Here are some questions that reveal how difficult it is to reach firm conclusions about the relationship between forgiveness and sacrifice:

How did it work in practice? During the post-exilic period the only legitimate place for sacrifice was the temple in Jerusalem. What good did these rituals do for a person living in Galilee, who may never have reached Jerusalem?

Forgiveness of unintentional sins seems to have been expensive. A goat for every sin?

If Milgrom is correct in his translation of 'aŝem as "feel guilt," rather than the usual "incur guilt" (Milgrom 1991, 339–45, 378), could these provisions be interpreted as a "pastoral" effort by the priests to relieve the consciences of those for whom the message of God's forgiving nature did not suffice? This perhaps naive question may be justified by the fact that once a year the Day of Atonement assured forgiveness for everything to the repentant person. Were the rituals of Leviticus 4–5 for the hypersensitive, then?

The studies of ritual alluded to above, with their emphasis on the restoration of normalcy, support taking the priests' references to forgiveness as including at least reconciliation between God and Israelites whose behavior had disrupted the relationship. The fact that a ritual for forgiveness of certain deliberate sins (Lev 6:1–7) required both restitution and payment of a 20% fine shows that the forgiveness the ritual assured did not mean relief from punishment (but see Lev 19:20–22). As for inner change, the use of "cleanse" with reference to the Day of Atonement is more likely a reflection of the priests' concerns for ritual purity than a claim that personal transformation might occur.

Two Other Forgiveness Passages

In Numbers 30 the subordinate status of a young woman to her father or a married woman to her husband with reference to a vow that the woman might make is clarified. In either case, the man could nullify the vow, if he wished, and the law specifies, "the LORD will forgive her" (vv. 5, 8, 12). If the man did nothing, she was bound by her vow, and in all cases widows and divorced women were bound by their vows (v. 9). Forgiveness in this case seems to require no ritual, and must mean simply relief from the penalty that would otherwise be incurred.

Murder was such a serious crime that it had to be dealt with somehow, even when the identity of the killer was unknown. There was guilt in the air that might lead to serious consequences for the inhabitants of a town nearest to the place where a body was found in the open country, so Deut 21:1–9 provided a way for them to claim their innocence. They took a young heifer to a wadi with running water, broke its neck, washed their hands, and declared, "Our hands did not shed this blood, nor were we witnesses to it. Absolve (*kipper*), O LORD, your people Israel, whom you redeemed; do not let the guilt of innocent blood remain in the midst of your people Israel" (v. 8). The law assured them, "Then they will be absolved of bloodguilt." Note that this is one of the passages where *kipper* has taken on the meaning "forgive" and forgiveness here means protection from the potential but undeserved effects of bloodguilt.

Reflections on Divine Forgiveness in the Old Testament

In the introduction to this book I approached forgiveness by asking about the human needs to which it responds, and found three: physical—relief from punishment, personal—the need for cleansing, i.e., inner change, and relational. It may be useful at this point to make a brief comparison of George Caird's description of "The Experience of Sin" in the New Testament, noted in the Introduction, with what we have found in the Old Testament. He approached sin by asking what God has done about it, and came to similar conclusions, using the vocabulary of the New Testament. Thus, a) sin involves guilt to be cancelled, which God does by justification, b) a stain to be erased, calling for consecration, c) an enmity to be dispelled, requiring reconciliation, and d) a servitude to be abolished, needing redemption (Caird 1994, 87–90). It will be seen that the first three correspond to the human needs that I described in other terms. We found, when we read Psalm 130, that redemption from iniquity appeared only there, as Caird also noted, so that way of describing God's work will appear as a distinctly New Testament subject.

It is of some interest to compare the metaphors Old Testament writers used with Caird's choices of typically New Testament language. As we do so, it will be helpful to recall (when possible) verses where the metaphors are used in parallel with the verbs *salah* and *nasa'*. As to canceling guilt (a), Paul's term "justify" is to some extent reflected by "take away" (*he'avir*) guilt or iniquity, as in Job 7:21: "Why do you not pardon (*nasa'*) my transgression and take away my iniquity" (cf. 2 Sam 12:13; 24:10=1 Chr 21:8; Zech 3:4)? "Covering" sin may have been another way that guilt has been nullified, as in Ps 85:2: "You forgave (*nasa'*) the iniquity of your people; you pardoned (*kasah*) all their sin" (cf. Neh 4:5; Ps 32:1). If God no longer remembers sin, obviously no guilt remains, as when God promised, "I will forgive (*salah*) their iniquity, and remember their sin no more" (Jer 31:34; cf. Pss 25:7; 79:8; Isa 43:25; 64:9; Ezek 33:16). Psalm 32:1–2 adds that idea to the idea of covering: "Happy are those whose transgression is forgiven (*nasa'*), whose sin is covered. Happy are those to whom the LORD imputes (*hašav*) no iniquity, and in whose spirit there is no deceit." Emphatic is *mahah*, wiping away or blotting out, as in Jer 18:23: "Do not forgive (*kipper*) their iniquity, do not blot out their sin from your sight" (cf. Neh 4:5; Pss 51:9; 109:14; Isa 43:25; 44:22). In a few cases, then, Old Testament authors may have thought of forgiveness in a way similar to Paul's notion of justification; i.e., that God declares the guilty to be innocent. There is a difference in that the sinner is the object of "justify," whereas sin is the object of the verbs just noted.

Both Testaments speak of something done to the sinner by erasing the stain that has corrupted oneself, using verbs of washing. So, "I will cleanse (*tahar*) them from all the guilt of their sin against me, and I will forgive (*salah*) all the guilt of their sin and rebellion against me" (Jer 33:8; cf. Lev 16:30; Ps 51:2, 7, 10; Ezek 36:33). Healing belongs here as well, for it seems to refer to inner change in Isa 6:10; 53:5; 57:18–19; Jer 3:22; Hos 6:11b-71; 14:4. The cleansing and healing metaphors included both past and future, for they expressed at least the hope that divine forgiveness would overcome one's sinful nature and make righteous living a true possibility. This will become a major theme in the New Testament.

Reconciliation, which we have found to be a major aspect of divine forgiveness, is not denoted so much by the metaphors we have traced as by the contexts in which forgiveness appears, and by references to God not hiding his face, to God no longer being angry, to God turning to the one who turns to him, and also to God no longer remembering sin. We have found forgiveness language to be so intimately associated with reconciliation in the Old Testament that the familiar, negative definition that confines it to something like "remission of sin" seems to apply to only a part of what Old Testament authors intended when they used the terms we have traced.

The idea that the sinner incurs a debt that needs to be repaid somehow appears in the New Testament, and is a common one to this day, but we did not find any metaphor for forgiveness in the Old Testament that suggested God was canceling a debt.

Throughout the Old Testament there is a strong emphasis on God's initiative, on God's desire to forgive, which led to the offer of forgiveness to the unrepentant. Since true forgiveness involved reconciliation, the restoration of a broken relationship, it could not be completely one-sided, so repentance was essential. An important contribution of the Old Testament is the insight that the ability to accept the fact that one is guilty, and thus to repent, may come about only when one is convinced that forgiveness is possible and has been offered.

2

We Forgive One Another

THE MOST OBVIOUS DIFFERENCE BETWEEN THE TESTAMENTS IN THE teaching about forgiveness concerns human relationships. The Old Testament says very little about forgiving one another, but it is a key element in the teaching of Jesus. Later, we shall consider why that may be, but at this point will just gather the little material there is in the Old Testament, with some reflection on various ways of restoring peace when there has been an affront, which may not involve forgiveness.

Jesus instructed his followers to be forgiving (Matt 6:12–15; 18:21–22). There is no comparable command in the Old Testament. Perhaps the nearest to it is Lev 19:18, "You shall not take vengeance or bear a grudge against any of your people, but you shall love your neighbor as yourself." Vengeance (*naqam*) was violent action outside the law directed against an offender, and the word translated "grudge" involves actual anger as it is used elsewhere. This verse concludes a passage (vv. 11–18) that forbids a series of actions that would disrupt harmony within the community. It adds to action the kind of attitude toward one's neighbors that will always disturb the peace, anger that lasts and the desire to get even. A hateful attitude (v. 17) needs to be corrected by a loving one. This might involve full forgiveness, but not necessarily so, and it may be significant that the partial quotation, "love your neighbor as yourself," which is so important in the New Testament, is not used there as part of a command to be forgiving.

There are four requests for human forgiveness in the Old Testament, each one using the verb *nasa'*. No one responds using a verb of forgiving, although two of the responses are positive. Did the Old Testament authors then think that forgiveness was something that only God can grant? They do not say (although consider Mark 2:7; "Who can forgive sins but God alone?"), so perhaps the best we can do is look to see how people tended to settle grievances. The book of Genesis is useful for this purpose, since it contains one of the explicit forgiveness passages.

After Jacob left Laban's household, both of them claimed to be the aggrieved party (Gen 31:17–55). Laban had lost his daughters and, in Jacob, a worker who had enriched him by his energy and skill. So, when he caught up with Jacob he claimed, "The daughters are my daughters, the children are my children, the flocks are my flocks, and all that you see is mine" (Gen 31:43). But Jacob, having reminded Laban of the ways he had enriched him, claimed, "If the God of my father, the God of Abraham and the Fear of Isaac, had not been on my side, surely now you would have sent my away empty-handed" (v. 42). There is no suggestion that either one ever forgave the other, but they did agree to separate in peace. Laban proposed that they make a covenant (v. 44), which someone has called a "non-aggression pact," for the gist of it was an appeal to God to watch over them to assure that each one behaved (vv. 49–50). The appeal to God as witness and the distance they promised to maintain from one another resolved an issue where it was unlikely that the two parties would ever be able to live together harmoniously.

Jacob was certainly the offender in the relationship with his brother Esau, having stolen Esau's birthright (Genesis 27). He fled from his brother's anger, so for years distance kept him safe, but when, after leaving Laban, he returned to Esau's territory, the old quarrel was potentially a source of great danger to him. He made careful plans to try to preserve at least part of his company (Gen 32:3–21), then the brothers met face-to-face. It was at least a more pleasant meeting than the one with Laban. Esau embraced him and kissed him and they wept (v. 4). We do not know whether Esau actually forgave Jacob; the author does not use that kind of language. He is remarkably gracious toward his devious brother, as the story is told, suggesting that his people and Jacob's journey together (vv. 12–16). If it truly was an offer of forgiveness, Jacob could not accept it, however; evidently because he was still afraid of Esau and was not willing to trust him. Full reconciliation did not happen, then, and once again distance took its place.

Distance would not solve the problem for Joseph's brothers. They had moved to Egypt with their father Jacob and lived there under Joseph's protection until Jacob died, but with their father gone they worried about whether Joseph might be ready to get even with them for selling him into slavery long ago (Gen 50:15). Unlike the characters in the previous story, they confessed their guilt and asked forgiveness, claiming that Jacob had told them, "Say to Joseph, I beg you, forgive the crime [*pesha'*] of your brothers and the wrong [*hatta'th*] they did in harming you" (v. 17). Once again there were tears and Joseph did not say explicitly that he forgave them, but the elements of forgiveness seem to be present. "Do not be afraid!" he said; there would be no punishment. He offered to provide for them and their children, reassuring them and speaking kindly to them, so it seems that the author intends to present a scene where forgiveness is truly accomplished.

We are led next to the stories about David because one of them contains another request for forgiveness that is granted. To abbreviate a fairly detailed story, after David had lost favor with Saul he and his men had for a time offered protection to the shepherds of Nabal (1 Samuel 25). When David asked a kindness in return, that they share in the feast Nabal had prepared for his shearers, Nabal refused, with insults, enraging David, who determined to slaughter every male of the household. Nabal's wife Abigail, however, who was as wise as he was foolish, quickly prepared an abundance of gifts and went to meet David. Her address to him is a gem of diplomacy, combining humility and flattery. First, she took responsibility for the insult, probably safely since David knew better, but by doing so she made herself the party that he ought to deal with. "Upon me alone, my lord, be the guilt" (v. 24). Pay no attention to Nabal, whose very name means "fool." Then she offered the present she had brought, asked forgiveness, and continued with a rather florid prediction of David's future success (vv. 26–31). "Please forgive the trespass of your servant," the NRSV reads, but the Hebrew uses a strong word, *peša'*. This was a transgression of the strict rules of hospitality of that period, but Abigail had made things right, and David responded graciously. "Blessed be your good sense, and blessed be you who have kept me today from bloodguilt and from avenging myself by my own hand!" He did not speak of forgiveness, but concluded with "Go up to your house in peace; see, I have heeded your voice, and I have granted your petition" (vv. 33, 35). The grievance was resolved this time by restitution, which was accepted. The encounter led to a bit more than forgiveness, for soon afterward Nabal died, and David married Abigail.

Johannes Pedersen's evaluation of David's character reveals that he is scarcely to be taken as an example of a forgiving person, in spite of numerous occasions when he refrained from violent action against someone who had offended him, so we shall just remind ourselves of some of them without going into detail (1940, III–IV:526–32). Pedersen began his paragraph concerning David and Abigail with this sentence: "The dread of interfering in a way that might provoke Yahweh's anger is the leading motive in the whole of David's conduct." So he spared Saul's life twice (1 Samuel 24 and 26) because, "who can raise his hand against the LORD's anointed and be guiltless" (1 Sam 26:9)? He left it to Solomon to carry out judgment, after David's death; against Joab and Shimei for the wrongs they had done to him (1 Kgs 2:5–9). Pedersen says that rather than being motivated by a forgiving spirit, "always we meet with this fear of doing something that might offend Yahweh through natural self-assertion; coincidental with it is the satisfaction that Yahweh himself undertakes the revenge which the man desires but dare not carry out himself for fear of Yahweh" (1940, 530). David's leniency toward his children ("His father had never at any time displeased him by saying, 'Why have you done thus and so?'" 1 Kgs 1:6) represents more a weakness of character than willingness to forgive, as his treatment of Absalom, a murderer, indicates (2 Samuel 13–14). So, the lengthy narratives in 1–2Samuel essentially fail us in our effort to find examples of forgiveness as a way of settling differences.

There are two other requests for forgiveness in the narrative material, both of them rejected. They are addressed to people, but divine forgiveness is involved in both cases. The pharaoh, of all people, confessed his sinfulness to Moses and Aaron, asking them to forgive him and pray to Yahweh that the plague of locusts be ended (Exod 19:16–17). Actually, Moses did pray and the plague was lifted, but it seems unlikely that we are expected to take repentance of the pharaoh very seriously, and the plagues did continue.

Saul's plea, addressed to Samuel, is to be taken seriously, for the refusal to forgive him led to the loss of kingship and his life (1 Samuel 15). Saul had been instructed to wipe out the Amalekites and destroy all their possession (v. 3), and he did not do that. When Samuel confronted him with a dire word of judgment (vv. 22–23), Saul confessed that he had sinned and asked Samuel to pardon him (vv. 24–25), but Samuel refused, and we are to understand this to be a refusal of divine forgiveness, even though the request was addressed to a person.

There is one Old Testament text that commends human forgiveness—probably. The NRSV translates Prov 17:9, "One who forgives an affront fosters friendship, but one who dwells on disputes will alienate a friend." The word translated "affront" is the strong sin-word *peša‘*, so the proverb refers to a serious matter. The verb translated "forgive" is *kasah*, literally "cover," and this might be taken to recommend keeping silent about a transgression, rather than exposing the sinner (McKane 1970, 508). Taking *kasah* to refer to true forgiveness, as it does elsewhere (Neh 4:5; Pss 32:1; 85:2), seems to be the more likely reading. So, although the Old Testament contains no command to forgive, it is at least commended in the wisdom literature.

The Old Testament thus offers remarkably little to provide a scriptural basis for Jesus' emphasis on human forgiveness. The evidence is too scanty for us to draw any conclusions about forgiveness in daily life in ancient Israel. All we can say is that human forgiveness was not a subject that interested the authors of the Old Testament books.

PART TWO

The New Testament

This is my blood of the covenant, which is poured out for many
for the forgiveness of sins.

—Matthew 26:28

3

God Forgives Us

Judaism in the Time of Jesus

THE NEW TESTAMENT MESSAGE CONCERNING FORGIVENESS DIFFERS considerably from what we found in the Old Testament, so it seems appropriate to ask whether, by the first century A.D., changes had occurred in Jewish thought that might account for any of the differences. The Intertestamental Literature for the most part contains only scattered references to forgiveness, so it does not seem helpful for us to survey all of it. A century ago, Henry J. Wicks located the references to forgiveness in the literature in his *The Doctrine of God in the Jewish Apocryphal and Apocalyptic Literature* (1915). A thorough, recent study appears in *Justification and Variegated Nomism*, volume 1, *The Complexities of Second Temple Judaism* (Carson 2001). We shall focus on two of the most instructive Jewish sources, with occasional references to other works. One book of the Apocrypha, Ecclesiasticus, or the Wisdom of Jesus son of Sirach, represents the continuation of traditional Jewish wisdom teaching. Sectarian Judaism will be represented by the documents from Qumran, which speak often of forgiveness. We shall approach both sources asking three questions, then will be able to draw some conclusions that we will need to keep in mind as we read the New Testament. The questions are these: 1. What elements of continuity with the Old Testament do we find? 2. What new elements appear? 3. Is there anything here that seems to anticipate New Testament teaching?

Sirach

This book was written in Jerusalem, probably between 190 and 180 B.C. It was written in Hebrew and parts of the original text survive, but it appears in the Apocrypha in a Greek version that was made by the author's grandson. We thus have some access to the original terminology used of forgiveness, but the translator's choice of Greek words will also give us some insights into Jewish thought around 100 B.C.

1. Sirach's theology is in most respects very similar to that of the Old Testament authors. The righteous God expected righteousness from his people: "He has not commanded anyone to be wicked, and he has not given anyone permission to sin" (15:20). He was the stern judge of unrighteousness: "Even if there were only one stiff-necked person, it would be a wonder if he remained unpunished. For mercy and wrath are with the Lord; he is mighty to forgive—but he also pours out wrath" (16:11). As in the Old Testament, God was both the judge of sin and the merciful one, willing to forgive. "For the Lord is compassionate and merciful; he forgives sins and saves in time of distress" (2:11). God's mercy is in part motivated by his awareness of how weak we are and how short our lives are: "He sees and recognizes that their end is miserable; therefore he grants them forgiveness all the more" (18:12); this without any explicit reference to sin. Compare Ps 103:13–14 and all of Psalm 90.

Mercy is not to be equated with indulgence, however. People are to strive for righteousness: "Before judgment comes, examine yourself, and at the time of scrutiny you will find forgiveness" (18:20). Since sin is inevitable ("remember that we all deserve punishment" 8:5b), repentance is essential (17:25–29; 21:6).

> Do not say, "I sinned, yet what has happened to me?"
>   for the Lord is slow to anger.
> Do not be so confident of forgiveness
>   that you add sin to sin.
> Do not say, "His mercy is great,
>   he will forgive the multitude of my sins,"
> for both mercy and wrath are with him,
>   and his anger will rest on sinners.
> Do not delay to turn back to the Lord,
>   and do not postpone it from day to day. (5:4–7a)

Here, Sirach echoes the warnings of the prophets against the assumption that being God's people means freedom from responsibility. Elsewhere he reminds us of their judgments of those who think sacrifices without justice will please God: "The Most High is not pleased with the offerings of the ungodly, nor for a multitude of sacrifices does he forgive sins. Like one who kills a son before his father's eyes is the one who offers a sacrifice from the property of the poor" (34:2–24; cf. 7:9; 35:14–15 and recall Isa 1:1–17; Amos 5:21–24; Micah 6:6–8). (Büchler, 1922/23; 1923/24; Sanders 1977, 329–46.)

2. Sirach speaks of human acts of atonement in ways that do not appear in the Old Testament, where it was a ritual act, carried out by the priest, that led to divine forgiveness. Sacrifice continued to have atoning value for Sirach (45:16), but righteous behavior seems to function the same way for him. "As water extinguishes a blazing fire, so almsgiving atones for sin" (3:30). The comparison suggests that charity could wipe out the effects of sin, with no need to refer to divine forgiveness as a separate act. A similar comment appears in Tobit 12:9, "For almsgiving saves from death and purges away every sin," so this was not an idea unique to Sirach. We cannot tell whether anyone would have associated a single act of almsgiving with a specific sin that had been committed, as a single sacrifice would be. Other texts suggest instead that this is an example of a righteous life that has continuing atoning value. "Those who honor their father atone for sins, and those who respect their mother are like those who lay up treasure" (3:3–4). The saying clearly refers to one's way of living rather than any specific act, and this is supported by the general statement in 35:5: "To keep from wickedness is pleasing to the Lord, and to forsake unrighteousness is an atonement." A rather odd saying also speaks of atonement: "Those who cultivate the soil heap up their harvest, and those who please the great atone for injustice" (20:28). The awesome nature of the ritual described in Leviticus, involving the blood of a sacrificial animal, has been lost when giving alms can be called atonement, but something has been added to the word as it is used here, for it seems that one can actually acquire forgiveness by one's actions, without need for reference to an act of God.

The same word, *exilaskomai*, is used in the Greek version of the book both for divine forgiveness (3:4–6; 16:7, 11; 17:29; 18:12, 20) and for human acts of atonement (3:3, 30; 20:28; 35:5; 45:16, 23). Where the

Hebrew text is available it shows that the word was usually a translation of *kipper*, as elsewhere in the Septuagint. Earlier, we saw that although *kipper* usually refers to ritual carried out by humans, occasionally, when God is the subject, it simply means "forgive," and this accounts for the two uses of the Greek word in Sirach (Lyonnet & Sabourin 1970, 124–32). By the time he wrote, it seems that the fact *kipper/exilaskomai* could mean "forgive" when God was the subject influenced uses of the word with reference to people's actions. E. P. Sanders has called attention to the use of "atone" in the rabbinic literature, saying the Rabbis used "a kind of terminological short cut," so that the word included both the human act and God's forgiveness (1977, 160–61). The same usage appears in Sirach and we shall find it in the Qumran literature as well. When we turn to the New Testament, we shall encounter a significant difference at this point, for forms of this verb are seldom used, and only with reference to the work of Christ. Human acts that might atone for sin are never mentioned.

Sirach speaks of vicarious atonement at one point. In his account of the great men of the past, he claimed that Phinehas's violent act against idolaters, which brought a plague to an end, was "atonement for Israel" (45:23). This also moves beyond Old Testament uses of the idea, for even Moses is not said to have succeeded in his hope to make atonement for Israel (Exod 32:30–33). It reappears in the Qumran literature.

3. There is one passage in Sirach that might be said to foreshadow the New Testament. We found that the Old Testament says little of human forgiveness, so Sirach's advice, which links it with divine forgiveness, seems important. "Forgive (*aphes*) your neighbor the wrong he has done, then your sins will be pardoned (*luthesontai*) when you pray" (28:2). He emphasized the point with "If one has no mercy toward another like himself, can he then seek pardon [lit. "pray"] for his own sins" (28:4)? Verse 2 is so similar to Jesus' teaching in Matt 6:12,14–15 that the question has been raised whether this might be a Christian interpolation into the text, but most scholars accept it as original. An even more striking teaching appears in *Testament of Gad* 6:3–7, which advises that one should even forgive the unrepentant:

> If anyone confesses and repents, forgive him. If anyone denies his guilt, do not be contentious with him, otherwise he may start cursing, and you would be sinning doubly. . . . But even if he

is devoid of shame and persists in his wickedness, forgive him
from the heart and leave vengeance to God.

Since there is strong evidence that *Testaments of the Twelve Patriarchs*
has been reworked by Christian editors, we cannot be as sure that this
reflects Jewish, rather than Christian, teaching.

Documents from Qumran

Two of the Dead Sea Scrolls will provide for us some insights into
beliefs concerning forgiveness held by a group of sectarian Jews during the period between the writing of Sirach and the New Testament.
For our purposes we need not enter into the debate over the identity
of the group—Essene or otherwise—and only a few of its distinctive
characteristics will be important for us. It was an eschatological community, who believed themselves to be living in the last days. They saw
themselves as the true Israel, recipients of the new covenant, and dedi-
cated to strict adherence to the Torah as they interpreted it. They had
separated themselves from worship at the Jerusalem temple, which they
considered to be illegitimate under the present priesthood, and so they
tended to spiritualize terms that originally referred to sacrificial ritual
(Ringgren 1995, 120–26; Sanders 1977, 298–305). The scrolls chosen for
treatment here are the *Rule of the Community* (also called the *Sectarian
Document* or the *Manual of Discipline*) and the *Thanksgiving Hymns*
(*Hodayot*). They cannot be dated with any exactness, but may have
reached their present form during the first century B.C. We shall ask of
them the same three questions that we asked of Sirach.

1. Although the sectarians insisted on strict obedience to the Torah,
considered themselves to be the only people truly faithful to God, and
all others to be hopelessly lost, their literature emphasizes their dependence on the mercy of God. The familiar language of the Old Testament
reappears in their praise of God for his graciousness to them, with forgiveness one of his gracious acts, done solely for his own sake (1QH
4:37; 11:10). Those who strive for perfection are likely to be either self-
deceived or subject to despair, but the writers of these documents both
acknowledged their imperfections and rejoiced in the all-sufficiency of
the God of Israel. Paul Garnet concluded, "Indeed the works themselves
[produced by the spirit] are not really counted as merits at all even for

the salvation of the doer, for the utter unworthiness of the author is greatly stressed in the immediate context of both passages concerned" [i.e. 1QH 16:11; f2:13]. "Atonement continues to imply an end of God's wrath and full acceptance of the sinner. Its real basis is God's goodness alone" (Garnet 1977, 56, 80).

> In my afflictions you had mercy on me.
> I delight in forgiveness (*slḥ*),
>   and I am comforted concerning former transgression;
> for I know that there is hope in your loving kindness.
>   (1QH 9:13–14. Translations of the Dead Sea Scrolls are by
> the author)

Two of the Old Testament's favorite words used in praise of God appear frequently in the hymns of Qumran, as in this example:

> I depend on your loving kindness (*ḥsd*)
> and on the abundance of your compassion (*rḥmm*),
> for you forgive (*kpr*) iniquity,
> to cleanse man from guilt with your righteousness. (1QH 4:37)

Note that these authors, like the Old Testament and Sirach, used *kipper* to mean "forgive" when God was the subject. They frequently added "righteousness" to their descriptions of God's mercy, using the word in its salvific sense, as we also found it in the Old Testament.

> In the righteousness of his truth he will judge me,
>   and in the greatness of his goodness he will forgive (*kpr*) all
>   my iniquities.
> By his righteousness he will cleanse (*thr*) me of the defilement
>   of man and of the sins of the children of man,
> for the praise of God's righteousness. (1QS 11:14–15)

Forgiveness was frequently called cleansing, as we have seen in 1QH 3:21 and 1QS 11:14–14. Ritual washing seems to have been practiced (1QS 5:13–14), but it was of no value apart from spiritual cleansing (1QS 3:4–5) and it is the latter that is emphasized:

> By the spirit of holiness, to unite himself with his truth, he shall
>   be cleansed from all his iniquities,
> and by a spirit of uprightness and humbleness his sin shall be
>   forgiven (*kpr*).

By the humbleness of his soul toward all the statutes of God
    shall his flesh be cleansed,
to sprinkle with water of purification and to make holy with
    water of purity.
(1QS 3:7–8)

Inner cleansing that makes it possible to live a righteous life, such
as the author of Psalm 51 prayed for, was clearly a major aspect of divine
forgiveness in the Qumran literature (cf. 1QS 4:21; 1QH 1:32; 6:8–9;
11:10, 30; 16:12). This divine gift, through the agency of the Holy Spirit
(1QS 3:7; 4:21; 1QH 16:12), made it possible for one to live as a member
of the holy community:

You have cleansed a corrupt spirit from great transgression
    so that it may take a place with a host of holy ones,
and enter into the community with the congregation of the
    sons of heaven. (1QH 3:21)
For the sake of your glory you have cleansed man from
    transgression,
to sanctify himself for you from all abominations of impurity
    and guilt of disloyalty;
to become united with the sons of your truth,
    and with the lot of your holy people. (1QH 11:10; cf. 6:8–9)

The hymns suggest that the members of the community tended
to live with a strong sense of sinfulness, even though (or perhaps because) they were convinced that they alone were God's elect. The Old
Testament message that God is merciful and ready to forgive seems
thus to have been a more vital part of their faith than it may have been
for more optimistic Jews, who spoke of forgiveness less often.

2. As in Sirach, references to human acts of atonement appear in the
Qumran literature, and we shall consider three passages in the *Rule
of the Community*. Sirach mentioned a few times the atoning value of
righteousness, for one's own sins, and once claimed that Phinehas made
atonement for Israel. The Qumran community, having rejected as illegitimate the acts of atonement by sacrifice offered in the Jerusalem
temple, took it upon themselves to act as the true priesthood and to
atone for those who accepted their way by "justice and uprightness and
charity and modesty in all their ways" (1QS 5:4). Thus,

> . . . to make atonement for all the members of the community, for holiness in Aaron and for the house of truth in Israel and those who join with them in the community; and to try and judge the wickedness of all who transgress a statute. (1QS 5:6–7)

There would be no atonement and forgiveness for those outside the community. Elsewhere, however, they spoke of atoning for the Land (1QS 8:6–10). Since the Torah spoke of sin bringing guilt on the Promised Land (e.g., Deut 24:4), it appears that the community hoped by its righteousness to lift the curse under which the Land had lain because of Israel's perennial sinfulness. They went beyond Sirach, who added atonement by righteousness to atonement by sacrifice, and substituted the former for the latter.

> They shall atone for the guilty rebellion and for sins of unfaithfulness that they may obtain loving-kindness for the Land without the flesh of holocaust and the fat of sacrifice. And prayer rightly offered shall be as a delectable free-will offering. (1QS 9:4–5. On the translation of this text, see Lichtenberger 1980, 159–72)

The community expected that when they became victorious, their priests would offer sacrifices acceptable to God in the Jerusalem temple (1QM 2:5–6).

After the destruction of the Jerusalem temple in A.D. 70 made atonement by sacrifice no longer possible, the Rabbis found justification in Scripture for assuring Jews that repentance is the essential prerequisite for forgiveness, and is fully acceptable to God in lieu of sacrifice (e.g., 1 Sam 15:22; Hos 6:6). (Schechter 1961, 293–343; Moore 1971, I: 507–34). The Qumran community had reached a similar conclusion earlier; forgiveness was accessible without sacrifice at a time when they believed the Jerusalem ritual was ineffective.

3. The attitude toward forgiveness found in the in Qumran literature in no way foreshadows that which appears in the New Testament. Both continue to affirm the Old Testament message about God's forgiving mercy, but whereas Jesus extended that mercy to those lives were far different from what was required of good Jews, at Qumran it was restricted only to members of their community. A part of their ritual was a curse on those who refused to accept their teaching, including, "May God not heed when you call on Him, nor pardon you by blotting

out your sin! May He raise His angry face towards you for vengeance"
(1QS 2:8–9)! It is thus not surprising that we do not find anything like
the New Testament emphasis on human forgiveness in this literature.

Both Sirach and the Qumran sectarians were convinced of the
pervasiveness and inevitability of human sin, taking with the utmost
seriousness the Old Testament message concerning the righteousness
of God and contrasting that with human behavior as they experienced
it. They were also convinced of the truth of the Old Testament's strange
message that the same God who stands in stern judgment of all unrighteousness is also willing to forgive, so that not all the consequences
of sin must be suffered. As we compare their teachings with what we
found to be the consequences of forgiveness in the Old Testament, we
find that forgiveness as remission of punishment is certainly present,
although not emphasized at length. The sectarians differ from Sirach
in their regular equation of forgiveness with cleansing. Internal change,
brought about by the divine spirit, which makes holy living possible, is
a central subject in the hymns. Life in the holy community convinced
them that forgiveness brought about reconciliation with God (e.g., ". . .
purifying me by your holy spirit and drawing me near to you by your
grace" 1QH 16:12). Sirach does not speak so often in personal terms, but
he reminds us of Psalm 25 when he moves from forgiveness to the gift
of wisdom which brings about the internal change he desires and brings
him close to God. He wrote of the scribe:

> He sets his heart to rise early
>   to seek the Lord who made him,
>   and to petition the Most High;
> he opens his mouth in prayer
>   and asks pardon for all his sins.
> If the great Lord is willing,
>   he will be filled with the spirit of understanding;
> he will pour forth words of wisdom of his own
>   and give thanks to the Lord in prayer.
> The Lord will direct his counsel and knowledge
>   as he meditates on his mysteries.
> He will show the wisdom of what he has learned,
>   and will glory in the law of the Lord's covenant. (39:5–9)

As to the human contribution to forgiveness, Sirach emphasized
repentance, and the Qumran literature speaks of it only as essential for

entrance into the community. The atoning value of righteous acts will eventually be elaborated in Judaism, but one can scarcely speak of this literature as teaching "works salvation."

In the past, scholars have often depicted the Judaism of Jesus' time as a religion that had replaced free access to God with a burden of regulations—the Law—in order to define what was new about the ministry of Jesus. The detailed studies of the Jewish literature of the period made in recent years by Sanders and others have shown that the Old Testament promise of forgiveness by the grace of God had in no way been compromised by the increasing emphasis on the Law (Sanders 1977; 1985). Our two examples represent what is generally found throughout the literature: that there is no claim that one can, or must, deserve forgiveness by gaining merits through obeying the law, and no sense of despair because of one's inability to live a fully righteous life. Repentance was always possible, and even the ability to repent was a gift of God, the acceptance of the forgiveness that God offers. What, then, was truly new about the New Testament's offer of forgiveness through faith in Jesus Christ? That question will guide our approach to the earliest Christian witness.

The Apostolic Preaching

The writers of the New Testament have a great deal to say concerning what God has done about human sinfulness, but the word "forgive" does not appear with great frequency in English translations of those books. Eventually we shall have to deal with "justify," "reconcile," and other terms, but we shall begin with passages that use *aphiemi*, the word chosen by the Septuagint translators to represent Hebrew words for forgiveness; for example, *nasa'* in Exod 32:32; Pss 25:18 (Greek 24:18); 32:1, 5 (Greek 31:1, 5), *salah* in Lev 4:20, 26, 31, 35; 5:10, 13; Num 14:19, and *kipper* in Isa 22:14. The logical approach would seem to be at first to begin with Jesus, and with John the Baptist as his predecessor, then to move to the various elaborations of the message of forgiveness through Jesus Christ in the rest of the New Testament. On second thought, however, the Gospels contain some difficult passages, but the sermons in the book of Acts state very explicitly what is new about forgiveness in the New Testament: "Everyone who believes in him receives forgiveness of sins in his name" (Acts 10:43). Thus it seems best to begin with them. According to Luke, the forgiveness of sins and the gift of the Holy Spirit were the first results of the death and resurrection of Christ to be proclaimed by the apostles. Forgiveness thus became a more complex subject in the New Testament, where it is said to become possible through faith in a man, Jesus. Had it not always been possible because of God's graciousness, according to what Jews believed? There is nothing like this in the Old Testament—interposing faith in a person into the way of obtaining God's forgiveness—so it seems that we ought to begin with the message the apostles proclaimed so confidently, and to see how much we can learn about what persuaded them of this, from Scripture and from the career of Jesus. Then, since Luke's Gospel says more about forgiveness than the others, it will be a natural move to turn from Acts, his second volume, to his first as our basis for work with the Synoptic Gospels.

According to Luke, the risen Christ showed his disciples evidence in Scripture that the Messiah would suffer and die and be raised from the dead (Luke 24:26–27, 46), thus accounting for what had happened to him as part of the plan of God. He then instructed them that "repentance and forgiveness of sins is to be proclaimed in his name to all nations" (24:47). He does not explain the connection between his death and resurrection and the preaching of forgiveness, however, except for the phrase "in his name." Luke offers no "theory of atonement" at the conclusion of his Gospel, and so we turn to the apostles' interpretation, as he recorded it in the book of Acts. We do not think that he has given us a word-for-word record of the early preaching, but there are good reasons for taking his accounts of the early sermons to be good reflections of the thinking of the earliest Christians shortly after Jesus' resurrection. They contain none of the developed theology that we find in the New Testament letters. Luke was a companion of Paul, whose ministry long preceded the writing of Acts, but he does not allow Paul's theology to influence the sermons he composed to represent the earliest preaching (Dodd 1936, 19–21). We shall be guided, then, by C. H. Dodd's description of the *kerygma*, the preaching of the church at Jerusalem in an early period, which contained these elements: 1) "The age of fulfillment has dawned." 2) "This has taken place through the ministry, death, and resurrection of Jesus." 3) "By virtue of the resurrection, Jesus has been exalted at the right hand of God, as Messianic head of the new Israel." 4) "The Holy Spirit in the Church is the sign of Christ's present power and glory." 5) "The Messianic Age will shortly reach its consummation in the return of Christ." 6) "The *kerygma* always closes with an appeal for repentance, the offer of forgiveness and of the Holy Spirit, and a promise of 'salvation,' that is, of 'the life of the age to come,' to those who enter the elect community" (Dodd 1936, 21–23).

When Peter began his first sermon, on the day of Pentecost, with a quotation from Joel, its introduction, "In the last days . . ." indicates that Peter was claiming that the outpouring of the Holy Spirit that they had just experienced was a sign that the *last days* promised by the prophets were in fact upon them. The eschatological tone of the sermon is the first key to our understanding of its promises. We can move quickly over Peter's argument, from Scripture and the fact of the resurrection, that God had made Jesus "both Lord and Messiah [Greek: Christ]" (Acts 2:36), for our interest is in the results of that divine vindication. Peter states them in one sentence: two things to do and two gifts that are offered. "Repent, and be baptized every one of you in the name of Jesus Christ so that your sins may be forgiven; and you will receive the gift of the Holy Spirit" (Acts 2:38). When we compare this sentence with the other sermons in Acts, we find that as Luke knew the earliest preaching, this was the essence of the gospel: God raised Jesus from the dead; therefore your sins may be forgiven and you may receive the Holy Spirit. The Gospels and Acts 1 tell us that Jesus had promised the disciples that they would receive the Spirit after he left them (Luke 24:49; Acts 1:8; cf. John 14:15, 26; 16:13). The early sermons do not explain how they concluded that forgiveness was the result of resurrection, however. The commentators on Acts that I have consulted show no great interest in forgiveness (baptism and the Spirit are rightly important for them) and ask no questions about its prominence here, but perhaps if we ask a question we may learn something important.

First, let us note the consistency of references to forgiveness in the sermons. They all include a reference to forgiveness, five times using *aphiemi* (2:38; 5:31; 10:43; 13:38; 26:18), once "wipe out" (*exaleiphthēnai*, 3:19), and once "wash away" (*apolousai*, 22:16). In those seven passages, "repent" occurs four times, baptism is called for three times, and the Holy Spirit is mentioned twice. There is one reference to forgiveness of a different kind, in Acts 8:22, when Simon is advised to repent of his desire to buy the power to bestow the Holy Spirit. This is forgiveness of one specific sin, after he had been baptized (v. 13), so it represents a kind of forgiveness we shall need to consider later. There are at least two passages where we might have expected to hear the *kerygma*, but it is missing, so they do not help with our study. Philip baptized the Ethiopian eunuch (8:26–40), but nothing is said of repentance, forgiveness, or receipt of the Holy Spirit. When the jailer in Philippi asked Paul, "Sir, what must I do to be saved?" he was likely to be hoping only to avoid being punished by his superiors, but all that Luke records of Paul's response is, "Believe on the Lord Jesus, and you will be saved, you and your household" (16:30–31), a quite different sort of salvation. There must have been much more to the occasion, but we are told only of baptism.

In our effort to understand what was new about the offer of forgiveness in these early sermons, let us ask of each of them how it is related 1) to the resurrection and present status of Christ, 2) to repentance, 3) to baptism, and 4) to the gift of the Holy Spirit.

1. In every case, it is the resurrection that is the basis for the good news that now can be proclaimed. Dodd called our attention to the fact that the preachers say nothing of the saving power of Jesus' death (Dodd 1936, 25). They do not say Christ died for our sins. The cross is still a scandal, and all they can do with it is blame it on the leaders of the Jews, then affirm that God has vindicated Jesus by resurrection (2:23–24; 3:14–15; 5:30; 10:39–40; 13:29–30). Of Jesus' new status, they say he is exalted at the right hand of God (2:33; 5:31), glorified (3:13), made both Lord and Messiah (2:36), and ordained as judge of the living and the dead (10:42). Once, they spoke of a return from heaven at the time of universal restoration (3:21). They do not call Jesus the Son of God, additional evidence that Luke is reporting an early stage in the efforts to understand Jesus' true relationship to God.

2. The call to repent in 2:38; 3:19; 5:31 results naturally from the preacher's claim that the listeners are guilty of the death of Jesus. A general call for repentance does not appear in Peter's address to Cornelius (ch. 10), or Paul's sermon in the synagogue at Antioch of Pisidia (ch. 13). Paul did allude to repentance as part of his ministry to the Gentiles in 26:20.

3. "Repent and be baptized" occurs just once, in 2:38. Baptism occurs elsewhere in connection with forgiveness in 10:43–44, 48 and 22:16.

The origins of Christian baptism have been widely discussed. It has been compared with Jewish proselyte baptism, but there is no strong evidence that this was practiced as early as the first century A.D. (Taylor 1997, 64–69). The ritual washings at Qumran have been of interest as possible parallels, but the differences between that community's practices and what Peter called for from a motley crowd in Jerusalem at Pentecost are profound. The parallels with John's baptism are striking, however, and it seems likely that Jesus' disciples knew his practices and took them over at the time when a major act of repentance for putting Jesus to death was called for. John is reported to have proclaimed a baptism of repentance for the forgiveness of sins (Luke 3:3; cf. Mark 1:4), and so did Peter, adding "in the name of Jesus Christ," and the promise of the Spirit. Even the latter has its parallel in John's preaching, for he said that while he baptized with water, one was coming who would baptize with the Holy Spirit (Mark 1:8; Luke 3:16). Luke's account of Pentecost thus puts it in direct continuity with the ministry of John the Baptist, providing an explanation for the sudden appearance of baptism, which played no role in Jesus' ministry.

The relationship between baptism and forgiveness has also been much discussed. Did the rite bring about forgiveness, as the sacrificial blood on the altar brought about atonement? There is general agreement that both for John and for Peter the answer was negative. Joan Taylor's work on John makes a persuasive case for understanding the meaning of his baptism as follows:

"(1) One repents and practices righteousness; (2) one's sins are remitted (=one is cleansed inwardly); (3) one immerses; (4) one's immersion is considered acceptable by God, and one becomes outwardly clean. Remission of sins comes from repentance and its proof in righteous behavior, as defined by John—not from immersion" (Taylor 1997, 98; for the full discussion, see Taylor 1997, 49–100.).

For Christians, especially in the Gentile world, the ritual cleansing of the body, which was important for Jews, soon became unimportant, but it may well have been part of the understanding of baptism at Pentecost, although it would have been of no interest to Luke when he wrote. Eventually baptism would become a rite of initiation into the church, with the forgiveness of sin associated with it. Acts is not very explicit about that, but it is suggested by the accounts in chs. 8, 10, and 16.

4. The Spirit had fallen on the followers of Jesus, and when Peter interpreted that with reference to Joel's prophecy he had a basis for assuring those who would repent that they also would receive the Spirit. Soon we shall find reasons to account for Peter's two-fold promise: forgiveness and the Spirit.

We may look at a few details that appear in the accounts of the other sermons, then will return to ch. 2 with more questions. When the lame man was healed in the gate of the temple and a crowd gathered, recognizing that this person they had often seen now could walk, Peter took advantage of the opportunity once again to preach the gospel. He had a natural point of contact with the ministry of Jesus: "and by faith in his name, his name itself has made this man strong, whom you see and know; and the faith that is through Jesus has given him this perfect health in the presence of all of you" (Acts 3:16). As in his Pentecost sermon, he directly accused the crowd of killing "the Author of Life," whom God raised from the dead (vv. 13–15). Without quoting Scripture this time, he claimed that Jesus' death had been foretold in Scripture (v. 18) and his later reference to Jesus as God's servant (v. 26) suggests he was alluding to Isaiah 53, a text we shall consider a bit later. Then two of the four elements that interested us in the Pentecost sermon appear: "Repent therefore, and turn to God so that your sins may be wiped out" (v. 19). He spoke of forgiveness as cleansing (*exaleiphthēnai*), using one of the metaphors we found in the Old Testament; then, instead of promising the Holy Spirit or calling for baptism, he looked forward to the return of Christ (v. 20). In this sermon, the power ("the name") of the risen Christ is associated directly with healing—easily understandable—but the references to repentance and forgiveness do not afford any clue as to how Peter connected them with Jesus' death and resurrection, unless he did in fact elaborate on Isaiah 53.

When Peter and the other apostles were brought before the high priest and the council, having been ordered not to teach in the name of Jesus (Acts 5:27–32), they dared to accuse these leaders of the Jewish people of killing Jesus, insisting not only that God had raised him from the dead, but also that God had exalted him at his right hand as Leader and Savior (v. 31). As a result, "he [God or Christ?] might give repentance to Israel and forgiveness of sins." Peter did not offer baptism to the high priest, but perhaps he would have if his words thus far had not led the council to become enraged (v. 33). For now, we just note that as in

Acts 2 Peter moved directly from resurrection to forgiveness, without explanation.

His message to Cornelius and his friends followed the same pattern as the earlier ones (Acts 10:34–43), with the addition of some information about Jesus' ministry that may not have been known to these Gentile "God-fearers" (see 10:1–2). Jesus' death is referred to briefly, and his resurrection with more detail, with the risen Christ this time called "judge of the living and the dead" (v. 42). Judges are not usually associated with forgiveness, so this addition to what Peter had said about Christ being exalted at the right hand of God does not seem to lead logically to his assurance, "All the prophets testify about him that everyone who believes in him receives forgiveness of sins through his name" (v. 43). Once again, two themes that we will need to examine have appeared: the prophets, and "through his name." Repentance is not mentioned, since Peter had no time to call for it. While he was still speaking the Holy Spirit fell upon those Gentiles (v. 44). Peter evidently took this as proof that they should be admitted into the Christian community, represented by the "circumcised believers" who were present, for he concluded that people who have received the Spirit should be baptized (vv. 44–48). Baptism appears to function essentially as an initiation rite here, as it is not said to have any causal effect on either forgiveness or receipt of the Holy Spirit.

The pattern of the *kerygma*, the preaching of the Jerusalem church as outlined by Dodd, reappears in Luke's account of one of Paul's sermons (Acts 13:16–41). Having been invited to speak in the synagogue at Antioch of Pisidia, he began with a reminder of Old Testament history from David to Jesus, although not referring to Jesus as Messiah (the descendent of David who would rule as king in the last days), but as Savior. Having cited the testimony of John the Baptist, he then accused the leaders in Jerusalem of responsibility for Jesus' death and testified to Jesus' resurrection. The effect of the resurrection is, as always, "through this man forgiveness of sins is proclaimed to you; by this Jesus everyone who believes is set free from all those sins from which you could not be freed by the law of Moses" (vv. 38–39).

The Jews in that synagogue might have been puzzled by that last clause. From what sins could they not be freed by the law of Moses (which included the Day of Atonement)? This may be Luke's one effort, in the whole speech, to reflect something of Paul's problem with the law, for we recognize that the language of the sermon is Luke's, and not what we know from Paul's letters. Once again, Luke found an occasion to repeat and expand the early *kerygma* as he had learned it, and forgiveness is the single result of God's vindication of Jesus that he sees fit to mention.

Finally, in one of Paul's accounts of his Damascus road experience, he reports that the risen Christ sent him to the Gentiles, "to open their eyes so that they may turn from darkness to light and from the power of Satan to God, so that they may receive forgiveness of sins and a place among those who are sanctified by faith in me" (Acts 26:18). Forgiveness is not typical of Paul's vocabulary, but for Luke it clearly was of the essence of the earliest Christian message, even including Paul's preaching.

This leads to my naive question. I call it naive because I have not found any commentator on Acts asking it. They discuss baptism and the Holy Spirit, and seem to find nothing about forgiveness that needs to be explained. Here is the background to my question, or questions: Peter's first three sermons are addressed to Jews. The Jews already believed in divine forgiveness, so who needed forgiveness from a new source? We have seen that the call to repent and be baptized for the forgiveness of sins is explainable as a continuation of John's ministry, and could thus have been understood as such by the Jerusalemites. But Peter connects forgiveness with the death and resurrection of Jesus, and that leads to my question. Why did he conclude that because a man had been crucified and raised from the dead, some new kind of forgiveness of sins was now available through him? If, today, we heard that someone had been tortured to death, but had miraculously reappeared alive, would we immediately conclude: This means our sins are forgiven?

I did find a church historian asking a similar question about the apostles' conclusions. Johannes Weiss commented,

> It is a permanently impressive fact that the disciples not only drew the conclusion, from the appearances of the Lord, that he still lived; but that they went on at once to the further inference; he is also now the Messiah (Acts 2:36). Taken by itself, one does not readily see why the Messiahship of Jesus must have followed from his resurrection or restoration to life. If a dead man were to reappear to his friends, they would scarcely draw any other conclusion than that the departed was still living and that in spite of the separation he was still near them. . . . but this was

> by no means a proof of Messiahship, for and in itself. (Weiss 1959, I:31)

But Weiss did not comment on the offer of forgiveness. More surprising—Peter told them it was a man they had murdered who would make forgiveness possible for them.

Luke's only explicit answer to the question appears in the conclusion to his Gospel. They preached forgiveness in Jesus' name because he had instructed them to (Luke 24:47; cf. Matt 28:19–20, which says nothing of forgiveness). This is too simple, for we want to know whether they understood what they were saying. There are hints that they did, in what we might call a preliminary way since Acts is far removed from offering a theory of atonement. We begin with two features of Luke's presentation: the indications that the apostles believed they were living in the last days, and the several references to their arguments from Scripture.

We have seen that Peter began his first sermon, with his quotation from Joel, claiming that the last days were upon them. Arguing from the fact of Jesus' resurrection, as he knew it, he moved to the eschatological claim that Jesus was the Messiah (2:36). In his second sermon he spoke, rather vaguely, of "times of refreshing" that may come if they repent, and those times are associated with the return of Jesus (3:20–21)—futuristic, rather than realized eschatology this time, although we know that Christ's return was expected very soon (cf. Matt 26:29; 1 Thess 4:13–18). Luke has both Peter and Paul declare that what has happened in their time has fulfilled the promises of the prophets (3:18, 24; 10:43; 13:23, 27, 32). If we had full accounts of their preaching, no doubt we would find many texts quoted and expounded, but since we do not have them we must trace the hints that are provided.

We think, then, about Old Testament promises of forgiveness in the last days, and there are good reasons to turn first to the promise of a new covenant in Jer 31:31–34. The passage is quoted at length in Heb 8:8–12 and briefly in Heb 10:16–17, and we shall consider its use in Hebrews later. The most important use of it for our present concerns is at the Last Supper. Jesus' words have been preserved for us four times, in 1 Cor 11:23–25, Mark 14:22–25, Matt 26:26–29, and Luke 22:17–20. The exact wording of each of them differs considerably from the others. A likely explanation is that each reflects the wording used in celebrations of the Lord's Supper in the region where the document was written

(Davies 1955, 242–50). The four accounts seem to represent two traditions, both of which agree in identifying the bread with Jesus' body and in associating the cup of wine with blood and a covenant. The following comparison includes only the words essential for our purposes:

Matthew 26:26b–28	*Mark 14:22b–24*
Take, eat:	Take;
this is my body	this is my body
. . . .	. . . .
this is my blood of the covenant	This is my blood of the covenant
which is poured out for many	which is poured out for many.
for the forgiveness of sins.	

Luke 22:19b–20	*1 Corinthians 11:24b–25*
This is my body,	This is my body
which is given for you.	that is broken for you.
Do this in remembrance of me.	Do this in remembrance of me
. . . . .	. . . . .
This cup that is poured out for you	This cup
is the new covenant in my blood.	is the new covenant in my blood.

Mark's version apparently does not indicate what the blood of the covenant would accomplish; saying just that it is poured out for many. Luke and Paul explicitly associate Jesus' shed blood with the new covenant promised in Jeremiah, and Matthew does so in his own way, by adding "for the forgiveness of sins."

Most of the issues that scholars discuss with reference to these accounts need not concern us, for it is just the reference to *covenant* that may have led to the emphasis on forgiveness in the early preaching. All agree that the association of the covenant with blood is an allusion to the ritual described in Exod 24:3–8, for of the Old Testament covenants, only the one made at Sinai was sealed with blood. But what could Jesus have meant by associating his impending death with the Sinai covenant? The answer is to be found in the word "new," cited by Paul and Luke. The term "new covenant" appears only once in the Old Testament, in Jer 31:31–34, and there it is contrasted with the one made at Sinai. The new covenant will be written on the heart, so that all will know the Lord. The climax of the promise was "I will forgive their iniquity, and remember their sin no more" (v. 34). As we have seen earlier, this forgiveness goes beyond what Israel had experienced, for it is associated with the internalizing of the law, evidently making it possible to be perfectly obedient, so that full knowledge of God would be possible. We have seen, also, in Jer 50:20, that he may have thought of eschatological forgiveness as including a transformation so complete that forgiveness would never again be needed.

Jesus' reference to Exodus 24, with the words "my blood of the covenant" (Matt 26:28; Mark 14:24) or "covenant in my blood" (Luke 22:20; 1 Cor 11:25) becomes meaningful if he is referring to Jeremiah's new covenant, which, like the Sinai covenant, will be sealed with blood. The record of his words in Luke and 1 Corinthians makes that explicit. Mark's record makes Jesus' death a sacrifice of some sort, but without offering much help as to what it would mean. Commentators usually claim that Matthew's "for the forgiveness of sins" is not to be taken as part of Jesus' original words, but as the evangelist's interpretation, but it shows Matthew also believed "the blood of the covenant" initiated Jeremiah's new covenant, by citing the climax of the promise—forgiveness.

"The days are surely coming," Jeremiah had said, and the records of the Last Supper indicate that Jesus announced to his disciples that with the shedding of his blood that day would come, the day of eschatological forgiveness, with the law to be written on the heart. The disciples clearly did not understand that at the time, but the early sermons suggest that a first step in their understanding was their recollection of Jesus' reference to the new covenant the night before his death, and the prominence of forgiveness in Jeremiah's promise led to the prominence of forgiveness in their preaching. It was something new, then; more than the restoration of a broken relationship with God which had always been available to repentant Jews, but the beginning of a perfect and permanent relationship with God.

Luke does not quote Jeremiah, however. Does this raise a serious question about the suggestion that the new covenant promises directly underlay the emphasis on forgiveness in the apostolic preaching? It certainly raises a question, but perhaps there is an answer in Acts, supported by evidence from the letters. The outpouring of the Spirit did produce dramatic changes in the lives of people who came to believe in Jesus Christ as Savior, and it quickly produced a new community marked by love and generosity (e.g., Act 2:43–47; 4:32–37) and a power-ful sense of the presence of the Risen Christ among them. It was a New Age for them, but it soon became apparent that the personal transfor-mations they had experienced were real, but not complete. They found the power to live better lives, but they still sinned, still needed forgive-ness. Luke records that in a matter-of-fact way in his account of Simon's effort to buy the power to bestow the Holy Spirit by the laying on of his hands (Acts 8:9–24). He had believed and been baptized, but Peter rebuked him, calling for repentance and prayer for forgiveness. The case of Ananias and Sapphira, who lied to the church and thus to the Holy Spirit—according to Peter—is recounted without any reference to the possibility of forgiveness (Acts 5:1–11). When accused by Peter they died immediately. Stroke or heart attack, we might think, but evidently it was taken as God's direct act of judgment, since "fear seized the whole church" (5:11). Luke does not say so; he reports the incident probably because it was well known, but it should not have happened, so he of-fered no explanation.

Perhaps this is why Luke does not quote extensively the Old Testament's eschatological promises that the early preachers may have used, such as Jeremiah 31 and Ezekiel 36, but tells us only that they cited the prophets. Luke is recording a success story, but it was not perfect. Promises had come true, but not all of them. We shall find Paul and the author of Hebrews struggling with that, but Luke found it possible not to discuss it. So, it is possible to argue that his failure to quote Jeremiah 31 is not evidence against making the connection with Jesus' words at the Last Supper that has been done here.

Our work with Acts has revealed immediately what is different about the New Testament message of forgiveness. Its direct association of forgiveness with the gift of the Holy Spirit indicates that for the fol-lowers of Jesus forgiveness in his name was a part of the New Age that his death and resurrection introduced, and the indwelling of the Spirit did bring about the personal, internal change, making full obedience to God possible, that Old Testament authors longed for and hoped for. That in fact it was not perfect after all did not lead them to reject the idea that the Risen Christ was truly the source of new life for them, for the changes that did occur were real. So far, we have looked back to the Last Supper as evidence, at least, that the apostles believed Jesus himself intended to be the one who would initiate this new age, and it seems very unlikely that they could have come up with such an idea unless they had heard it from him. But now, we must turn to the Gospels to look for the role of forgiveness in Jesus' words and deeds.

The Synoptic Gospels

Forgiveness is referred to in a variety of ways in Matthew, Mark, and Luke, and each of them raises questions that will need to be taken seriously if we are to understand the relationship between Jesus and forgiveness that the evangelists intended to convey. One important feature is almost new—instruction concerning human forgiveness—and we shall reserve discussion of those passages for the section "We Forgive One Another." We shall approach the subject of divine forgiveness this way: First, just a list of all the passages in each Gospel, noting parallels and the types of literature used, including human forgiveness at this point; then a detailed study of each text, following Luke, who has the most to say about the subject.

Mark does not say a great deal about forgiveness, and has only one saying that is unique. His evidence:

A report about John's preaching (1:4; also Luke 3:3)

A healing story: the paralytic (2:1–12; also Matt 9:2–8; Luke 5:17–26)

A warning: blaspheming the Holy Spirit (3:28–30; also Matt 12:31–32; Luke 12:10)

Interpretation of a parable—the sower (4:12; cf. Matt 13:15)

Instruction on prayer (11:25; also Matt 6:14–15; Luke 6:37)

Mark's one unique occurrence is not particularly significant. Where Matthew 13:15 quoted Isa 6:10 literally, using "heal," Mark 4:12 interpreted the verb correctly as meaning "forgive." Luke 8:10 omitted that part of the verse. We shall also consider a verse that does not speak explicitly of forgiveness, as we look for evidence of how the evangelists thought forgiveness came about as a result of the death of Christ. It is, "For the Son of Man came not to be served but to serve, and to give his life as a ransom for many" (Mark 10:45; Matt 20:28).

Matthew adds:

The Lord's Prayer, with its petition, "And forgive us our debts as we also have forgiven our debtors" (6:12; also Luke 11:4)

Instruction on human forgiveness (18:21–22; also Luke 17:3–4)

A parable—the unforgiving debtor (18:23–35)

An announcement—"This is my blood of the covenant, which is poured out for many for the forgiveness of sins" (26:28)

Luke adds:

A prayer (1:77)

A story and parable—the sinful woman and the two debtors (7:36–50)

Parables—the lost sheep, the lost coin, and the prodigal son (15:3–7, 8–10, 11–32); the Pharisee and the tax collector (18:9–14). Matthew also has the parable of the lost sheep (18:23–25), but does not associate it with repentance.

A story of repentance—Zacchaeus (19:1–10)

A word from the cross—"Father, forgive them; for they do not know what they are doing" (23:34)

The commission to the disciples (24:47)

The list makes it clear that we can deal with most of the forgiveness passages in the Synoptics by focusing on Luke, comparing the parallels in Matthew and Mark. Commentators call attention to the importance of forgiveness in that Gospel. In addition to the number of relevant passages, which we have just noticed, he begins and ends his work with references that do not occur in the other Gospels. The hymn attributed to Zechariah, father of John the Baptist, repeats the hopes for Israel found in Old Testament psalms—deliverance from their enemies (1:71, 74) that they might live in holiness, righteousness, and peace (1:75, 79). The salvation (1:67, 77) of which he spoke was thus essentially deliverance from physical distress, as the word is used in the Old Testament, but this did not come as a result of John's or Jesus' work. Zechariah modified "salvation," however, in a way that pointed to what John and Jesus really did: "to give knowledge of salvation to his people by the forgiveness of sins" (v. 77). That this was a key word for Luke's understanding of Jesus' work is indicated by its reappearance at the end of the Gospel, in Jesus' commission to the disciples: "repentance and forgiveness of sins is to be proclaimed in his name to all nations, beginning from Jerusalem" (24:47). We have seen how he continued that emphasis in Acts, forgiveness offered in a new way, "in his name," and not only for the Jews, but for all nations.

After Luke's unique material concerning the births of John and Jesus (chs. 1–2), he mainly follows the order of Mark, one of his primary sources, for several chapters, with the addition of some unique passages, of which 4:16–30 is clearly of major importance for the evangelist. Jesus went to worship in the synagogue at Nazareth, and having read Isa 61:1–2a, "The Spirit of the Lord is upon me, because he has anointed me to bring good news to the poor. He has sent me to proclaim release to the captives and recovery of sight to the blind, to let the oppressed go free, to proclaim the year of the Lord's favor," he declared, "Today this scripture has been fulfilled in your hearing" (4:21). This is Luke's introduction to the ministry of Jesus, and it leads very naturally into the next section of the book, in which he uses Mark's accounts of a series of healings (4:31–5:26; cf. Mark 1:21–2:12), the last of which is the healing and forgiving of the paralyzed man.

> One day, while he was teaching, Pharisees and teachers of the law were sitting nearby (they had come from every village of Galilee and Judea and from Jerusalem); and the power of the Lord was with him to heal. Just then some men came, carrying a paralyzed man on a bed. They were trying to bring him in and lay him before Jesus; but finding no way to bring him in because of the crowd, they went up on the roof and let him down with his bed through the tiles into the middle of the crowd in front of Jesus. When he saw their faith, he said, "Friend, your sins are forgiven you." Then the scribes and the Pharisees began to question, "Who is this who is speaking blasphemies? Who can forgive sins but God alone?" When Jesus perceived their questionings, he answered them, "Why do you raise such questions in your hearts? Which is easier, to say, 'Your sins are forgiven you,' or to say, 'Stand up and walk'? But so that you may know that the Son of Man has authority on earth to forgive sins"—he said to the one who was paralyzed—"I say to you, stand up and take your bed and go to your home." Immediately he stood up before them, took what he had been lying on, and went to his home, glorifying God. Amazement seized all of them, and they

glorified God and were filled with awe, saying, "We have seen strange things today." (Luke 5:17–26)

The story appears early in each of the three Gospels, introducing almost at the beginning of Jesus' ministry the question of his relationship to divine forgiveness. Has God authorized him to *announce* what God has done, or does Jesus actually have the *power* to forgive—something only God can do? The story ends with that question, but the way it is told—mostly what it omits—leads to many other questions, most of which cannot be answered. We shall not learn all that we wanted to learn, but we will be able to be sure about what the evangelist wanted this story to teach.

The commentaries tend to focus on two kinds of questions, which we might call issues of integrity and of authenticity. Integrity: Is this a combination of two originally distinct stories; one about healing and another about forgiveness? Recent discussions of the matter have concluded that the two subjects were most likely part of the same story from the beginning, and the reasons given are convincing enough that we need not delay over that issue (Bock 1994, 470; Fitzmyer 1970, 579; Marshall 1978a, 211; Bovon 2002, 245). Authenticity: Did Jesus really say what he is here reported to have said? This is not a question we can answer, as much as we would like to know. I am skeptical of all efforts to get behind the texts we have in order to discover who Jesus really was, what he could and could not have said and done, even what he really thought. All of those efforts are too highly subjective to be satisfying to one who always asks, "What is the evidence?" We were not there, and all we have are these texts. What they record may or may not have happened. My understanding of the inspiration of Scripture does not include an insistence on the complete accuracy of everything in it. We can be certain about this, however: They do tell us what the earliest followers of Jesus believed about him. That is not enough for many, but it is enough for many others, since in fact it has not been the original, authentic words and acts of Jesus that have brought people to faith in him and sustained the church over the centuries. We have never had them. It has been this earliest testimony that has done so. I shall be satisfied, then, if I think I have accurately discerned what the evangelists wanted their readers to know about Jesus.

We still have many questions about the story, and if we resist the temptation to fill in the gaps with guesses we shall find that it does not tell us as much about forgiveness as we had hoped to learn. There is considerable variety in the ways the three authors recount the story, but it is not the variations but the consistent elements that raise the questions. A man so severely paralyzed that he cannot walk was carried by his friends (Matthew doesn't mention "four") to the house where Jesus was teaching. Neither he nor his friends are allowed to say anything, as the story is told, but an assumption seems acceptable here: They hope Jesus will heal him. Jesus "saw their faith." Who is included in "their"? Certainly the friends; probably also the paralytic. But, if so, what does his faith include? He says nothing. He does not ask for his sins to be forgiven, and this is rather important, for there is nothing in the story that suggests repentance on his part. Forgiveness without prior repentance? We did see something of that in the Old Testament.

What sins did Jesus forgive? We are not given a hint. Capernaum was a small town, and he may have known or known of the man, so this might have been a quite specific forgiveness, but we are not told that. The suggestion that Jesus was forgiving the man's fallen state as a member of the human race strikes one as a tacit admission that we do not know exactly what happened here.

Commentators emphasize Jesus' use of the passive voice, "your sins are forgiven" (Matt 9:2; Mark 2:5; Luke 5:20); i.e., they have been forgiven by God. The sentence then might be read as only a claim by Jesus to possess the authority to know when God had forgiven someone's sins. But it could mean that Jesus himself had done the forgiving. The former claim might well be accepted without serious reservations, but the latter would create a major issue. Mark and Luke tell us that this is the way the scribes (and the Pharisees, in Luke) heard it. "It is blasphemy! Who can forgive sins but God alone" (Mark 2:7)? (The second sentence is identical in Luke 5:21, except for one word). It seems surprising that Matt 9:3 includes only, "this man is blaspheming," but Matthew had abbreviated the story at several other points, and his understanding of the meaning of the event is not different, as we shall soon see. In later rabbinic teaching, the charge of blasphemy was restricted to one crime, speaking the personal name of God (Mishnah, *Sanhedrin* 7:5), but there is evidence that at this time the word was used more broadly (cf. Mark 14:64). The question, "Who can forgive sins but God alone?" suggests they were thinking of something even more serious—claiming to be God.

Jesus did not defend himself against such a potential charge, but reinforced the shocking nature of what he had said. His challenge, comparing two "impossible" things with "which is easier?" would not prove anything to a person unwilling to believe, but it represents the true climax of the story for the evangelists, emphasized for us by the fact that this is one of the few sentences in the three versions where the wording is almost identical: "But that you may know that the Son of man has authority on earth to forgive sins—" (Matt 9:6; Mark 2:10; Luke 5:24). Jesus uses the term Son of man in various ways in the Gospels, and it has been questioned whether he is always referring to himself (Hare 1990, 257–82; esp. p. 274), but it seems certain that the evangelists intended their readers to understand it as his self-designation. What would be the climax in another story of healing is not so important compared with what Jesus had just said. He healed the man, who took up his bed and went home. Luke does add that he joined the others in glorifying God (Luke 5:25), but that is all we know of him. In other healing stories that would be enough, but with our interest in forgiveness we wish we could have known more about him.

In our study of forgiveness thus far we have been seeking to learn what difference it makes for a person's life to have one's sins forgiven by God. Here we have encountered what seems to be the first important forgiveness passage in the Synoptics, a vivid story of a man let down through the roof of a house, surprised (we assume) by being told his sins are forgiven, then having attention diverted from him and his physical distress, but finally having it alleviated, not so much out of concern for him (it seems), but to prove a point about Jesus. Then he gets up and goes home. What did it mean to him to be forgiven? We are not told, but as a kind of excursus to our main interest something should be added here about sin and sickness. Some interpreters point to the widespread tendency to blame sickness on sin, and may even suggest that Jesus connected this man's disability with his sinfulness (Branscom 1934). The story does not exactly say that, however. Jesus compares forgiveness with healing, as to difficulty, and does not make one the cause of the other. Most interpreters point out that forgiveness did not produce healing; they were separate acts. They also remind us of Jesus' challenges elsewhere to the notion that suffering is always the result of sin (Luke 13:2; John 9:2–3). So, the simple but inadequate answer to the question of what forgiveness meant to the man—it healed him—seems to be no answer. We knew nothing about the man as a person at the beginning (everyone has sinned in some way) and at the end we still know nothing, except that Luke says he glorified God. Have the evangelists failed us, then? In one respect they have, for we want to know more about what forgiveness does for a person, but it is clear that they intended to make a different point. What they omitted and included all contribute to that point, namely, *who Jesus was*. There is a remarkable amount of variety among the three ways this short story is told, but at certain points the three authors agree on almost identical wording, and this must mean they agreed that these are the key sentences in the story.

Your sins are forgiven.

Who can forgive sins but God alone?

The Son of man has authority on earth to forgive sins.

The story, placed early in each Gospel, makes an astonishing claim for this man who had been known thus far as a healer. The evangelists knew a tradition that said Jesus once claimed for himself the ability to forgive sins, and it was a valuable one for them because it contributed to one of their chief aims in writing. It means that in Jesus, somehow the very power of God was present on earth. Note that their inclusion of that final phrase—on earth—is not unimportant: "authority on earth to forgive sins." There is an answer, then, to our question about why this story and the next one we shall read do not tell us all we want to know. The evangelists tell us what *they* want us to know, and they focus only on that. Their primary aim was to explain *who Jesus was*, and certain traditions about Jesus and forgiveness helped them to do that.

By the time the Gospels were written, people far beyond Palestine had experienced the gift of the Holy Spirit, changing them for the better, when they came to believe that the death and resurrection of Jesus was proof both of God's love for them and his power to forgive their sins. The presence of the Spirit with them was proof of this, but who, in truth, was this Jesus? Paul and others called him Son of God, which for Jews could just mean a righteous man, and for Gentiles was likely to mean a semi-divine being, like Hercules. What "son of God" meant with respect to Jesus remained to be defined, and at first it must have been hard to uphold. Jesus' career seemed to end in failure, with crucifixion; so, as we have seen, resurrection had to be, from the first (e.g., Acts 2) central to the explanation of who he was. But those who had been changed by belief in him needed to know more, and in the Gospels were gathered memories of him that contributed to the writers' insistence that in Jesus God was somehow personally present on earth. (Recall Matthew's use of Isa 7:14: Immanuel—God is with us; Matt 1:23.) So, they focused on miracles, on Jesus' claims to authority (over Sabbath-observance, to be able to announce forgiveness, to teach with originality), and his acceptance of the cross as the completion of his work on earth, rather than resisting it. Each story, then, might have ended as some do: "Who is this?" and the evangelists intended their readers to answer as Matthew did: "This was God with us." This approach suggests an answer to the disinterest in what became of those who were forgiven. Once some evidence of forgiveness has been provided the point of the story has been reached: This is One who has the power of God to forgive sins.

There are two more accounts, in Luke only, that involve Jesus and forgiven people. We shall find that they also raise some challenging questions. The first is the story of a woman who interrupts a dinner to anoint Jesus' feet, leading to a parable and more statements about forgiveness. Whereas the account of the paralytic began and ended as a healing story, with its real point in the middle, where it became a controversy story, Luke 7:36–50 is a controversy story throughout, with the parable in the middle essential to its development.

> One of the Pharisees asked Jesus to eat with him, and he went into the Pharisee's house and took his place at the table. And a woman in the city, who was a sinner, having learned that he was eating in the Pharisee's house, brought an alabaster jar of ointment. She stood behind him at his feet, weeping, and began to bathe his feet with her tears and to dry them with her hair. Then she continued kissing his feet and anointing them with the ointment. Now when the Pharisee who had invited him saw it, he said to himself, "If this man were a prophet, he would have known who and what kind of woman this is who is touching him—that she is a sinner." Jesus spoke up and said to him, "Simon, I have something to say to you." "Teacher," he replied, "Speak." "A certain creditor had two debtors; one owed five hundred denarii, and the other fifty. When they could not pay, he canceled the debts for both of them. Now which of them will love him more?" Simon answered, "I suppose the one for whom he canceled the greater debt." And Jesus said to him, "You have judged rightly." Then turning toward the woman, he said

to Simon, "Do you see this woman? I entered your house; you gave me no water for my feet, but she has bathed my feet with her tears and dried them with her hair. You gave me no kiss, but from the time I came in she has not stopped kissing my feet. You did not anoint my head with oil, but she has anointed my feet with ointment. Therefore, I tell you, her sins, which were many, have been forgiven; hence she has shown great love. But the one to whom little is forgiven, loves little." Then he said to her, "Your sins are forgiven." But those who were at the table with him began to say among themselves, "Who is this who even forgives sins?" And he said to the woman, "Your faith has saved you; go in peace." (Luke 7:36–50)

Erich Auerbach, in his book *Mimesis*, compared the poetry of Homer, in which everything has to be explained, with the stories in Genesis, which he called "fraught with background." He called attention to the way Hebrew authors focused so narrowly on the point of their stories that they tended to omit every unnecessary detail (Auerbach 1953, 1–20). The same comment can certainly be made about this story, and so it is that every interpreter attempts to find a history for this woman, since it seems as though that is necessary if we are to understand it. But suppose we assume that Luke knew exactly how to accomplish what he intended, and his story is fraught with background because he included all that was necessary, and no more. If we attempt to read it that way we shall still, inevitably, be confronted by many questions, but if the text does not provide clear answers, we shall try to avoid filling the gaps imaginatively.

The scene is the house of a Pharisee, where Jesus had been asked to dine. The dinner was interrupted by the extravagant behavior of a woman who was clearly not of the household, and had gained entrance to the place somehow. We are told only that she was "of the city," with the place not named, and that she had learned where Jesus was. The scene can easily be pictured, knowing that at a formal meal guests would have reclined on one side, with the feet projecting away from the table. Kenneth Bailey, whose years of experience in the Middle Eastern countries have made him a master interpreter of the parables, has provided examples of every detail of such banquets from his own observations and those of early travelers (Bailey 1983, 3–6). The woman approached Jesus weeping profusely, her tears wetting his feet, leading her to dry them with her hair, a shocking sight at any dinner party. Bock (1994,

695) points out that the verb for weeping is used of rain showers elsewhere, so this was no mere whimpering (Matt 5:45; Jas 5:17; Rev 11:6). She then anointed his feet with ointment, also a most unusual act, but because of his position at the table she could reach his feet and so she did what she could.

Like the paralytic, she has no name and says nothing, but it is she rather than Jesus who is active this time. Luke does not tell us why she came, although he will let Jesus tell us something about her later. Luke identifies her only as a sinner (7:37) whose bad reputation was known to the Pharisee (v. 39). Interpreters have never been satisfied with this, and for centuries she has been called a prostitute, some even saying "undoubtedly." But Luke does not say that, and there are other sins. She might have been a thief, but we will not speculate, and if the nature of her sin had been important Luke would have told us.

What does seem important is the question why she came and did what she did. Various explanations have been proposed. At first, one might take her weeping to be a sign of repentance for whatever she had done wrong and the anointing of Jesus as an act of repentance, which then led Jesus to pronounce her forgiven. But for what sin would anointing feet be an appropriate act of repentance? Had she sinned against Jesus? In fact, this is the wrong course to take, for Jesus calls what she had done an act of love, i.e., gratitude, so to see the event as a repentance-forgiveness scene does not work.

Some have found the reference to John the Baptist shortly before this story (7:18–35) to be significant. Luke has said that Pharisees refused to be baptized by him (v. 30), unlike others, including even tax collectors (v. 29), so it has been suggested that this woman had been baptized by John and received forgiveness. The story thus is intended to illustrate the contrast between those who accepted John and those who did not. This approach fails to make an adequate connection between Jesus and her baptism by John, which would account for such an emotional response to Jesus.

That response immediately suggests that there must have been an earlier encounter between Jesus and the woman in which he assured her that her sins were forgiven. If so, designating her "a sinner" would refer to her past life and her reputation rather than her present status with God and her new life. That Jesus had in fact forgiven her earlier is supported by his parable, which speaks of love (gratitude) as a result of forgiveness, and then applies it to the woman. This reading of the parable has been questioned because of the wording of two of Jesus' statements at the end of the story. "Your sins are forgiven" (v. 48) suggests that something new has just happened. Just before that, "her sins, which are many, are forgiven, for she loved much" (RSV, v. 47) has been taken to mean that it was her love of Jesus that somehow made her deserving of forgiveness. The grammar of the sentence makes that reading possible, but not necessary, for *hoti* need not mean the reason why she was forgiven, but instead the evidence that she has been forgiven, so NRSV translates it "hence she has shown great love" (Fitzmyer 1970, 687). We will make an assumption, then, about one thing that Luke does not tell us, for the parable supports it. The woman and Jesus had met before, and she had already experienced forgiveness as a result of his presence.

Before turning to the parable and its application, let us note that this could have been a story about ritual defilement. The Pharisee's thought, "If this man were a prophet, he would have known who and what sort of woman this is, for she is a sinner" (v. 39), might have led Jesus to a comment about what really defiles a person, similar to those that appear in Matt 15:1–20; Mark 7:1–23; and Luke 11:37–41, but instead he defended the woman's strange behavior with a parable about forgiveness. Luke has been very concise in the way he has told most of the story, but at two points he became wordy, which means, pay attention; this is the important part. First is the detailed description of what the woman did (vv. 37–38), repeated by Jesus and compared with what Simon did not do (vv. 44–46), and second is the parable, a story about forgiveness, which might never have been expected from the way the passage began. Interpreters debate how negative Jesus intended his references to Simon to be, but that is a side issue as the story concludes, for the focus is entirely on the woman and Jesus. The point of the parable was so obvious Simon could not question it. One is far more likely to be grateful for forgiveness of a great debt than a small one. It can be applied in only one way. The woman (like the debtor) has been forgiven her many sins, and her reaction to Jesus (who thus must have been the forgiver, anticipating vv. 48–49) has been appropriately extravagant. Jesus' powerful words, "Your sins have been forgiven" (v. 48) may thus be taken as a reassurance, and not as news to her, although likely it was to Simon. As in the story of the paralytic, Luke does not allow the reader to think Jesus was only announcing God's forgiveness, for he quotes the others at dinner, who say among themselves, "Who is this, who even forgives sins" (v. 49)? That wondering question once again explains why we are told so little about the paralytic and the woman; what they were like before and what forgiveness meant to them. For Luke, what was important was evidence, in the traditions passed on to him, that Jesus forgave sins, meaning that in him the power of God was personally present on earth. This time, Jesus does not make the claim himself, as he did in ch. 5, but he dismisses the woman with a blessing containing words that are important for Luke: "Your faith has saved you; go in peace" (v. 50).

"Peace" points to the new life that is open to her. The state of forgiveness is now called salvation, a term used of rescue from physical distress in the Old Testament, but now used of rescue from sin. The human contribution to the receipt of divine forgiveness is now called "faith." Recall that Jesus was led to pronounce forgiveness over the paralytic "when he saw their faith." Nothing has been said of repentance in either story, and it is not easy to see repentance as a part of what is meant by faith. It is not that repentance is unimportant for Luke. Rather, in these stories he has added a new element, which becomes more obvious in Acts. A personal relationship with Jesus Christ—faith—brings about a personal relationship with God the Father that transcends everything in one's life that has damaged that relationship in the past.

The next story also occurs only in Luke. It does not contain words for repentance or forgiveness, but unlike the previous two it focuses on repentance. It concludes with an assurance of "salvation," a term we have just noted in the conclusion of the story of the sinful woman.

> He entered Jericho and was passing through it. A man was there named Zacchaeus; he was a chief tax collector and was rich. He was trying to see who Jesus was, but on account of the crowd he could not, because he was short in stature. So he ran ahead and climbed a sycamore tree to see him, because he was going to pass that way. When Jesus came to the place, he looked up and said to him, "Zacchaeus, hurry and come down; for I must stay at your house today." So he hurried down and was happy to welcome him. All who saw it began to grumble and said, "He has gone to be the guest of one who is a sinner." Zacchaeus stood there and said to the Lord, "Look, half of my possessions, Lord, I will give to the poor; and if I have defrauded anyone of anything, I will pay back four times as much." Then Jesus said to him, "Today salvation has come to this house, because he too is

a son of Abraham. For the Son of Man came to seek out and to save the lost." (Luke 19:1–10)

The story of Zacchaeus differs in many ways from those we have just read. This time it is important that we know something about him; he was a chief tax collector and very rich. Unlike the paralytic and the woman he had power, but like them his reputation was poor. The Roman system of taxation, which allowed collectors to keep all that they could extract over and above what the government expected, made tax collecting attractive to the most greedy and merciless, and so it is that the Gospels link "tax collectors and sinners" (e.g., Matt 9:10–11; 11:10). Jesus had drawn a crowd as he passed through Jericho, and as the story is told Zacchaeus just seems to have been curious about him. Luke will not tell us whether he knew anything of Jesus' teachings, so that he might have been looking for a way to ease an already uneasy conscience. All we know is how he reacted when Jesus insisted on becoming a guest in his home. Luke reminds us of the way Jesus' willingness to associate with the most despised people in the community shocked those who expected a teacher to keep himself pure.

At any rate, the story has the tax collector suddenly deciding to reverse the direction his life has taken. "Zacchaeus stood there and said to the Lord, 'Look, half of my possessions, Lord, I will give to the poor; and if I have defrauded anyone of anything, I will pay back four times as much'" (19:8). (For various laws concerning restitution, see Exod 22:1, 4, 7; Lev 6:5; Num 5:7.) Almost all scholars understand this to be a gesture resulting from true repentance, which must involve restitution, where that is possible, and a sincere commitment to living a changed life. There are some, however, who see a problem with the fact that Luke has him use the present tense: "I give," and "I pay back." They claim this must mean Zacchaeus was not repenting, but was defending an already virtuous life. Jesus' words, "Today salvation has come to this house," thus did not refer to forgiveness but to his vindication of a man whose reputation had been unjustly impugned (Fitzmyer 1970, 1220–22). In Greek, a present tense may be used to refer to the future, however, and it may be that Luke chose that tense here to reflect a usage in the original Aramaic that suggested a "futuristic present" (Wilson 1965–1966; Salom 1966–1967). Furthermore, a story of a virtuous tax collector defended by Jesus would be so contrary to everything else that Luke has written that it is hard to imagine why he would have included it. Jesus' announcement that salvation has come would scarcely fit merely the possibility of gaining a better reputation.

That Luke does not speak of forgiveness here does not mean that this is not a story of forgiveness. Since scholars always note that save/salvation is a favorite theme of this author, this seems to be an appropriate place to consider what he says people may be saved from. In Zechariah's psalm the word is used as it is in the Old Testament, saved from one's enemies (1:71), but as we have already noticed, later it is in parallel with forgiveness (1:77). Elsewhere Jesus speaks of saving life, opposite to destroying or losing it (6:9; 9:24). At the cross, "save" also refers to physical life (23:35, 37, 39). An important group of texts associates salvation with faith. As we have seen, when Jesus assured the woman, "Your faith has saved you" (7:50), salvation meant forgiveness. He said the identical words to the woman who had been healed of hemorrhage (8:48), although *sōzō* is regularly (and appropriately) translated "healed" here. He also assured the leper (17:19) and the blind man (18:42) with the same words. The account of the raising of Jairus's daughter is similar: "Only believe, and she will be saved" (8:50). Without reference to faith, the demoniac is also said to have been "saved" (8:36), so the most prominent uses of the word in Luke make it equivalent to healing. It seems to be used in a quite different sense in a few places, namely being saved for eternal life. In the parable of the sower and the seeds, the seeds that fall on the path represent people from whom the devil takes away the word from their hearts, "so that they may not believe and be saved" (8:12). The disciples asked, "Will only a few be saved?" (13:23), and the question took on a more critical form after Jesus' saying, "Indeed, it is easier for a camel to go through the eye of a needle than for someone who is rich to enter the kingdom of God." Then the question became, "Then who can be saved" (18:26)? Just a few paragraphs after Jesus' answer, "What is impossible for mortals is possible for God" (18:27) we read the story of a rich man, Zacchaeus, to whom he says "Today salvation has come to this house, because he too is a son of Abraham. For the Son of Man came to seek out and to save the lost" (19:9–10). For Luke, salvation could mean for eternal life, and that would be appropriate here, but this seems to be a forgiveness story, and that may be at the foreground of the word in this context. If so, then Jesus' reference to saving the lost would mean restoration of the relationship with the God of Israel which that son of Abraham had lost because of his choice of an unjust way of life.

Once, Jesus directly asked God the Father to forgive; to forgive those who were murdering him (Luke 23:34). It seems most unlikely that any early Christian would have created those words and attributed them to Jesus, so this is one case where skepticism seems unwarranted and we may take the words to reflect something of what Jesus believed about forgiveness. Once again, however, we have come to a text that raises many questions for us. It is one sentence in the midst of the extended narrative of Jesus' trial and crucifixion, and the context offers nothing to help us interpret it. The interpreter must begin with some very basic questions: Did Luke write it? Did Jesus say it? Then we shall move to some that are very profound.

The question of Lukan authorship would not arise if it were not that the sentence is missing from some of the earliest and most reliable manuscripts. That scarcely settles the matter in favor of it being a later addition, however, for it is present in other very early and reliable manuscripts, so one must consider whether it is more likely that an early scribe omitted the sentence or whether one added it. Raymond Brown has surveyed the discussion in a most helpful way and argues, as do many other commentators, for its originality (1994, 979–80). It is suggested that, given the hard feelings that existed between Jews and Christians from the second century A.D. on, there were some who could not believe that Jesus had forgiven the Jewish leaders for plotting his death, so the verse was dropped from some manuscripts. It seems far less likely that those early Christians would have wanted to invent a saying that claimed Jesus forgave either Jews or Romans. Given the special interest in forgiveness that we have found in Luke it seems sound to conclude that the verse was part of the original Gospel.

As to whether Jesus himself said it, once again, caution seems appropriate. All four Gospels tell us that followers of Jesus were present, watching the crucifixion from a distance, so Luke could have heard of this saying from one who was there, but this is a possibility, not a certainty. It is essentially a very shocking saying, however. Why should those unrepentant people, whoever they were, be forgiven? As such, it is in keeping with other shocking sayings of Jesus—"Love your enemies," "If anyone wants to sue you and take your coat, give your cloak as well" (Matt 5:44, 40)—so it seems more likely that these words came from him than from anyone else. They should be of special importance, then, but what do they mean?

Serious questions: First, who were "they," whom Jesus asked the Father to forgive, since they did not know what they were doing? The discussions focus on the Roman soldiers and the Jewish leaders. Two opinions: Calvin said that Jesus had pity on the Jewish people and the soldiers because of their ignorance, and interceded for them, but that it would have been in vain to pray for the scribes and priests. But Joseph Fitzmyer would exclude the soldiers, since they are not mentioned explicitly until v. 36 (1985, 1503). Is there any way that we can identify "them"? What limits might there have been on Jesus' mercy? Let us begin at the cross and work backward; to see where readers think they must stop.

The soldiers: They did not know what they were doing, in executing an innocent man, for Jesus had been condemned to death by the governor. As far as they knew they were exacting justice, and there would have been little or nothing in their experience to teach them that inflicting such pain on anyone was wrong. What they did was wrong, but the one they tortured might ask God to forgive them.

The bystanders who mocked him: They had no excuse for such behavior, but the evangelists want us to know that in their ignorance they spoke the truth. "He saved others; he cannot save himself" (Mark 15:31). They obviously enjoyed their cruelty. Would Jesus have prayed for them?

Pilate: He knew what he was doing, but only partly. He knew Jesus was the source of trouble in Jerusalem, or potential trouble, and keeping the peace was all that mattered for him. He was willing to condemn to a terrible death a man whom he decided was innocent of any crime (Luke 23:4, 14–15, 22). But he did not know who Jesus really was. Was he included in Jesus' prayer?

The priests: I believe that they also saw Jesus as primarily a political danger, likely to stir up trouble with the Romans. As Jews who knew their law they might have had serious qualms of conscience about seeking the death of a man for those reasons, but John claimed to know how they reasoned, quoting the high priest Caiaphas as having said, ". . . it is better for you to have one man die for the people than to have the whole nation destroyed" (John 11:50). Here, also, he spoke more truth than he realized, for this one man died for the people in a way Caiaphas could not have foreseen. Unless they truly did believe the charge of blasphemy, which was subject to the death penalty in Jewish law, the guilt of the priests seems heavier, for their standards were different from those of Pilate and the soldiers, and they had a greater potential for understanding Jesus, but in fact they did not understand him, and did not realize all that they were doing.

Peter and the Ten: They did not fully understand Jesus, either, and they were just weak, without courage enough to try to help their friend. They also needed forgiveness. But here is something different. John records a scene in which the Risen Christ evidently forgave Peter (John 21:15–19), and in none of the resurrection appearances does Jesus refer to the ways his disciples had failed him.

Judas: The way to the cross began with him, and did Jesus ask forgiveness for Judas? We do not know why he betrayed Jesus, so will not use space to discuss the various theories. All that Luke can tell us is that Satan entered into Judas (Luke 22:3). According to Matthew, however, he also did not know what he was doing, for when he saw that Jesus was condemned he repented, saying, "I have sinned by betraying innocent blood" (Matt 27:4). He is the one person in all this cast who is said to have repented. Did Jesus pray for his forgiveness?

The discussions of Jesus' prayer usually refer only to the soldiers and the priests (sometimes also the people), but I thought that reflection on what Jesus meant by forgiveness ought to be more inclusive, for there was a lot of guilt involved with his death. We cannot answer the questions asked above, for we cannot get into the mind of Jesus, but asking them leads us to reflect on what forgiveness really means, and this leads to more questions.

Calvin's concern for upholding the justice of God leads us to wonder whether he thought Christ's prayer was not answered. "For when Christ was moved by a feeling of compassion to ask forgiveness from God for his persecutors, this did not hinder him from acquiescing in the righteous judgment of God, which he knew to be ordained for reprobate and obstinate men. . . . Yet knowing that God would be an avenger, he left to him the exercise of judgment against the desperate." He seems to find in the passage Christ's merciful feelings, but not true forgiveness.

Suppose "they," whoever they may be, really were forgiven, then let us ask our next question. What would forgiveness have meant for any of them? The only people we know of who were forgiven in the sense that we found in the work of the most perceptive of the Old Testament authors were the Eleven (and perhaps also those priests mentioned in Acts 6:7, but we know nothing more of them). Peter and the others were not held accountable for their failure, according to the resurrection narratives. Their relationship with Jesus was restored and they were personally transformed. Come to think of it, was that why their earliest preaching focused on forgiveness? They had been forgiven, but we will leave the question open, for the resurrection texts and the Acts sermons do not explicitly say that.

What could forgiveness have meant for the others on our list? Judas was dead, and there is no evidence that many of the others ever had a relationship with the Risen Christ, or even knew that they needed to be forgiven. Calvin does remind us of the Jewish people who became followers. The question as to what forgiveness meant in this and the preceding stories we have considered is seldom asked, probably because it is assumed that it meant remission of punishment after death, at the Last Judgment. If Judas, and even Pilate, may have been included in Jesus' prayer (and not everyone may agree with that), then what else could forgiveness mean? Or, let us ask it about the paralytic and the sinful woman, whom we know to have been forgiven. Did it refer only to judgment after death, or did it change them, as the Old Testament authors hoped forgiveness would do? The stories did not tell us, and although the Gospels refer to the Last Judgment they do not say much about forgiveness in connection with it.

Now readers will see why it was better to begin with Acts than with the Gospels. The early sermons testified in a straightforward way to the belief of the first Christians that a new kind of forgiveness had become available through faith in the Risen Christ, but it had much in continuity with what was said about forgiveness in the Old Testament, for it promised a new life here and now. That happened to the disciples and the many others who came to believe in Christ, but we do not know what became of the paralytic and the woman and Zacchaeus. It is more difficult with the word from the cross. Did Jesus really pray for those who did not and would never repent? If so, and his prayer was answered, what would it mean? We recall that the Old Testament did speak of God's forgiveness of the unrepentant, and that must be important. However, that forgiveness, as in the case of the golden calf and Israel's refusal to enter the Promised Land (Numbers 14), made possible the continuation of a seriously damaged relationship. For Pilate and others in our list there was no relationship, before or after Jesus' death, so if there was forgiveness for them it could refer only to remission of punishment after death. We have no access to any information about that (although many claim that we do), but we can see that this would not correspond to the fullness of what the Old Testament writers said about forgiveness. That will be true of the other New Testament writers as well.

These reflections, which so far have seemed very inconclusive, do lead to a conclusion, after all. Forgiveness may begin entirely by the initiative of the injured party, but it can never achieve what is intended unless it can be accepted by the guilty one. The Old Testament emphases on the restoration of relationship and on healing (cleansing) as essential parts of the forgiveness God offers provide a way for us to respond to our questions about who may have actually been forgiven by Jesus' words on the cross. All that we know of him from the Gospels tells us that he longed for all of those on the list to be forgiven, but for most of them it did not happen, for there was no new relationship with God and no cleansing.

Twice our reflections on "Father, forgive them" have reminded us of the preaching of forgiveness in Acts. In Hengel's helpful book, *The Atonement*, he asks the question we considered in our study of Acts: "How were the disciples able to justify this new assurance of forgiveness after Easter, beginning with the first eyewitness, Simon Peter, who denied his master, through James, who untrustingly had opposed his physical brother (cf. John 7,5), to the last of them all, Saul-Paul, who hated the Messiah and persecuted his followers" (1986, 69)? He points out that between Jesus' death and their preaching of forgiveness through him there must have been a time of "awareness of their utter failure and deep guilt" (1986, 67). One might have expected to find at least one more forgiveness scene in the Gospels, but the resurrection appearances look ahead rather than backward. The Risen Christ accepts the disciples, even in spite of continued unbelief (e.g., Matt 28:17; Luke 24:11, 25, 38; John 20:24–29), and commissions them to continue his work. The incident with Peter in which three times Jesus asks, "Do you love me?" (John 21:15–19) is the closest we have to a forgiveness scene. That the disciples knew Christ had forgiven them in the fullest sense of the word is the essential background to all their activity in the book of Acts, however.

In two passages Jesus spoke of his impending death in ways that contribute to our search for the meaning of forgiveness in the New Testament. We have already considered one of them, his words at the Last Supper, in our effort to understand the prominent emphasis on forgiveness in the early preaching of the Apostles. We shall return to that passage shortly, but first must take up a unique saying that appears in Mark 10:45 and Matt 20:28. In response to the request of James and John to be granted the right to sit on his right and his left when he comes in glory, Jesus offered his own definition of greatness. "Whoever wishes to become great among you must be your servant" (Mark 10:43). Then he added, "For the Son of Man came not to be served but to serve, and to give his life a ransom for many" (Mark 10:45).

The context of the saying is significant. Three times Jesus had foretold his death and resurrection (Mark 8:31; 9:30–32; 10:32–34) without explaining what that might mean. After the first, he claimed, "For those who want to save their life will lose it, and those who lose their life for my sake, and for the sake of the gospel, will save it" (8:35). After the second, he offered another paradoxical saying: "Whoever wants to be first must be last of all and servant of all" (9:35). After the third came another reference to servanthood, cited above, plus the ransom saying. These three sayings insisting on reversal of what everyone considers to be normal are thus connected each time with his unacceptable message concerning his own death. It would have to be this way for Jesus' followers because it would be this way for him, and Mark 10:45 finally adds something of an explanation of his chosen route. The life he would give up would be a ransom for many. The fullest extent of his service would be the gift of his own life, but this would not be the result of weakness but of power, for the word "ransom" (*lutron*) referred back to Old Testament passages concerning the great power of God's ransoming/redeeming acts.

This is essentially a new concept for us. We found one passage in the Old Testament that spoke of ransom from iniquity (Ps 130:8), so we are justified in taking Jesus' words as a reference to forgiveness. New Testament authors also use the word explicitly in that way, as we shall see. The terms "ransom" and "redeem," which mean the same thing, became part of the rather large New Testament vocabulary used to explain the meaning of Jesus' death, and we shall return to this theme when studying other New Testament authors. The Old Testament concept of ransom/redemption provides the essential key for interpreting the rather cryptic saying in Mark 10:45. Two Hebrew words, *padah* and *ga'al*, are instructive. A third, *kopher*, is less important. In daily life, to redeem or ransom meant to gain release or to set free, usually by payment of some kind (e.g., Exod 21:8; 34:20; Lev 25:25–32; Jer 32:7–8). The idea of setting free was so prominent in the two words that they became standard ways of referring to God's mighty acts by which he liberated the Hebrew slaves from bondage in Egypt (e.g., Deut 7:8; 9:26; 13:5; 15:15; 24:18; Mic 6:4). It is important that this involved no payment of any kind, emphasized in Isa 52:3: "For thus says the Lord: 'You were sold for nothing, and you shall be redeemed without money.'" Nothing should be made of the verse, "I gave Egypt as your ransom, Ethiopia and Seba in exchange for you" (Isa 43:3). This is extravagant poetry extolling the power of Yahweh over all the nations without reference to any real exchange. Although the use of the terms in human affairs thus suggests that payment should be involved, as "salvation language" their entire emphasis is on setting free without payment, and it is important to keep this in mind when interpreting Mark 10:45, for the questions that have been asked, "What was the price, and to whom was it paid?" are probably irrelevant and distracting.

Our focus on the meaning of forgiveness also enables us to avoid some of the other widely discussed questions about the verse, since they do not contribute to our subject. Once again, our emphasis on the message of *Scripture* means we can leave to one side the question whether Jesus really said this. Discussions of its origin are helpful to the extent that they provide evidence it was part of the church's earliest witness (Hengel 1986, 53–75). The extended debate over the possible relationship with Isaiah 53 is not helpful to us (Moulder 1978), since nothing like the key word *lutron* (ransom) appears in that chapter. Claims that it corresponds to *'asam* (guilt-offering) in Isa 53:10 have nothing to support them (Barrett 1959; Hill 1967, 79; Hooker 1959) so readings of the verse that introduce sacrificial language should be avoided. Since ransom/redeem is not a sacrificial term, some caution also seems appropriate in using references to the deaths of Jewish martyrs as atoning for Israel's sins (e.g., 2 Macc 7:37–38; 4 Macc 6:28–29; esp. 17:21–22). This kind of atonement, the idea that suffering somehow pays for one's sins, was a new idea in Judaism at the time, and vicarious atonement of the kind affirmed in 4 Maccabees appears in only a few references during this period. The idea may be significant as background to the way the earliest Christians interpreted Jesus' death, but to introduce atonement into the interpretation of Mark 10:45 adds something to the meaning of *lutron* (*padah/ga'al*) that does not appear in any of its uses in the Old Testament.

The use of *padah* with *'awon*, "iniquity," in Ps 130:8 suggests an understanding of sin and forgiveness that we did not find elsewhere in the Old Testament, but will find developed explicitly in the New Testament. That is, as God set Israel free from bondage in Egypt, so also he sets Israel free from bondage to sin. We have thought of forgiveness as remission of punishment, as restoration of a broken relationship, and of inner transformation, but this is a different idea. Sin can now be thought of as a master to which one can become enslaved. Personal responsibility is certainly still involved, but the likelihood of being able to restore what had been destroyed through sin by one's own efforts is diminished when one is called a slave of sin. Only a greater power can change that, and it is God's overwhelming power that scripture celebrates. Note Ps 130:7: "with him is great power to redeem."

In the New Testament, various forms of the word *lutron* are both identified with forgiveness ("in whom we have redemption [*apolutrōsin*], the forgiveness of sins" Col 1:14; cf. Eph 1:7) and with being set free from the power of sin:

You know that you were ransomed from the futile ways inherited from your ancestors . . . (1 Pet 1:18)

He it is who gave himself for us that he might redeem us from all iniquity and purify for himself a people of his own . . . (Titus 2:14)

. . . a death has occurred that redeems them from the transgressions under the first covenant. (Heb 9:15)

As George Caird wrote: "More commonly sin in one or other of its many forms was the enemy; the human race needed to be set free not only from the individual slavery of habit and deeply entrenched attitudes, but also from the corporate slavery of sin embedded in the practices, institutions, conventions, and ethos of the old order" (Caird 1994, 157). This idea of having been set free from being enslaved by sin as a result of the work of Christ was expressed with other verbs, as well: "you, having been set free [*eleutherōthentes*] from sin, have become slaves of righteousness (Rom 6:18; cf. 6:22; 8:2). "He has rescued [*errusato*] us from the power of darkness and transferred us into the kingdom of his beloved Son, in whom we have redemption, the forgiveness of sins" (Col 1:13–14).

We see that when the New Testament used as a forgiveness term the Old Testament concept of ransom/redemption, which referred to God's powerful acts to deliver his people, a deeper, more threatening concept of sin then appears. The human dilemma discovered by Jeremiah and Ezekiel, inability to repent and do right (cf. Jer 5:1–5; 13:23; Ezek 36:26), takes on a threatening form in the New Testament as a power that must be defeated if forgiveness can take place. This darker concept of sin is a major reason for the church's proclamation of forgiveness through Jesus Christ as something new. Sin is evidently a power so great that for God to take it on must involve the life of the Son of Man himself. The power set loose by the gift of that life is associated with those paradoxical sayings that preceded Mark 10:45, for it is death, the ultimate weakness, that will defeat the power of sin.

This reminds us of one of the theories of atonement, called the classic, or *Christus Victor*, theory, which emphasizes Christ's conflict with and triumph over the powers of evil (Aulén 1951). Fortunately, we do not have to become mired in a discussion of the various theories of atonement, for they do not make essential contributions to our concern—what forgiveness means (Boyd 2006). We will do well to agree with Plummer's comment on this verse, "The way in which this ransom sets men free is beyond our comprehension" (1910, 280).

Now, if we look again at Jesus' words at the Last Supper, we see that a different Old Testament tradition from that of ransom lies behind them. It is the covenant relationship. Mark's version, "This is my blood of the covenant, which is poured out for many" (14:24), does not tell us much about what Jesus meant by his own death, for it just recalls the sealing of the Sinai covenant by sprinkling the blood of burnt offerings and peace (or well-being) offerings over the people (the many?) in Exod 24:8. Matthew's addition, "for the forgiveness of sins" (26:28) takes us to Jer 31:31–34, where forgiveness is said to be the result of the new covenant, to be written on the heart. The reference is explicit in 1 Cor 11:23–26 and Luke 22:17–19; Jesus' blood establishes the new covenant. Implicit, then, in all but Mark's version, is a reference to Jeremiah's promise that forgiveness must and will involve an inner transformation, which will make obedience possible. If that sense of forgiveness is primary in these words, then they also help to explain the two-fold emphasis in the early sermons in Acts—forgiveness of sins and the gift of the Holy Spirit. There may also be a certain parallel to what "ransom" says about forgiveness, in that both Old Testament traditions speak of God's work to overcome the human inability to avoid sinning. Ransom, in a sense, defeats the power that attacks from without. Transformation, often denoted by cleansing language, provides power to resist sin from within. Note the way Titus 2:14 brings the two together: "He it is who gave himself for us that he might redeem us from all iniquity and purify for himself a people of his own who are zealous for good deeds."

We turn now from Jesus as one who forgives to Jesus as one who teaches about forgiveness. There are four relevant parables in Luke, with a parallel to one of them in Matthew. They are the Lost Sheep (Luke 15:3–7; Matt 18:12–14), the Lost Coin (Luke 15:8–10), the Prodigal Son (Luke 15:11–32), and the Pharisee and the Publican (Luke 18:9–14). The word "forgive" does not appear in any of them, but each one is a commentary of some sort on divine forgiveness.

Oddly, it would seem, sin and repentance appear in the interpretations of the first two, although sheep and coins do not sin. The connection is made with the words "lost" and "found," and those words also appear in the third parable, which does describe an act of repentance, as does the fourth, although neither uses the word repent. "Sin" appears in all four, and we are led to think that each needs to be interpreted with reference to the others.

All four parables include attacks on the attitude of self-righteousness, an approach to the subject of forgiveness that we have not seen before. It appears in glaring ways in the Pharisee and the Publican and in the final paragraph of the Prodigal Son. In both cases, that attitude leads to disdain for the unrighteous, and it links these parables with the other two (Luke 15:3–10), which are responses to the criticism of scribes and Pharisees, that Jesus received sinners and ate with them (15:2). Jesus then used the "deserving"—righteous people who took undue pride in their righteousness—as a foil against which to present his message of God's mercy toward the undeserving.

> He also told this parable to some who trusted in themselves
> that they were righteous and regarded others with contempt:

"Two men went up to the temple to pray, one a Pharisee and the other a tax collector. The Pharisee, standing by himself, was praying thus, 'God, I thank you that I am not like other people: thieves, rogues, adulterers, or even like this tax collector. I fast twice a week; I give a tenth of all my income.' But the tax collector, standing far off, would not even look up to heaven, but was beating his breast and saying, 'God, be merciful to me, a sinner!' I tell you, this man went down to his home justified rather than the other; for all who exalt themselves will be humbled, but all who humble themselves will be exalted." (Luke 18:9–14)

It is likely that real Pharisees would have highly disapproved of the imaginary one Jesus created for this parable. He chose a Pharisee because they were known for their commitment to righteous living, and then makes of him an extreme example of pride in one's own righteousness. The prayer ascribed to this one is a caricature of what sincere prayer should be (although such prayers may really be offered at times), for the Pharisee thanks God not for what God has done for him, but for how good he is, and especially in comparison with the obviously sinful. The tax collector standing at a distance, whom he knows, provides an excellent example with whom to contrast himself.

Did this self-glorifying pride make the Pharisee a sinner, also in need of forgiveness? Jesus does not say that, explicitly. It certainly does not make him admirable, and Jesus' reference to justification in v. 14 indicates he also is a needy person. It is the tax collector, who does not get as many lines, who is the central character in the parable, however, as the verse just alluded to indicates. We need not dwell on the Pharisee's boasting, then, for it is the tax collector's prayer and Jesus' evaluation of it that are useful for our purposes. The prayer is regularly translated, "God, be merciful to me, a sinner," but it uses an interesting verb, *hilastheti*. Forms of this verb occur only eight times in the New Testament (elsewhere, Matt 16:22; Rom 3:25; Heb 2:17; 8:12; 9:5; 1 John 2:2; 4:10), but it appears quite often in the Septuagint, usually as the translation of *kipper*, "to make atonement." The tax collector's choice of this unusual word (for the New Testament) is thus nothing else than an explicit plea for forgiveness. Because the prayer takes place in the temple, Bailey has suggested that he is asking God to make atonement for him (1983, 154). We have seen, however, 1) that it was the priest, not God, who made atonement, and 2) that when *kipper* did appear with God as subject it just meant "forgive."

Then, Luke used another distinctive word, "justified." This sounds like Paul rather than Jesus, but once we note that two forms of the same Greek word occur in the parable, at the beginning and the end, we can see why Jesus would have said this. He addressed the parable to "some who trusted in themselves that they were righteous [*dikaioi*]," and at the end declared the tax collector to be "justified [declared righteous, *dedikaiomenos*]." How could he be declared righteous, rather than the Pharisee? It was because he asked God to remove the barrier between them caused by his sin. (Recall what we learned about the function of atonement in the Old Testament.) The Pharisee, instead, created a barrier, self-righteousness, disrupting his relationship with God, which had to be dependent on God's goodness, not his. Jesus' emphasis in this parable is on the necessity for all people to recognize their neediness, with the assurance, emphasized by his choice of a despised tax collector, that God is always ready to respond to the appeals of the needy. This is Jesus' own distinctive way of reaffirming the Old Testament message that God graciously offers forgiveness to those who in no way can claim to deserve it.

He found another striking way to speak of God's graciousness in the three parables in Luke 15, each with the theme of rejoicing that the lost has been found. Criticism of Jesus' own graciousness in being willing to eat with sinners is used by Luke to introduce the parables, and the final one concludes with the older son criticizing his father for his graciousness in welcoming the prodigal back. The chapter is consistent, then, in illustrating variously God's desire to restore sinners to relationship with him. Since Jesus had come to carry out that work, and was misunderstood because of it, the parables take the rather extreme position of depicting righteous people in not a very good light, as we have seen in the Pharisee and the Tax Collector, will see in the Prodigal Son, and as the remarkable saying indicates, "There will be more joy in heaven over one sinner who repents than over ninety-nine righteous persons who need no repentance" (Luke 15:7). Another of Jesus' surprising sayings parallels this: "Those who are well have no need of a physician, but those who are sick; I have come to call not the righteous but sinners" (Mark 2:17; Luke 5:32 adds "to repentance").

The parables of the lost sheep and the lost coin can be considered together, as they are variations of the same theme. They are introduced as Jesus' response to the criticism, "This fellow welcomes sinners and eats with them," claiming that the repentance of even one sinner makes that worthwhile. Sheep and coins would not seem to be very appropriate choices for the parables, for they cannot sin, repent, or accept forgiveness, but Jesus was able to use them by paralleling sin and forgiveness with being lost and found. It did not matter so much that they were not human, for the focus of the parables was not the sinner, but God, as each of them concludes with reference to joy in heaven.

> Which of you, having a hundred sheep and losing one of them, does not leave the ninety-nine in the wilderness and go after the one that is lost until he finds it? When he has found it, he lays it on his shoulders and rejoices. And when he comes home, he calls together his friends and neighbors, saying to them, "Rejoice with me, for I have found my sheep that was lost." Just so, I tell you, there will be more joy in heaven over one sinner who repents than over ninety-nine righteous persons who need no repentance. Or what woman having ten silver coins, if she loses one of them, does not light a lamp, sweep the house, and search carefully until she finds it? When she has found it, she calls together her friends and neighbors, saying, "Rejoice with me, for I have found the coin that I had lost." Just so, I tell you, there is joy in the presence of the angels of God over one sinner who repents. (Luke 15:4–10)

Two elements hold the parables together, the extreme measures that are taken in order to retrieve what has been lost and the extreme rejoicing once the lost has been found. The first reflects the reality of Jesus' life, his willingness to put himself into positions that were shocking to the good people around him, in order than he might bring forgiveness to those who needed it most. Bailey's knowledge of the customs of the Middle East corrects an assumption that Jesus created a foolish shepherd in the first parable, who left ninety-nine sheep untended while he went to search for one. Flocks as large as one hundred were always cared for by two or three shepherds, so Jesus' listeners would not have imagined a flock left by itself (1983, 149). The search for one sheep and the labor involved in carrying it home are nothing compared with the joy of finding the lost sheep, so that all the neighborhood are invited to join in. The theme of rejoicing then constitutes the second element, Jesus' claim that his association with sinners is God's work. The conclusion to the first parable puts it more emphatically than the second by comparing what produces the most joy in heaven. God's concern for sinners is so intense that repentance leads to more joy in heaven than goodness (v. 7). If that verse in itself is not striking enough, note that Jesus' use of "lost" and "found" in the parables associates, in the interpretation, repentance with being found; repentance itself a part of God's saving act (Bailey 1983, 155; Tannehill 1996, 238).

The parable of the Prodigal Son might better be called the parable of the Two Sons, as Jesus in fact introduces it, for the full meaning of the story comes through only when the final act is considered. By then we realize it is really a story about the father. The words "lost" and "found" plus the theme of rejoicing connect this parable with the preceding ones, but it is a far more powerful story.

> There was a man who had two sons. The younger of them said to his father, "Father, give me the share of the property that will belong to me." So he divided his property between them. A few days later the younger son gathered all he had and traveled to a distant country, and there he squandered his property in dissolute living. When he had spent everything, a severe famine took place throughout that country, and he began to be in need. So he went and hired himself out to one of the citizens of that country, who sent him to his fields to feed the pigs. He would gladly have filled himself with the pods that the pigs were eating; and no one gave him anything. But when he came to himself he said, "How many of my father's hired hands have bread enough and to spare, but here I am dying of hunger! I will get up and go to my father, and I will say to him, 'Father, I have sinned against heaven and before you; I am no longer worthy to be called your son; treat me like one of your hired hands.'" So he set off and went to his father. But while he was still far off, his father saw him and was filled with compassion; he ran and put his arms around him and kissed him. Then the son said to him, "Father, I have sinned against heaven and before you; I am no longer worthy to be called your son." But the father said to his slaves, "Quickly, bring out a robe—the best one—and put it on him; put a ring on his finger and sandals on his feet. And get the fatted calf and kill it, and let us eat and celebrate; for this son of mine was dead and is alive again; he was lost and is found!" And they began to celebrate. Now his elder son was in the field; and when he came and approached the house, he heard music and dancing. He called one of the slaves and asked what was going on. He replied, "Your brother has come, and your father has killed the fatted calf, because he has got him back safe and sound." Then he became angry and refused to go in. His father came out and

began to plead with him. But he answered his father, "Listen! For all these years I have been working like a slave for you, and I have never disobeyed your command; yet you have never given me even a young goat so that I might celebrate with my friends. But when this son of yours came back, who has devoured your property with prostitutes, you killed the fatted calf for him!" Then the father said to him, "Son, you are always with me, and all that is mine is yours. But we had to celebrate and rejoice, because this brother of yours was dead and has come to life; he was lost and has been found." (Luke 15:11–32)

This is universally recognized to be one of the masterpieces of Jesus' storytelling ability, with a few words bringing to light the true character of each of the three participants. Here, as elsewhere, Ken Bailey's insights drawn from his experience in the Middle East bring to life aspects of the story that Western readers would otherwise miss. He cites evidence that shows how very wrong was the younger son's request. A father *might* decide to divide his property among his sons before his death (not a wise choice, Sirach advises, 33:20–24), but for a son to ask for his inheritance while his father still lived would have been interpreted as wishing his father's death (1983, 161–65). It is doubtful that in real life any father would have granted such a request, but Jesus has this father do so, for the point of his story requires it. That the son has fully rejected his home and family then becomes clear when he sells the property and takes the proceeds with him to some distant country, where he then wastes all that he has.

Every aspect of the story is extreme, the son's rebelliousness, the father's acceptance of an outlandish request, the son's new lifestyle, and now his shockingly low state, suffering from hunger, and of all things, living with pigs.

Did he repent? Maybe, and maybe not. Regret is not the same as repentance. His motive is clear—hunger—and he realizes there may be a way to alleviate that. It would involve a confession that he had sinned against his father, but no request to be accepted into the family again. Bailey suggests that "treat me like one of your hired hands" indicates he desired to retain his independence, working for his father as a "contractor" and living wherever he chose (1983, 173–76). If that reading is acceptable, then the story is another example of what we found in the Old Testament, of God's desire to forgive preceding and surpassing the desire to be forgiven, for the father's desire is to welcome him back as a son. What in real life this would have meant for the family's finances we need not think about, for Jesus certainly meant the story to go no further than what he gave us.

The first indication of the father's unwillingness to resent or condemn his son's churlish behavior appears in the notice that he saw the returnee while he was still far off. Interpreters cannot resist imagining him daily looking down the road in the hope that he might see his son on the way back. Then he ran to meet him, and dignified men do not run, Bailey informs us (1983, 181). As he hugged and kissed his son, the latter began his prepared speech, but it was interrupted by orders to prepare to celebrate. "This son of mine was dead and is alive again; he was lost and is found."

Had this willful, inconsiderate, and unloving son truly learned a lesson from his mistakes? He returned to his father, and that is part of repentance, but had he really changed? That is essential to repentance. Would he be able to accept his father's forgiveness? If not, forgiveness cannot really work. Jesus does not tell us any of that, and now we are reminded of the paralytic and the sinful woman, whose lives after forgiveness are not recorded. We saw the reason for it in those stories; that they are really about the forgiver. The same is certainly true here, for it is the father's willingness to forgive one who is completely undeserving that is the point of Jesus' story.

His graciousness to both sons marks the conclusion of the parable. Another unlikable character appears. The elder son, who now stood to inherit the whole estate ("all that is mine is yours"), had lost nothing as a result of his brother's behavior, but may well have been angered by the way the brother had treated their father. He certainly had done nothing to deserve a celebration. Who knows what he might do next? As we recreate such a family situation we may find it hard to be as judgmental of the elder brother as interpreters usually are. But once again, Jesus' emphasis is on the father. He does not rebuke his son for his hard feelings, but reminds him of their close relationship. "Son, you are always with me, and all that is mine is yours" (v. 31). In real life there would be difficult times ahead in that family, but it does not suit Jesus' purpose to continue the story. He gives us a father who joyfully puts all that is past behind him and accepts without conditions the one who had been lost. We may wonder whether Jesus had Psalm 103 in mind as he created the parable. This is his fullest comment on divine forgiveness. We have seen that it is not the whole story, in that it focuses on the forgiver and does not speak of all that is involved in receiving forgiveness. For that, as we work through the New Testament, we are still recalling what we learned from the Old Testament, and we will find nothing to change that.

The Lord's Prayer introduces something new, human forgiveness related to divine forgiveness, so we shall need to consider it here and again in the section "We Forgive One Another." So far, we have encountered in the New Testament only one example of someone praying to be forgiven, the tax collector in the parable of the Pharisee and the Publican, so we have several new elements to consider here, although the Lord's Prayer continues the Old Testament practice of praying to God for forgiveness.

The first new element is the fact that Jesus instructed his disciples in the way that they must pray (Matt 6:5–8). Prayers for divine forgiveness were thus to be an essential part of Christian life. Second is the relationship between divine and human forgiveness, which we shall consider at more length later. Third is the use of a term we have not seen before, debts (*opheilēma*), and this suggests another approach to forgiveness that deserves attention.

Two forms of the Lord's Prayer appear in the New Testament, in Matt 6:9–13, where the forgiveness petition reads, "And forgive us our debts, as we also have forgiven our debtors" (v. 12), and in Luke 11:2–4, where it reads, "And forgive us our sins, for we ourselves forgive everyone indebted to us" (v. 4). It seems likely that Luke has substituted the ordinary Greek word for sin, *hamartia*, for the original but less familiar "debt," to make the prayer more easily understandable for his Hellenistic readers. Scholars generally account for "debt" by assuming Jesus' word was the Aramaic *hoba'*, which means both sin and debt. There must have been a good reason for Matthew's choice of a Greek word that explicitly means debt, so it seems appropriate for us to think about forgiveness in the different way the word suggests.

Interpreters emphasize the essential relationship between the two parts of the Lord's Prayer. At first we speak of God, then of ourselves, and only those who make the affirmations in the first part have any right to offer the imperatives in the second.

"He permits us, he commands us to pray, as we are invited to do in these first three requests, for the success of his cause. He invites us to participate in his work, in the government of the Church, of the world. If we pray: 'Hallowed be thy name. Thy kingdom come, Thy will be done,' we place ourselves at God's side, nothing less than that.... On these first three requests hang the freedom, the joy, the alacrity, and the certitude of the other petitions" (Barth 1952, 38).

Then come the three petitions which, taken together, involve laying all our needs before God, acknowledging that we are needy (daily bread), fallible (forgive us), and vulnerable (deliver us) people, and affirming our complete dependence on him. Interpreters regularly take the request for daily bread to refer to more than food, but to all of our physical needs, so that life itself may be sustained from day to day. The prayer reminds us that we have no control over how long our lives may last or what the quality of life may be, and the appeal "give us" comes from our awareness of our absolute dependence on God for life itself.

Forgiveness, that will restore and reconcile, is essential. Physical health and security are by no means enough for us to be truly human. The prayer for forgiveness, which we shall consider more thoroughly, moves to our relationship with God and with people. In neither case are they what they should be. From the smallest offenses to the most grievous harms that we have committed we have brought pain, hatred, and grief to others (and to ourselves), and God, who is *against* all that, also bears the offense. Healing and reconciliation thus must begin with God, but not end there.

Jesus warned that there is evil in this world (called Satan, or here, the evil one) that cannot be blamed on our sinfulness. This is an evil that would separate us completely from God, and thus from all that is good, if it could. Although God has made us his own, through the death and resurrection of Jesus Christ, Satan still has the ability to lie (John 8:44), and if the great lie is believed it would, to quote Barth, "utterly and irrevocably degrade us to the level of beasts" (1952, 74). But with the prayer we put ourselves into the hands of the One who has already defeated the enemy and will protect us from all that might spiritually destroy us.

The prayer thus speaks of our physical needs and of the most dire threat to our spiritual being. As to our relationships with God and people only forgiveness is mentioned. The implications of that are sweeping. We always need to be forgiven and to forgive. We have not found the subject in a large number of passages in the Gospels, but its place in the prayer seems to justify Norman Perrin's claim: "If one asks the natural question: In what way is the kingly activity of God primarily known? then the answer of the teaching of Jesus is abundantly clear: In the forgiveness of sins. According to the gospel tradition, this is the central, specific aspect of Jesus' proclamation of the Kingdom, and we have every reason to accept the impression created by the tradition at this point. This is particularly the case since the tradition is here supported by the central petition in the Lord's Prayer and by a major group of parables" (1967, 90).

The unique terms, debt and debtors, in Matthew's version of the prayer and in part of Luke's version, thus should be taken seriously. They come from the realm of law and commerce, and we shall find Hans Dieter Betz's careful study to be a helpful guide as we consider forgiveness as removal of a debt (1995, 400–404). Jesus spoke of forgiveness in that way in the parables of the Two Debtors (Luke 7:41–42) and the Unforgiving Servant (Matt 18:23–35), but these were stories about actual monetary debts. Here, sin itself is called a debt, conveying the idea that we owe something to ones that we have wronged, and need to pay them back so as to undo the harm that was done. The idea may thus have roots in the requirement of restitution, which had its place in law. Exodus contains a series of laws concerning property by which a crime could, in effect, be undone by making restitution, sometimes with a fine added (Exod 21:33—22:15). The law for the guilt offering in Lev 6:1–7 specifies that crimes of this kind can be forgiven only after repayment plus twenty per cent had been made. The same principle is repeated in Num 5:5–8 in general terms, as if it might apply to any crime, but of course there are many that cannot be "undone." We thus accumulate an ever-increasing burden of debt, for which reparation is impossible. Since unpaid debts are instances of injustice, God, as the upholder of justice, is also involved.

These are debts we cannot repay, but Jesus' use of the idea in his parables reminds us that a creditor can, in fact, cancel a debt. So the Lord's Prayer, taken at that level, asks God to take upon himself the burden of what we owe. Jesus did not talk about the cost to the creditor of writing off a debt, so we probably should not speculate too much about what this costs God. Would it be appropriate, however, to think of the gift of the Son of God to suffering humanity (and not just Jesus' death) as God's way of making the reparations for human sin that we cannot make?

Thinking in these terms reminds us that when someone forgives us, it will cost that person something to do so. We introduce more injustice into the world if we expect to be forgiven without also being willing to bear the cost of forgiving others. So, the addition, "as we also forgive" cannot be omitted, when sins are thought of as debts. More on this later.

This legal way of thinking about forgiveness is different from what we have found earlier. Forgiveness is not declaring a guilty person to be innocent (and thus not subject to punishment), or removal of bitterness and hatred so as to restore a harmonious relationship, or cleansing so as to make righteous living possible. It makes forgiveness a matter of mutual obligation, debts we owe one another. This concept involves declaring one to be free of an obligation that one has no possibility of repaying.

Neither Matthew nor Luke intended "debt" to replace the usual words for sin. Since Luke substituted *hamartia* "sin" in part of his version, "And forgive us our sins, for we ourselves forgive everyone indebted to us," it seems that he equated the two words. Matthew added an explanation of the second clause, using another sin-word, "trespasses" (*paraptōmata*), a stronger word than *hamartia*, meaning a false step or transgression (cf. Rom 5:15–20). They must have used "debt" because of a strong tradition associating it with Jesus' teaching.

Once, Jesus spoke of the possibility that God would not forgive sin. This was not a new idea. We found it more than once in the prophetic books, the declaration that at that time Israel had gone beyond the limits and it was too late for forgiveness. Judaism of Jesus' day emphasized God's readiness to forgive all who repent, however, and the calls for repentance in the preaching of Jesus and John were in keeping with the beliefs of the time. In one of the most troublesome sayings in scripture, however, Jesus spoke of something on the human side that would make divine forgiveness impossible—the "unforgivable sin," blasphemy against the Holy Spirit. The saying has produced great distress in Christians whose consciences have troubled them (we must say over-much) so this section should begin and end with the conclusion reached by every interpreter of the passage: Anyone who worries about having committed the unforgivable sin certainly has not done so.

Mark 3:28–29	Matthew 12:31–32	Luke 12:10
Truly I tell you, people will be forgiven for their sins and whatever blasphemies they utter; but whoever blasphemes against the Holy Spirit can never have forgiveness, but is guilty of an eternal sin.	Therefore I tell you, people will be forgiven for every sin and blasphemy, but blasphemy against the Spirit will not be forgiven. Whoever speaks a word against the Son of Man will be forgiven, but whoever speaks against the Holy Spirit will not be forgiven, either in this age or in the age to come.	And everyone who speaks a word against the Son of Man will be forgiven; but whoever blasphemes against the Holy Spirit will not be forgiven.

Matthew and Mark agree on the setting of the saying, which is crucial for understanding it. Luke has made a specific application of it. Robert Tannehill suggests that he made the saying refer to a time when a disciple who is in danger because of his faith, a time when the Spirit can be depended on to teach him what to say (see Luke 12:11–12), "refuses to be led by the Spirit and instead publicly reviles the Spirit given through Jesus" (1996, 302).

Mark and Matthew, however, connect the saying directly with an accusation that Jesus was possessed by Beelzebul (Mark 3:22; Matt 12:24), and that he derived his power to cast out demons from the prince of demons. After Jesus' basic defense, that what they have said is logical nonsense, "How can Satan cast out Satan?" (Mark 3:23), he added the doubly troublesome saying about blasphemy. On the one hand, in Matthew and Luke it seems as though it would be possible to oppose the Son of Man without blaspheming the Spirit. On the other hand, there seems to be a limit to God's grace, for blaspheming the Holy Spirit will not be forgiven.

Significantly different efforts have been made to explain the saying: 1) It has been claimed that the first part refers to non-believers, whose words against the Son of Man could be forgiven because of their ignorance. Blaspheming the Holy Spirit was then equated with apostasy on the part of those who had been believers. 2) A variation makes a chronological distinction: Before the outpouring of the Holy

Spirit words against the Son of Man were forgivable, but afterward there would be no excuse for them. 3) The widely accepted explanation refuses to identify blasphemy against the Holy Spirit with any one specific sin, or to confine it to words. It focuses on the nature of Jesus' defense, as recorded in Mark and Matthew. His attack on the charge that he derived his power from Satan was as extreme as the charge, for he claimed that his opponents had turned good and evil upside down. The refusal to believe that a powerful work for good could come from God and must instead be the work of Satan could be possible only for one who had become blinded to the difference between good and evil. Or, as Swete more effectively put it, "To identify the Source of good with the impersonation of evil implies a moral disease for which the Incarnation itself provides no remedy" (1909, 68).

This means that no single act can qualify as blasphemy against the Holy Spirit. There is no single act of which one could not repent and be forgiven. It refers to a mind-set that is not aware there is anything that needs to be forgiven, since the distinction between good and evil has been lost. In Jesus' time it referred to those who were so obstinate in their refusal to believe that God could be working through him that they resorted to the desperate measure of making the devil the author of good works. The possibility of breaking through that mind-set seemed hopeless. In our time, we might apply the saying to another kind of equally closed mind, to those for whom God is just a joke, sin and forgiveness just a joke, nothing to repent of, no change to be hoped for or rejoiced in.

We may conclude the section as we began. This saying is not to be taken as in any way contradicting scripture's consistent testimony to God's willingness to forgive anyone who sincerely desires it. Those who take their faults seriously then, and desire to be forgiven, cannot possibly have committed the unforgivable sin.

The Letter to the Hebrews

According to the Gospels, the power to forgive sins, which belongs to God alone (Luke 5:21), also belonged to Jesus of Nazareth, who claimed the right simply to announce, "Your sins are forgiven" (Luke 5:20; 7:48; compare the passive formula in Lev 5:10, etc.: "you shall be forgiven"). We have seen that the evangelists used stories of forgiveness as part of their evidence to show that the power of God was personally present in Jesus. We have also seen that they did not have much in the Jesus-tradition that would help to account for the early association of forgiveness with his death. We found only two references to the death of Jesus as something that makes forgiveness possible, the ransom-saying in Matt 20:28 and Mark 10:45, and the references to the new covenant in Matt 26:28 and Luke 22:20. The earliest Christian preaching, which we found reflected in Acts, was not projected back into the Gospel record, so we looked for reasons why the apostles seem to have immediately associated forgiveness with their proclamation of Jesus as Messiah. The material we have found so far suggests that the promise of forgiveness as a major part of the early preaching was based at least on Jesus' new covenant promise at the Last Supper and on the fact that the disciples found that the Risen Christ had forgiven them and indeed transformed them. We found that the sermons in Acts do not include, "Christ died for our sins," which soon became an essential part of the Christian confession of faith (1 Cor 15:3), along with "God raised him up" (Acts 2:24; 1 Cor 15:4, 20), and "Christ is Lord" (Acts 2:36; Phil 2:11). But Paul affirmed that the Christian confession he received, not long after the resurrection, began with "Christ died for our sins in accordance with the scriptures" (1 Cor 15:3).

But, what did this mean? Martin Hengel's helpful treatment of the question puts it in this forceful way: "How did it come about that the disciples of Jesus could proclaim that cruel disastrous execution of their master as the saving event *par excellence*" (1981, 1)? Christians have struggled to explain it to this day, with a variety of theories of atonement (Boyd 2006). We shall not go beyond what the authors of the New Testament explicitly say, although it may leave us unsatisfied, but we do find in the New Testament two major efforts to explain Jesus' death, in the writings of Paul and in the Letter to the Hebrews. They offer two, differently based claims for the all-sufficiency of the death of Christ as God's final way of dealing with sin. Each of them contrasts what Christ has done with the inadequacy of what Judaism has offered as an assurance of divine forgiveness, but there is very little overlap in their ways of dealing with Judaism.

For Paul, the key word was righteousness (Rom 1:17; 3:21–26). God gave to Israel the law, which defined what righteousness means and what is required to be righteous, but one cannot claim to be righteous if one breaks the law, and everyone does. This legal way of understanding one's relationship to God then leaves one without any humanly achievable possibility, so God has bypassed it with a gift—Jesus Christ—declaring us to be justified (somehow), apart from law, as an act of grace. This sketchy survey of his thought must be elaborated later. It is provided here in order to show the contrast between his approach and that of Hebrews.

For Hebrews the key words are purity and holiness, so whereas Paul emphasized the moral aspects of the law, it is the cultic provisions that interest Hebrews the most. The author begins with a more positive evaluation of Judaism than Paul does. The sacrificial cult did bring about purity and holiness, but only temporarily, for sacrifices had to be repeated. Focusing on cleansing (leading to purity), as we found it in the Old Testament, Hebrews insists that the sacrifice of animals cannot cleanse the conscience, but that Christ's death was another kind of sacrifice that could do so. In fact, when accepted by faith, it not only could cleanse one, but could make one holy and thus able to come into the very presence of God.

Since there seems to be more continuity with Judaism in Hebrews than in Paul's writings we shall turn to it next, even though it is later in date. Chronology is not a factor, since the thought of Hebrews is independent of Paul. It cannot be dated with any certainty, with A.D. 65–90 the generally accepted range for its composition. Since the author refers to the sacrificial cult as being presently in effect, the book may have been written before the fall of the Jerusalem temple in A.D. 70, but there is no general agreement on that. The book is anonymous, and although it has been ascribed to Paul, Barnabas, Silas, Apollos, and Priscilla, there is no actual evidence to support any of those claims. Even though Priscilla is on the list, for convenience we shall call the author "he," rather than the clumsy "he or she." More important than date or authorship for the answer to our questions about forgiveness would be the identity of the recipients of the letter, but here also there is very little to go on. A congregation in Rome is the favorite candidate, but rather than location we need to know as much as possible about the needs of the people who are addressed. We shall gather what information we can as we consider what the author wanted to assure them about forgiveness.

It may be present somewhere, but I have not found a discussion of the message of Hebrews that compares what it says about the work of

Christ with promises of divine forgiveness elsewhere. This is not surprising, for the author's choice of vocabulary and his unique approach do not suggest making such a comparison. Since forgiveness is our subject, we must attempt it, however. Hebrews says much about what God has done about sin, in a unique way. A first step, then, toward appreciating the special contribution of this book may be to gather some explicit statements about how God has dealt with sin, then to move from observations about the vocabulary used there to a survey of the way he develops his case. Then we shall find it necessary (and we hope possible) to make our comparisons.

Key Terms

In our survey of vocabulary we shall encounter a) forgiveness, b) atonement (or expiation), c) cleansing, d) sanctification, and e) perfection.

a) The word "forgiveness" (*aphesis*) appears only twice in the book, so it is evident that the author found other terms to be more useful for his purpose. He uses it in two sentences that summarize important parts of the message, however. The first introduces us to his use of the sacrificial system of the Old Testament as the basis of his entire argument: "Indeed, under the law almost everything is purified with blood, and without the shedding of blood there is no forgiveness of sins" (9:22). It is clear already that blood is another of the book's key words. It was an essential part of the rite of forgiveness in the Old Testament cult, and the blood of Christ has completed, he will argue, what those sacrifices could do only imperfectly.

Evidence for that finality could be found in Jeremiah's promise of the new covenant, which the author quoted in full in 8:8–12 and in part in 10:16–17. After he quotes, "I will remember their sins and their lawless deeds no more" (10:17; Jer 31:34) the author adds, "Where there is forgiveness of these, there is no longer any offering for sin" (10:18). This has happened as a result of Christ's death. These two verses that speak of forgiveness already point us toward the center of the author's thought. Christ's death was not a terrible mistake corrected by the resurrection, or a heroic demonstration of faithfulness, as the martyrs died. It was the gift of a human life as a sacrifice that accomplished something for the forgiveness of sin that no other sacrifice could do. Exactly what it accomplished remains to be seen. That it was all-sufficient is explained at length, but is summed up in one sentence a couple of times; for example, "But as it is, he has appeared once for all at the end of the age to remove sin by the sacrifice of himself" (9:26b; cf. 10:12). Here the author used a general term, "remove" (*atheteō*), which will be worth further comment later.

b) There is just one use of the term *hilaskomai*, which the LXX typically uses to translate *kipper* (make atonement) in the Old Testament. The verb appears with reference to Christ's work as high priest in 2:17: "Therefore he had to become like his brothers and sisters in every respect, so that he might be a merciful and faithful high priest in the service of God, to make a sacrifice of atonement for the sins of the people." The word occurs in various forms only a few times in the New Testament; in Luke 8:13 (the tax collector's plea for forgiveness); Rom 3:25; 1 John 2:2; 4:10; and as a term for the lid of the ark of the covenant ("mercy seat") in Heb 9:25. It is clearly not a key word for Hebrews, since Christ's sacrifice is referred to many times without using it. It is of some interest, then, to recall the standard formula for the rite of forgiveness in Leviticus, "Thus the priest shall make atonement on your behalf for the sin that you have committed, and you shall be forgiven" (Lev 5:10). One might think the author could have rewritten it, "Christ has made atonement on your behalf for the sin that you have committed, and you have been forgiven," but he did not. The reason may be that although he refers to the priests several times, his main interest is the high priest and his work on the Day of Atonement (9:7, 25) as the type fulfilled by Christ.

c) The first reference to sin in the book speaks of cleansing, purification: "When he had made purification for sins, he sat down at the right hand of the Majesty on high . . ." (1:3b). Here is one of the author's favorite terms, *katharizō* "cleanse, purify." Forgiveness is sometimes called cleansing in the Old Testament (e.g., Ps 51:2, 7, 10; Jer 33:8; Ezek 36:33), and the most important of the passages for our author was probably Lev 16:30, where the high priest's activities on the Day of Atonement are summed up in this way: "For on this day atonement shall be made for you, to cleanse you; from all your sins you shall be clean before the LORD." He makes extensive use of the idea of the cleansing power of blood, emphasizing that it is superficial in the Old Testament, in order to compare and contrast the work of the priests with the power of Christ's blood to transform believers: "For if the blood of goats and bulls, with the sprinkling of the ashes of a heifer, sanctifies those who have been defiled so that their flesh is purified, how much more will the blood of Christ, who through the eternal Spirit offered himself to God, purify our conscience from dead works to worship the living God" (9:13–14; cf. 10:2, 22). It is the conscience that is cleansed, a new term for us, one that will be important as we attempt to understand the result of forgiveness in these terms.

d) Cleansing the conscience is accompanied by, or leads to, sanctification, being made holy (*hagiazō*). "And it is by God's will that we have been sanctified through the offering of the body of Jesus Christ once for all" (10:10; cf. 13:12). Here, the author uses another aspect of Old Testament thought, and it will be of great importance to him. People could move through four realms. They were, clean and unclean; holy and profane (or common). Daily life took place in the profane world, where one had to be ritually clean in order to participate in worship. But a priest had to be more than clean in order to enter the tabernacle (or temple). He had to fulfill the rites to make him holy (e.g., Exod 29:21). We shall see that in Hebrews the ability to come near to God will be upheld as the ultimate benefit of forgiveness, and he will spiritualize the movement from unclean to clean and clean to holy, saying both are the result of Christ's sacrifice for us.

Still at a preliminary level, we may note some parallels between this distinctive way of describing the work of Christ and what we have learned about forgiveness earlier. That divine forgiveness involves internal change (recall Psalm 51 and Jer 31:31–34) is affirmed with reference to the conscience and in other ways. That it restores one's relationship with God is expressed in a quite dramatic way as being granted entrance into the Holy of Holies (e.g., 10:19–22). Remission of punishment does not play a prominent role in the author's thought, although he will speak of the possibility of future punishment (e.g., 10:29–31), raising one of the major questions the book poses for us: What really is the status of those who have been transformed in such a final way as the author usually insists? The concept of forgiveness as liberation from the power of evil, which we found in Mark 10:45, appears at least once, another idea the author does not develop: "Since, therefore, the children share flesh and blood, he himself likewise shared the same things, so that through death he might destroy the one who has the power of death, that is, the devil, and free those who all their lives were held in slavery by the fear of death" (2:14–15).

e) Before turning to the way the author develops his understanding of the work of Christ, we must note another of his key terms that will be of great importance for our understanding of forgiveness, namely, "perfect." One quotation will suffice for now, followed by a question. "For by a single offering he has perfected for all time those who are sanctified" (10:14). Question: Is this saying that sin itself is a thing of the past, for believers, and if so, how does that correspond with real life? We are not ready to try to answer that question yet, for to do so will require us to follow the development of the author's argument as carefully as possible.

Christ's Work in Heaven: The Development of the Author's Case

The structure of the book is somewhat complex and one can become distracted while attempting to follow the author's thought. He presents a carefully worked-out argument for his claim concerning the all-sufficiency of the work of Christ, but there are several digressions from the main course of the argument. Fortunately, for our purposes, we need not reconstruct the entire theology of the book. We do need to follow his unique description of the heavenly work of Christ, then will focus on what he says about believers who have been "perfected" by his work.

The author claims to know a great deal about what has happened in heaven, and we must begin with the question, How does he know that? for such references are unusual in the Bible, apart from the book of Revelation. Unlike the author of Revelation he does not claim to have experienced visions of heaven. Instead, he develops his message mostly as an exegete. We can see essentially two sources for his message: the apostolic preaching (2:3) and a study of scripture guided by the assumption that the Old Testament spoke directly of Christ and by the generally accepted exegetical techniques of the time. A necessary part of his argument also was acceptance of the legitimacy of the sacrificial cult, in what it was competent to accomplish and what it foreshadowed of Christ's fully completed work.

The two most important parts of the apostolic preaching for the author were "Jesus is Lord," already an affirmation of his divinity, and "Christ died for our sins." He certainly believed in the resurrection, but does not refer to it often. By the time Hebrews was written, Jesus was called the Son of God, as the standard way of affirming his divinity, and the author begins his work with a group of texts that reinforce that belief (1:5 cites Ps 2:7 and 2 Sam 7:14; 1:6 cites the LXX of Deut 32:43; 1:8 cites Ps 45:6–7; 1:13 cites Ps 110:1). He does not need to persuade his readers of this; rather he offers a powerful statement of a belief that he and they hold in common. He moves on to reaffirm the humanity of Christ as another belief that they accept (2:10–18; 4:15–16), quoting Ps 22:22 and Isa 8:17–18, and with emphasis on his sufferings, pointing toward the main message of the book, the benefits of Christ's death. Already in 2:17 he is called a high priest, and in 4:14 one who has passed through the heavens. These are new ideas, and the author has derived most of them from his study of scripture. We shall trace his argument here as briefly as possible.

Since Jesus is Lord, Psalm 110 tells us he is also a priest (Heb 5:5–6). He was a Judean, not a descendent of Aaron, so not of the Levitical priesthood (Heb 7:14). Psalm 110, however, speaks of a priesthood "according to the order of Melchizedek" (v. 4), the priest-king of Salem, who appears elsewhere in the Bible only in Genesis 14. This is a superior order, for it existed earlier than the Levitical priesthood and Abraham himself even paid tithes to Melchizedek (Heb 7:1–10). Furthermore, since Genesis 14 offered no genealogical information about the king of Salem the rules of exegesis prevailing at that time allowed the author to conclude, "Without father, without mother, without genealogy, having neither beginning of days nor end of life, but resembling the Son of God, he remains a priest forever" (7:3). Christ's priesthood is thus eternal, "For it is attested of him, 'You are a priest forever, according to the order of Melchizedek'" (7:17), and he must, therefore, be exercising it in heaven. There is a temple (the true temple) in heaven, for Moses was told to build the tabernacle—"a sketch and shadow of the heavenly one"—according to "the pattern that was shown you on the mountain" (8:5; Exod 25: 9, 40).

Scripture has, thus far, revealed to the author that the Risen Christ serves eternally as a high priest in the heavenly temple. The fundamental belief, "Christ died for our sins," now can be understood as a sacrifice.

As high priest Christ has offered himself for our sins (9:11–14). The work of the Aaronic high priest on the Day of Atonement now becomes helpful, for the tabernacle's Holy of Holies, where one might come nearest to the presence of God, was off-limits to everyone except the high priest on that one day of the year (Lev 16:11–15; Heb 9:6–8). The author now affirms something for which he cannot cite scripture. Christ has "entered once for all into the Holy Place," the Holy of Holies of the heavenly temple, with his own blood, which is an all-sufficient sacrifice, never again needing to be repeated (9:11–14, 24–26; 10:12–14), for Christ died only once.

Along the way, the author interspersed another Old Testament tradition, which he could use to reinforce his message that Christ's death dealt with sins once and for all. It was Jeremiah's promise of a new covenant (Jer 3:31–34), which referred to the old covenant as inadequate since Israel had broken it. This was the Sinai covenant, which had been sealed with sacrificial blood, according to Exod 24:3–8. He does not quote Jesus' words at the Last Supper, but it would be strange if he did not know them, for as he elaborates on the redemptive power of Christ's blood in 9:11–10:18 he recalls Moses' words, "This is the blood of the covenant that God has ordained for you" (9:18–20), and he declares twice that the new covenant is now in effect, as a result of the work of Christ (8:6–13; 10:14–18). Jeremiah's promise is of special importance to him since it concludes with a sweeping reference to forgiveness, "I will remember their sins no more" (8:13; 10:17), the eschatological forgiveness that the author declares has now been accomplished by Jesus ("eternal redemption" 9:12; "eternal inheritance" 9:15; "perfected for all time" 10:14).

Perfection?

Here is the climax of the message about forgiveness, but do we not need to ask what this really means for the life of an ordinary Christian? Does it mean that it is not possible for a Christian to sin (moral perfection), or that sins committed in the future have already been forgiven in advance? Or, isn't there surely a better answer? We need a good deal of help with this, so will turn first to a selected group of interpreters for their comments before trying an approach of our own. We begin with a couple of statements that reflect the emphasis of Hebrews on the finality of Christ's work. William Lane wrote that the author used texts "demonstrating that God had announced a new arrangement to provide a decisive purgation for a defiled people and unrestricted access to the divine presence" (1991, cxxxiv–cxxxv). Obviously more needs to be said, but this sentence reflects numerous sentences in Hebrews that suggest there needs to be no more forgiveness for believers, for they have been cleansed, sanctified, and perfected. David Peterson's book on perfection in Hebrews includes statements such as this, "The *consummation* of men and women in a direct and lasting personal relationship with God is now a present possibility, through the finished work of Christ (10:14, *teteleiōken eis to diēnekes*)" (1982, 167; cf. 152–53). Comments such as this certainly reflect the language of Hebrews, but they do not include the whole of the Christian experience. What of believers who are well aware that they still commit sins?

We turn, then, to authors who comment on qualifications of those sweeping statements that appear in Hebrews. David deSilva finds a necessary modification of Hebrews' perfection language in the appearance of two tenses in 10:14:

"'By a single sacrifice he has perfected forever [perfect indicative active] those who are being sanctified [present passive participle].' The perfect tense indicates that the 'decisive ritual that cleanses and consecrates the believer is accomplished,' but the present participle means 'the longer rite of passage that surrounds the ritual and actually signals transition—continues for believers.' The hearers belong neither to their former, normal state (their status and at-homeness in Greco-Roman or Jewish society) nor yet to their final, normal state (their status and at-homeness in the unshakable realm of God's city and homeland)" (2000, 204).

One wonders whether the author of Hebrews thought his readers were sophisticated enough to understand the sentence this way, and what he thought it should tell them to think they should do about the fact that they still committed sins while the process of perfecting them continued.

John Scholer found that chapters 9 and 10 of Hebrews teach that "Perfection for the believers is the present access to God's heavenly sanctuary which they enjoy already, not at some future time when they die" (1991, 2000). He defines what access to the heavenly sanctuary means in this life as "a spiritual approach [to God], through worship and prayer" (ibid., 199). This reminds us of the importance of worship in the author's advice to his readers (10:24–25; 12:18–24). Scholer, like deSilva, finds evidence that this perfection is somehow still not complete, for earlier in Hebrews the author spoke of a "sabbath rest that still remains for the people of God," and urges the readers to "make every effort to enter that rest, so that no one may fall through such disobedience as theirs [the wilderness generation]" (4:9, 11). But, are they on their own, now, where disobedience is concerned? There are warnings that judgment still lies in the future (6:2; 9:27; 10:27, 30–31).

Craig Koester reflects our concern when he defines the primary issue that concerned the author as "the apparent contradiction between the glory that God has promised people and the fact that they do not see this promise realized in their own experience" (2001, 88). In addition to Koester's emphases on the perfecting of Christ's work and of the believer, he acknowledges that believers are still subject to sin, and that the promises of the new covenant have not been completely fulfilled, citing "Take care, brothers and sisters, that none of you may have an evil, unbelieving heart that turns away from the living God. But exhort one another every day, as long as it is called 'today,' so that none of you may be hardened by the deceitfulness of sin. For we have become partners of Christ, if only we hold our first confidence firm to the end" (3:12–14). (2001, 101, cf. 112, 392) Hebrews does not seem to go quite far enough, in passages such as these, leaving us asking whether we are on our own, after baptism. Koester helpfully calls our attention to a passage that tells us at least in part what the author had in mind, and we shall come back to it. In 7:25 we read, "Consequently he is able for all time to save those who approach God through him, since he always lives to make intercession for them." Here, as in Rom 8:34 and especially 1 John 2:1, is a picture of Christ still active in heaven, praying for the forgiveness of those who "approach God through him," i.e., removing the barrier between the sinner and the forgiving God, perhaps somewhat the way the priest's act of atonement in Lev 5:10 led to divine forgiveness.

This is helpful, but Hebrews emphasizes the completed work of Christ rather than his continuing work. Robert Daly puts it more bluntly than most authors. Having noted that Christ "made atonement for all by a single, perfect offering, . . . he continues to intercede for us," Daly adds, "Hebrews is unable, or perhaps just unconcerned, to resolve the apparent contradiction" (1978, 72).

Barnabas Lindars has approached the book with something like our question in mind from the beginning. He found enough clues in chapter 13 to enable him to conclude that the letter was addressed to Jewish Christians who were being tempted to go back to the synagogue. The reason was that baptism had dealt with past sins, but Christian teaching at that time was not explicit enough to assure them about forgiveness of sins committed after baptism, whereas Judaism's sacrificial system offered continuing assurance of forgiveness (1991, 2, 11–13, 124). Lindars' conclusion that the issue addressed by the letter is temptation to return to the synagogue on the part of Jewish Christians has not been widely accepted (see, e.g.,, deSilva, 2000, 2–7; Attridge 1989, 9–13), but since he approaches the book in a way that is more directly helpful to us his comments may be used with caution. We have asked what readers would understand of post-baptismal sin after reading the book. He proposes that the author of Hebrews knows their confidence concerning their relationship with God has been undermined by their awareness they continue to sin (9:9, 14; 10:20), and this is the problem he intends to resolve. The Christian life they had adopted did not give them anything practical to do about sins they still committed, unlike the Jewish way. The author's approach, then, was to show first the inadequacy of the sacrificial system, then the all-sufficiency of Jesus' sacrifice, (p. 59) then to add some practical advice about what they could do, which Lindars found in 10:23–25 (p. 104). They should hold fast to the confession, provoke one another to love and good deeds, meet together for mutual encouragement, and remember that "the Day" is near. Note that repentance and prayer are not mentioned, and we may wonder why. Daly, commenting on the same verses, is once again more blunt than other authors: "Living the Christian life has taken over the atoning function of the sacrificial cult" (p. 73). Would the author of Hebrews claim it as an answer to the question of post-baptismal sins? We are led to try another approach, to test what we have found thus far.

The Results on Earth of Christ's Work in Heaven

Let us approach the book now asking for explicit answers to our questions about the meaning of forgiveness for this author, if they can be found. We shall take a series of cross-sections through the book: First, what does the author say about the status of the readers before they heard the gospel? Second, what happened to them in their conversion experience? Third, how does he describe their present relation to God? Finally, what continues to damage that relationship, and how can it be remedied?

1) Hebrews does not contain an introduction typical of letters written at the time, which would have provided some information about the recipients. The conclusion (ch. 13), which does contain elements typical of letters, says nothing about the status of the readers before they heard the gospel, so we are left with only a few allusions in the body of the letter. All their lives they had been "held in slavery by the fear of death" (2:15). Since the belief in resurrection of the dead was widespread in Judaism at the time, the expression suggests that at least some of the readers were Gentiles whose religion had not offered a hope of life after death. In the very next sentence they are called descendents of Abraham, however (2:16), but this need not prove they were Jews, for converts to Christianity were considered to be "adopted" children of Abraham (cf. Gal 3:24). Little is said of their past life. We do not find expressions such as "enslaved to elemental spirits of the world" (Gal 4:3; cf. 4:8; Eph 2:2), or "dead through the trespasses and sins in which you once lived (Eph 2:1). Their past life is called "dead works" in 6:1 and 9:14. Since the author does not attack "works of the law," as Paul does, it seems likely that his expression just refers to their past way of life, which was leading to death rather than life. In 9:15 they are said to have been redeemed from "transgressions under the first covenant." Since he said earlier, "if that first covenant had been faultless, there would have been no need to look for a second one" (8:7), 9:15 would seem to refer to its inadequacies, now remedied by the new covenant. The evidence shows that the author has little interest in reminding his readers of what they have been saved *from*.

2) Externally, the readers' conversion had followed the pattern described in Acts and alluded to in other letters. The preaching of the gospel had led them to repent, believe in God and be baptized (6:1b–2a). Gifts of the Holy Spirit are referred to in 2:4, and 6:4 speaks of sharing in the Holy Spirit along with "signs and wonders and various miracles," so there was external evidence that God had acted on their behalf.

So, having confessed their faith, received baptism and the gifts of the Holy Spirit, what does the author say has really happened to them?

How have they been changed? Having established that Christ now serves as high priest in heaven and has become the mediator of the new covenant (8:6), which promised, "I will remember their sins no more" (Jer 31:34; Heb 8:12), he speaks of the sacrifices offered by the Aaronic high priest, especially on the Day of Atonement, and of their inadequacy (9:6–10:14). They could bring about outward cleansing (9:13), but could not cleanse the conscience (9:9; 10:4, 11), and the evidence for that is the need to repeat them again and again (10:1–3, 11). Over against this evaluation of the sacrificial system the author creates a picture of a heavenly temple into which Christ, as high priest, has brought a perfect sacrifice, his blood having the power to cleanse the conscience. Furthermore, when he entered the Holy of Holies in heaven he made it possible for believers "to approach [God] with a true heart in full assurance of faith" (10:22). As we compare the author's message with what we have learned of forgiveness elsewhere we shall see that access to God, the restoration of a broken relationship, is a major interest.

They have access to God now, in spite of past sins, because the cleansing power of Christ's blood has changed them. The idea of cleansing is especially valuable to the author because of the double way it is used in the Old Testament. He and his readers both accept the idea that sacrificial blood produces ritual cleansing (9:13), and he has projected that idea into heaven, speaking of the true temple and Christ's perfect sacrifice. But the Old Testament also spoke of forgiveness as cleansing, so the idea of inner change was already associated with forgiveness. It was a natural move, then, to speak of the change Christ has brought about in them in this way: "How much more will the blood of Christ, who through the eternal Spirit offered himself without blemish to God purify our conscience from dead works to worship the living God" 9:14)! The conscience (*suneidēsis*) is a Greek concept that does not have an exact parallel in Hebrew. It has been defined as "percipient and active self-awareness," as "man himself aware of himself in perception and acknowledgment, in willing and acting." (Maurer 1971, 914) Hebrews speaks both of a good (or clear) conscience (13:18) and of an evil conscience (10:22). The evil conscience is "the painful reaction of man's nature, as morally responsible, against infringements of its created limits," the sense of guilt resulting in shame and fear (Pierce 1955, 108, 117). Cleansing the conscience, then, must refer at least to removal of the sense of guilt that oppresses the sinner and that has created a feeling of being defiled. The author says that worshippers who have been cleansed once for all would no longer have any consciousness of sin (10:2). For the sense of guilt rightfully to be gone, however, must mean that personal responsibility for one's sin must have been taken away somehow, and that must be what the author means by "take away [*aphaireō*] sins" (10:4, 11), "remove [*atheteō*] sin" (9:26), and by "redeem [*apolutrōsis*] from transgressions (9:15; cf. 9:12). "Redeem" is used as it is of divine redemption in the Old Testament, meaning simply "deliver, set free" without any suggestion of payment (Hill 1967, 68–69). The use of cleansing vocabulary thus seems to refer to forgiveness as the canceling of guilt. Hebrews does not put any emphasis on the remission of punishment as a result of that. The letter does speak of divine judgment, as we shall see, but not specifically as something eliminated by forgiveness. The author's interest is more on what forgiveness adds—access to God—than what it removes.

His use of ideas drawn from priesthood and the sacrificial system enables him to promise more than cleansing as assurance that access to God is possible. He can move beyond the realm of clean and unclean to the realm of holy and profane. Only priests were allowed to enter the holy place (except for the Passover sacrifice), and thus to come nearer to God than other people, as a result of their careful adherence to the procedures for their sanctification (e.g., Exod 28:43; 40:30–32). The high priestly work of Christ has not only made believers clean, it has made them holy, so that there are now no barriers between them and the Holy One. "And it is by God's will that we have been sanctified through the offering of the body of Jesus Christ once for all" (10:10). They already have the status of priests in heaven, then; an idea we have never seen associated with forgiveness before, but a dramatic way of assuring one of one's true relationship with God (Scholer 1991, 207). There is an echo here of Ezekiel's promise of a new heart and a new spirit, to follow God's sprinkling with clean water and cleansing from all uncleanness (Ezek 36:25–26). These gifts are to be received by faith, and have been made possible by Christ's establishment of the new covenant, just referred to in 10:15–17, with its promise, "I will remember their sins and their lawless deeds no more." The author makes this absolutely certain with his use of "once-for-all" language and the vocabulary of perfection. "For by a single offering he has perfected for all time those who are sanctified" (10:14). What needed to be done for believers has been done and nothing more is needed. They are holy. Nothing more needs to be done in order for sin to be forgiven. "Where there is forgiveness of these [sins and lawless deeds], there is no longer any offering for sin" (10:18). The eschatological forgiveness promised by Jeremiah and Ezekiel has become a reality. Believers have been transformed, as God had promised. As C. A. Pierce wrote, "Hebrews would unquestionably have regarded 'a Christian suffering from conscience' to be a contradiction." (1955, 110)

The expression "perfected for all time those who are sanctified" (10:14) seems to be saying that there is no longer any need for forgiveness, for believers. With that in mind, one could take 10:18, "no longer any offering for sin," to mean offerings for sin are no longer needed because forgiveness is no longer needed. The author never calls his readers sinless, however, and we shall find several indications that he knows they may give in to temptation, although he does not speak explicitly of a need for forgiveness in the future. Obviously, there is still more to be done as we try to be sure of what he does and does not mean by these extravagant statements.

In order not to misunderstand sentences such as those just quoted, we need to be clear about what the author means by "perfecting." The terms have been studied at length in a book by David Peterson (1982). The briefer studies by Koester, deSilva, and Scholer are also helpful (Koester 2001, 122–25; deSilva 2000, 194–204; Scholer 1991, 185–200). Koester's use of "complete" in his translation is in keeping with the conclusions reached by other scholars. That is, as deSilva concludes, it is better to translate the verb "to perfect," meaning to end a process, than "to make perfect," i.e., imparting a quality (2000, 195). This helps us to understand what the author means when he uses the term with reference to Jesus. When he wrote that Jesus was made "perfect through suffering" (2:10), that "being made perfect he became the source of eternal salvation to all who obey him" (5:9), and that he "has been made perfect forever" (7:28), he was referring not to any change in Jesus himself, but to the completion of his work. It means he has cleansed and sanctified believers once and for all (10:2, 14), and yet the author can write, "let us also lay aside every weight and the sin that clings so closely" (12:1). Note that he includes himself. If resisting sin is still a challenge, for him and his readers, why does he use such extravagant language of finality? We did not find that Lindars' hypothesis was quite satisfactory, so might try another assumption concerning the needs of the readers, in order to see whether it might be a likely explanation for the author's apparent overemphasis. The problem must have been something fundamental. Having experienced conversion to faith in Christ, they are now beginning to wonder whether they had been mistaken. They realize that the message that had wrought such a remarkable change in them is in fact hard to understand. How could the death of a crucified man actually bring about the forgiveness of their sins? They had experienced something that had at first seemed life-changing (6:4–5), but now they are not so sure about their relationship with God as they had been at first. Perhaps the trials they were experiencing as a result of being Christian had something to do with their worry that they might have been mistaken. David deSilva's description of the system of honor and shame in the Roman world adds detail to the situation we are imagining (2000, 7–20). So it may be that the key words the author has chosen, which could be taken to mean that Christians will be sinless in the future, were chosen because of the readers' present state of insecurity, to inspire in them certainty that the death of Christ means they can be *sure* their sins are forgiven. To paraphrase his message: "You *are now* in a relationship with God that is in no way distorted by sinfulness." The extravagant language thus focuses on *now*. The future for each individual is in fact not so completely certain, as we shall see the author acknowledging several times. The expression "perfected for all time those who are sanctified" would then best fit with the message of the whole letter if it refers to the complete sufficiency, the absolute dependability of the work Christ has done in order to bring about cleansing and sanctification, but not to a change in believers so thorough that they no longer should have any need to appeal to Christ for help after their conversion.

3) How does he describe the believers' present relationship to God, now that they have been cleansed and sanctified? Now we come to the evidence that there is still more to be done, but in this section we shall focus on the positive statements, reserving the issues that concern the author for the final one.

Believers can consider themselves to be partners with Christ (3:14), an idea that might have been elaborated helpfully, but the author does not do so. He adds an "if only." Human responsibility must be part of the relationship, but note that here it does not involve righteous living, but holding "confidence firm to the end." If our assumption is correct, that the author's chief concern is the difficulty the recipients are having in continuing to believe that Christ has really done all that is needed for their sins to be forgiven, then "confidence" would refer to that belief.

As we have already seen, a major emphasis in the letter is the gift—available now—of free access to God as a result of Christ's work. So, confidence moves to boldness in 4:16: "Let us therefore approach the throne of grace with boldness, so that we may receive mercy and find grace to help in time of need." It would seem as though "the perfect" would not still need grace and mercy, but the time of need that is referred to must be the physical trials they have faced and will face (10:32–39; 12:4; 13:3). We shall want to know what "approaching God" actually meant in daily life, but first there are other helpful terms used when the author speaks of this gift. It is associated with a better hope in 7:19, a hope that must refer to the new covenant's promise of forgiveness, to be introduced shortly, in 8:8–12. In 7:25 Christ is said to be able to "save those who approach God through him, since he always lives to make intercession for them." If they need Christ's intercession, then forgiveness must also still be needed in the future, although the author will not elaborate on that (cf. 9:24). "Confidence" reappears with the author's promise that believers now can actually enter the heavenly sanctuary, "in full assurance of faith" (10:19–22). There is no suggestion that the author is thinking of mystical experiences as he speaks of coming into God's presence, and he is not reserving this for the time after death. There are a couple of references that indicate he refers to "ordinary" Christian worship. The first appears immediately after he speaks of entering the heavenly sanctuary. It seems to remind him that he needs to admonish them not to neglect to meet together, as is the habit of some (10:25), and that must be meeting for worship. His impressive comparison of Israel's experience in God's presence at Mount Sinai with the present experience of Christians tells us the most about how he understood worship:

"But you have come to Mount Zion and to the city of the living God, the heavenly Jerusalem, and to innumerable angels in festal gathering, and to the assembly of the firstborn who are enrolled in heaven, and to God the judge of all, and to the spirits of the righteous made perfect, and to Jesus, the mediator of a new covenant, and to the sprinkled blood that speaks a better word than the blood of Abel" (12:22–24).

They do not *see* any of this yet, but it is most likely that he is claiming their simple worship services in one-another's homes are already a participation in that glorious heavenly celebration.

The author has focused so strongly on access to God as the result of the holiness Christ grants them that he says much less about righteous living than is typical for the New Testament letters. There are no lists of virtues and vices or extended discussion of ethical issues. A few words of advice about Christian living are added in 13:1–9, 16–17, but clearly it is what they believe rather than how they behave that is the issue for the community. That appears even in the "ethical" section: "let us continually offer a sacrifice of praise to God, that is, the fruit of lips that confess his name" (13:15).

4) What continues to damage the relationship with God that Christ has perfected, and how can that be remedied? This good news about the absolute dependability of what Christ has done was addressed to people who were not prospering because they had become Christians, and for some of them life had become more difficult. This had raised questions about whether they had believed the wrong thing, and even for those whose faith may not have been severely tested, morale was low. The author refers to these problems throughout the book.

> "Therefore we must pay proper attention to what we have heard, so that we do not drift away from it" (2:1).

> "Take care, brothers and sisters, that none of you may have an evil, unbelieving heart that turns away from the living God" (3:12).

> "Therefore, while the promise of entering his rest is open, let us take care that none of you should seem to have failed to reach it" (4:1).

> "For though by this time you ought to be teachers, you need someone to teach you again the basic elements of the oracles of God" (5:12).

> "Do not, therefore, abandon that confidence of yours; it brings a great reward. For you need endurance . . . "(10:35–36a).

> ". . . so that you may not grow weary or lose heart" (12:3b).

> "See that you do not refuse the one who is speaking . . ." (12:25a).

From God's point of view, our author insists, the problem has been solved, but for people that can be hard to believe. What still needs to be done is the Christians' responsibility; they need to strengthen their faith. The passages just cited are not of direct concern for us, then, as they do not speak of forgiveness, but there are two warning texts that are of direct relevance, and they have been the most difficult parts of the book for readers from early times until today.

> For it is impossible to restore again to repentance those who have once been enlightened, and have tasted the heavenly gift, and have shared in the Holy Spirit, and have tasted the goodness of the word of God and the powers of the age to come, and then have fallen away, since on their own they are crucifying again the Son of God and are holding him up to contempt. (6:4–6)

> For if we willfully persist in sin after having received the knowledge of the truth, there no longer remains a sacrifice for sins, but a fearful prospect of judgment, and a fury of fire that will consume the adversaries. Anyone who has violated the law of Moses dies without mercy "on the testimony of two or three witnesses." How much worse punishment do you think will be deserved by those who have spurned the Son of God, profaned the blood of the covenant by which they were sanctified, and outraged the Spirit of grace? For we know the one who said, "Vengeance is mine, I will repay." And again, "The Lord will judge his people." It is a fearful thing to fall into the hands of the living God. (10:26–31)

These texts seem to say, plainly enough, that sins committed after one has been converted to Christianity will not be forgiven. "It is impossible to restore again to repentance" (6:4a); "there no longer remains a sacrifice for sins" (10:26b). They have led some sincere Christians to fear that they may die unforgiven, have led others to delay baptism until as near death as they could risk it—since baptism would wash away all past sins, and they have led interpreters from the second century until today to search for ways to make the verses conflict less with the rest of scripture. The issues they raise and the explanations they have engendered are many. As we attempt to identify the most important, we shall follow, in part, Koester's helpful discussion (2001, 312–23).

First, various explanations have been offered of the "impossibility."

1. A favorite interpretation makes the impossibility the result of perennial sinfulness, which has so hardened the moral sense of the person that response to God is no longer possible. Koester points out, however, that another will seems also to be involved, because of the word "restore"—by whom?

2. Writers in the early church, from the second century on, took "restore" to refer to the church's decision concerning reception of lapsed members. "Impossible" led mostly to discussions of whether a second baptism was permitted, with the usual conclusion being that it was not (Haselhurst 1921, 42–51; Heen and Krey 2005, 164–66).

3. Some have suggested that the author believes the Last Judgment is so near that there will be no time for repentance (see 10:25).

4. The author's emphasis on divine judgment in 10:29–31 suggests that it is God who will not restore one who has fallen away, impossible not because God was unable to do it but because it would be incompatible with his character.

Amid the lengthy and complex discussions of these passages there is at least one point of general agreement: They do not speak of individual sins, but of apostasy, of repudiation of Christ as savior and of return to a life the church considers to be scandalous. But is it possible for a true believer, one of God's elect, to become an apostate, to lose the eternal salvation decreed by God? These texts seem to challenge the Reformed doctrine of the perseverance of the saints. Whereas the Arminian branches of Christianity will allow that people who have truly been converted may lose faith and lose their salvation, this is not acceptable in Reformed theology. In a recent discussion of the issue, from four points of view, two ways of reading these texts were proposed by Reformed theologians (Bateman 2007). One claimed that the words in 6:4–5, which seem to describe true Christian conversion, may speak of an *outward* experience that had not truly brought the person into a saving relationship with God (p. 217). Another concluded that the judgment proclaimed by the author was not eternal damnation, but just punishment, in this life, for the sins of the elect (pp. 366, 374). Most readers will probably find the latter view questionable in the light of the emphatic message of judgment in 10:29–31. As to the former, it seems to insist that the author has overstated his case, if he really referred to people who weren't truly converted, for he has been thorough and emphatic in his listing of the gifts God has bestowed on them: "who have once been enlightened, and have tasted the heavenly gift, and have shared in the Holy Spirit, and have tasted the goodness of the word of God and the powers of the age to come" (6:4b-5). The plain sense of his words indicates that he believes (or fears) that people who had truly been transformed by the gift of the Holy Spirit can rebel against what has been done for them, and if it is lost, he believes it can never be regained.

Recent commentators are close to agreement on what they think the passages mean, although they word their explanations variously. Koester suggests that God could offer to reinstate the apostate, if he chose to do so, but his offer would be the same gifts that had been rejected, so God permits the sinner's decision to stand (2001, 322). Attridge points back to the word "foundation" in 6:1. Since Christ's death is the only foundation of repentance, rejecting it leaves no other possibility (1989, 169). Lane's conclusion is similar: The apostate repudiates the only basis upon which repentance can be extended (1991, 142). DeSilva reads the passage with reference to the customs of patronage in the Roman world. The attitudes of patron and client are radically different. The patron should not expect to receive any benefits from what he does for lesser persons—they owe him nothing. The client, on the other hand, should consider himself to be more in debt than can ever be repaid. Hebrews speaks from the point of view of the client. Repudiating God's gracious gift is a crime against his goodness for which there are no remedies. DeSilva adds something that Hebrews does not: The patron [God] still has the right to be gracious, if he chooses (2000, 240–44). If these words in 6:4–6 represent the attitude of the Christian (i.e., the author of Hebrews) who has received so great a gift that in truth he cannot imagine turning away from it and then being allowed to return (rather than representing God's attitude to the matter), Karl Rahner's comment on repentance may be relevant:

> Just as one cannot love truly without excluding in the act of love the thought that it could be revoked and come to an end, so one cannot repent of one's guilt before the unconditioned that is God if this sorrow is not intended as irrevocable and once for

all. Only from the outside and by one who is not involved can it
be said that it could happen often. (1982, 82–83)

If we take the harsh words in this way, as the attitude of the forgiven sinner (the author; note the first person plurals in 6:1 and 10:26),
then his immediate words of assurance, that he does not expect any
such thing to happen among his readers (6:9–10), are not surprising.

Commentators agree that 10:26–31 also refers to apostasy, and
that is likely to be so, but our interest in all aspects of forgiveness and
our awareness of a problem that will appear in Romans leads us to look
closely at the exact wording of this text. Paul had to deal with serious
cases of sin among people in the church at Corinth who were claiming
to be Christians (e.g., 1 Corinthians 5), and when he wrote to the church
in Rome he thought it necessary to correct a serious misunderstanding
of his message, that since God justifies (declares righteous) the ungodly,
then one is free from moral responsibility (Romans 6). That people
claim to be devout Christians while living an immoral life has been a
problem for the church from that day to this, so although Hebrews is
not explicit about it, we may note that "if we willingly persist in sin after
having received the knowledge of the truth" (10:26a) might refer not
to the "falling away" of 6:6 but to so-called Christians who claimed the
right to do as they pleased. For the author of Hebrews that would mean
they had "spurned the Son of God, profaned the blood of the covenant
by which they were sanctified, and outraged the Spirit of grace" (10:29),
for such behavior would have been as scandalous as outright apostasy.

The understanding of divine forgiveness reflected in Hebrews thus
includes all the aspects we have found earlier:

1. Remission of guilt is emphasized by the expression "cleanse the
   conscience." Remission of the punishment warranted by guilt is
   not emphasized.

2. Restoration of one's relationship with God is strongly emphasized, with the author's distinctive assurance that Christians may
   with confidence enter the Holy of Holies in heaven. Indeed, this is
   more than restoration, for it means that a closer relationship than
   ever before has now become possible.

3. Cleansing and sanctifying surely must have involved for the author the kind of internal transformation hoped for by the author
   of Psalm 51 and promised by Jeremiah and Ezekiel, but he does

not describe the moral life of Christians in much detail. The transformation should be so complete that he cannot associate it with a Christian deliberately continuing to sin, and he cannot imagine it being undone and then repeated.

4.   Deliverance from the power of evil is mentioned as well, although not developed at length.

The new experience that had come about from believing the message, "Christ died for your sins," has led the author to conclude that what the prophets had promised about forgiveness had not fully been realized until now, but now it has come true.

The Apostle Paul

When I began to write on forgiveness I knew that the whole project might come to an end when I came to Paul. He does not discuss forgiveness or repentance. He introduced a new word as a part of his explanation of what Christ has done for us—justification. Readers of his letters have been trying to understand exactly what he meant by that, ever since. The decision that the writer of a book on forgiveness must make, then, is whether to let Paul take over and dominate the rest of the discussion, as he has tended to do in Christian theology, or whether one's defined topic, forgiveness, can be discussed without becoming mired in the continuing debate over what justification really means. One notes with appreciation that an author who identified himself as a person with a life-long affection for Paul wrote, as he approached the end of his book, "How does one escape the maze of Pauline scholarship" (Bird 2007, xiii, 113)? I shall attempt to discuss one aspect of Paul's work without entering the maze. There are hundreds of specialists in Pauline studies and systematic theologians who have written hundreds of books on justification, and there is still no agreement among them. I am not a specialist in Paul, and I have neither the inclination nor the ability to write another such study. In fact, if I attempted it, it would lead us away from the intent of this book, as I will try to show. My approach will begin with John Knox's critique of Paul on this subject:

> The absence of any emphasis whatever in Paul's letters upon these two concepts [repentance and forgiveness] is much more

than interesting or even curious—it is nothing short of astounding ...

But if Paul's neglect of many Old Testament passages is surprising, how shall we describe his apparent disregard of what is undoubtedly the most characteristic, constant, and pervasive feature of Jesus' own teaching? .. How could he have failed to make use of ideas so conspicuously present in Jesus' teachings and so suggestive of the whole character and quality of Jesus' life itself? (1950, 142–44)

Knox and others claim that Paul says almost nothing about forgiveness, and that is the route I will explore, but others claim he says a great deal, only with his distinctive vocabulary. It will be necessary for us, then, to survey briefly the range of opinions on that before taking up the questions I wish to pursue; namely, whether it is true that he did not write about forgiveness, and if so, why he did not.

We must begin with the data, vocabulary, once again. There are not many references to consider. As to repentance, the verb *metanoeō* occurs in 2 Cor 12:21, referring to members of the church who have not given up "impurity, sexual immorality, and licentiousness." The noun occurs two or three times. Paul speaks of repentance as Old Testament authors did: "Do you not realize that God's kindness is meant to lead you to repentance?" (Rom 2:4). But this has not happened. In 2 Cor 7:9–10 repentance can lead to salvation (not forgiveness), and in 2 Tim 2:25, which may or may not be the work of Paul himself, repentance can lead to knowledge of the truth. The familiar pattern, repentance/forgiveness, does not appear. It is evident that in daily life he had not rejected his heritage, the need for repentance, but he did not find a way to work it into his theology.

The verb *aphiemi* "forgive" appears only in Paul's quotation of the Septuagint version of Ps 32:1–2 (Rom 4:7). The noun *aphesis* "forgiveness" is used in parallel with redemption in Eph 1:7 and Col 1:14. Since many scholars question the Pauline authorship of these letters, we shall be cautious, turning to them eventually but without considering them to be proof of what Paul thought. Another verb, *charizomai*, which has the basic sense of a gracious gift, also means "forgive," at times. It refers to human forgiveness in 2 Cor 2:7, 10; 12:13, to divine forgiveness in Col 2:13, and is used to compare divine and human forgiveness in Eph 4:32 and Col 3:13.

Whether or not Paul wrote Ephesians, Colossians, and 2 Timothy, it is evident that he avoided the terms repent and forgive. He used other terms familiar to us from the rest of scripture: redemption, reconciliation, salvation, and sanctification, and added a term we have not found associated with forgiveness elsewhere (except in Luke 18:14)—justification; i.e., declaring one to be righteous. Note that to declare someone to be righteous has a wholly different sense from redeem, reconcile, save, or sanctify (make holy) so, although righteousness is a key Old Testament theme, Paul uses the concept in a new way. The data concerning word-use lead immediately to two questions, and there will be more. Why did Paul not use the word "forgive"? Why did he choose to use the word "justify"? It may be possible to find an answer to the former question without having to be sure of an answer to the latter, and if that can be done it may enable us to avoid most of the indecisive debate over justification.

Relatively few of the writers on the theology of Paul consider the first question. I surveyed a good many major works that contain indices and found that many of them did not include one reference to forgiveness. It is not a Pauline theme. Those that do refer to the word usually either identify forgiveness with justification, or say that forgiveness is a part of justification. For an example of the former, Anders Nygren wrote, "For Paul the essence of justification is the *forgiveness of sins*" (1952, 171). Douglas Moo states the latter view explicitly, "It is clear that forgiveness of sins is a basic component of justification" (1996, 266). Other scholars, however, find Paul's avoidance of the words forgive and repent to be significant, and look for an explanation. Rudolf Bultmann suggested that Paul offered a new promise—not release from the guilt of former sins (forgiveness), but release from *sinning*, the power of sin (1951, I: 287). E. P. Sanders offered a similar explanation. Paul found the traditional offer of divine forgiveness to be an inadequate response to our real plight, which is not transgressions but the lordship of sin (1977, 503, 507). Günther Bornkamm's view was the same: "The reason for this is that justification does not relate to actual sins committed in the past but to release from sin as a power which makes men its slaves" (1971, 151). James Dunn's explanation is slightly different: It may be that "in Paul's perspective, talk of repentance and forgiveness was too much tied up with the assumption that it was the language of the covenant, the privilege of the covenant member who, despite his various sins, nevertheless maintained his standing within the covenant by his loyalty to its distinctive claims (works)." So Paul developed his own focal terms (1988, I: 207). Here, then, are a few distinguished scholars who have found that there is something about Paul's non-use of these terms that calls for an explanation. Perhaps we can expand on their suggestions.

We begin with the widely accepted idea of Paul's "bad conscience" before his conversion, an obsession with sin that his Jewish faith and practice could not adequately assuage. In fact, there is little support for the idea in his own writings, and Krister Stendahl has credited him with a "robust conscience," instead (1976, 79–83). When Paul referred to his early life he said that he "advanced in Judaism beyond many among my people of the same age, for I was far more zealous for the traditions of my ancestors" (Gal 1:14). At that point he speaks of his conversion without reference to sin, but "so that I might proclaim him [Christ] among the Gentiles" (v. 16). He expressed his attitude toward his life before he met Christ more emphatically in Phil 3:4b-6:

"If anyone else has reason to be confident in the flesh, I have more: circumcised on the eighth day, a member of the people of Israel, of the tribe of Benjamin, a Hebrew born of Hebrews; as to the law, a Pharisee; as to zeal, a persecutor of the church; as to righteousness under the law, blameless."

There is no hint in either passage that he had been struggling with inadequacies in his former faith. The contrary seems to be indicated. In the past, Rom 7:7–25 was thought by some to be autobiographical and a confession of Paul's earlier "bad conscience," but that does not seem to be the most natural reading of those verses, and it has now been mostly given up (Jewett 2006, 441–45).

> In Philippians St Paul protests about his fidelity to the ideal of the Pharisees. This amounts to saying that justification was not in question when he was called. He lived at ease in his pharisaism. On the other hand we must discard the idea of considering Rom. 7 as a psychological description. If we have correctly understood his call, the Christian idea made an inrush upon his conscience through Christ's appearance, which was destined not to resolve a crisis of the soul, but to call him to a great mission, the greatest that a soul such as his could dream of. (Cerfaux, 1967, 375, n. 1)

The essence of Paul's conversion, then, seems not to have been a new experience of forgiveness, but an encounter with Jesus Christ that brought him into a relationship that transformed him and sent him forth to proclaim the message that this was a relationship available to *anyone* (Jew or Gentile) who believed in Christ. So, E. P. Sanders has spoken of the "solution as preceding the problem." (1977, 442–47) He summarized Paul's preaching in this way (not focusing, as most do, on Rom 3:23–25):

"... that Christ had died and that God had raised him, that Christ is Lord, that the Lord will return, that the *apistoi* [unbelievers] will be destroyed (II Cor. 4.3f), that the believers would be saved—if alive by having their bodies transformed and if dead by being raised in a 'spiritual body' (I Cor. 15.44)" (445–46).

He added, "Thus he did not begin with sin and the transgression of man, but with the opportunity for salvation offered by God (from which sin could exclude one)" (446, cf. 484, 499–500). He noted that classic texts such as Rom 3:25 and 2 Cor 5:19 speak of God's work in Christ without any reference to repentance or forgiveness (499). These observations led Sanders to discuss the absence of those words at greater length than most other scholars, so what follows here will be guided by his description of Paul's thought, without becoming embroiled in the debate over his "new perspective" on Paul (Dunn 1983, 95–122; Bird 2007).

It has been Romans 1–3, with the description of universal failure leading to "all have sinned and fall short of the glory of God" (3:23) that has been largely responsible for taking Paul's theology as the message concerning God's cure for sin. This is not what he mostly wrote about, however, as Sanders suggested in the summary quoted above. It was Paul's sense of oneness with Christ, which he assumed was available to others who believed, that reappears again and again, in various ways, in his letters. It was such a profound experience that he used the most extravagant language available to refer to it—dying and rising with Christ, and more; becoming part of a new creation.

"I have been crucified with Christ; it is no longer I who live, but it is Christ who lives in me." (Gal 2:19b–20a)

"For if we have been united with him in a death like his, we will certainly be united with him in a resurrection like his." (Rom 6:5; cf. 6:8)

"So if anyone is in Christ, there is a new creation: everything has passed away; see everything has become new." (2 Cor 5:17)

As if dying and rising with Christ and becoming a new creation were not striking enough as ways of speaking of the relationship with Christ Paul proclaimed, he used, many times, another group of expressions: "in Christ," or "in the Lord," "with Christ," "into Christ," and "the body of Christ" (Dunn 1998, 390–412; Sanders 1977, 453–63). Here are a few examples:

"There is therefore no condemnation for those who are in Christ Jesus." (Rom 8:1)

". . . to those who are sanctified in Christ Jesus." (1 Cor 1:2)

". . . all of you are one in Christ Jesus." (Gal 3:28; cf. v. 26)

"Therefore we have been buried with him by baptism into death." (Rom 6:4)

"As many of you as were baptized into Christ have clothed yourselves with Christ." (Gal 3:27)

For Paul these were more than metaphors. They referred to a reality for him that is not easy for many to comprehend; but that he thought of it realistically is indicated by his references to our physical bodies becoming parts of the body of Christ. He referred to suffering as "always carrying in the body the death of Jesus, so that the life of Jesus may be made visible in our mortal flesh" (2 Cor 4:10). His basis for condemning consorting with prostitutes was, "Do you not know that your bodies are members of Christ? Should I therefore take the members of Christ and make them members of a prostitute? Never!" (1 Cor 6:15). Somehow, he could speak both of being in Christ and of Christ within us: "But if Christ is in you, though the body is dead because of sin, the Spirit is life because of righteousness" (Rom 8:10).

Here we encounter a reference to sin and the victory over sin that is accomplished by union with Christ. Paul developed those themes at length in Romans 6, with v. 11 a key for us at this point: "So you must consider yourselves dead to sin and alive to God in Christ Jesus." "Christ died for our sins" was a major part of the gospel Paul had received from the church, and it had to become part of his theology, but as Sanders and others have shown, it comes in as one of the aspects of the wholesale transformation of the person that he experienced and taught. So, in addition to passages such as Rom 3:22b–25; 4:24b; and 5:6–9, he wrote:

> "For the love of Christ urges us on, because we are convinced that one has died for all; therefore all have died. And he died for all, so that those who live might live no longer for themselves, but for him who died and was raised for them." (2 Cor 5:14–15)

> "If we live, we live to the Lord; so then, whether we live or whether we die, we are the Lord's. For to this end Christ died and lived again, so that he might be Lord of both the dead and the living." (Rom 14:8–9)

Note that both passages do not speak of Christ dying for our sins but of a far more comprehensive gift that is the result of his death (and of course, his resurrection). In Romans 14 it is that he might be Lord of all, and Sanders has emphasized *transfer of lordship* as a key to Paul's theology.

"All of this can take place without reference to Christians' becoming convinced of their transgressions, repenting of them and being forgiven for them. . . . But the main conviction was that the real transfer was from death to life, from the lordship of sin to the lordship of Christ" (1977, 500).

Dunn made the same point; ". . . 'in Christ' denotes transfer of lordship and existential participation in the new reality brought about by Christ" (1998, 400). That new reality included freedom from the lordship of (or slavery to) sin, and in Paul's writings the word is usually singular, sin as a power, rather than plural, individual transgressions (Dunn 1998, 111–14). So, although he makes passing references to forgiveness of sins, without using the word, as in Rom 3:25 ("in his divine forbearance he had passed over sins previously committed") and 2 Cor 5:19 ("not counting their trespasses against them"), he is not very interested in that, compared with the new life in Christ. That means becoming "conformed to the image of his Son" (Rom 8:29) and even means that "in him we might become the righteousness of God" (2 Cor 5:21).

If true, then the new life bestowed upon believers had to reflect the righteousness of God. Paul offered specifics, in his ethical instruction, but he emphasized the positive so strongly that he had little to say about what to do when Christians failed—except to try harder. This brings us back to John Knox's comparison of forgiveness in Jesus' teaching with justification in Paul's. We have followed Sanders's explanation of Paul's lack of interest in forgiveness—not that he rejected that sacred belief but that it was overpowered by the experience of the new life in Christ. Paul knew very well that the transformation was not yet complete. The future hope was essential to his message (1988a, 461–98). For example:

> "I am confident of this, that the one who began a good work among you will bring it to completion by the day of Jesus Christ." (Phil 1:6)

> "And all of us, with unveiled faces, seeing the glory of the Lord as though reflected in a mirror, are being transformed into the same image from one degree of glory to another; for this comes from the Lord, the Spirit." (2 Cor 3:18; cf. Rom 8:19–25)

All this is completely positive. It seems to leave, not only our past inadequacies, but those of the present and future completely in the hands of the Lord—which is very good, but does that relieve us of responsibility for them? The question arose among those who, Paul insisted, misunderstood his message of justification by faith, so he dealt with it at length in Romans 6. This is where he might logically have written of repentance and forgiveness, but he did not. His answer was consistent with his basic message—dying and rising with Christ means dying to sin. We found that the emphasis on the completeness of Christ's work in heaven, in Hebrews, led to questions not fully answered about sin after conversion. Paul's different but related emphasis, on the thoroughness of Christ's work in the believer, led to the same questions, but he had to deal with outright antinomianism: "What then are we to say? Should we continue to sin in order that grace may abound?" (Rom 6:1). His response, you have died to sin, with Christ, and a dead person cannot sin (vv. 2, 7), had to be recast to be realistic. "So you also must consider yourselves dead to sin and alive to God in Christ Jesus" (v. 11). That the difficulty in doing this might lead to feelings of guilt and uncertainty as to what to do about them does not find a place in Paul's argument.

In spite of the dominant role that Paul played in the development of the church, Christians found that the old message of repentance and forgiveness could not be omitted from their lives. The Apostles' Creed reads, "I believe in the forgiveness of sins," not "I believe in justification by faith." Knowing what will come in Christian history leads one who has set out to write on forgiveness not to take justification as the last word on the subject, so this chapter has deliberately circled around that, for, in spite of the Reformers' emphasis on justification, in Christian experience "forgiven" has always been a more potent word than "justified." When John Knox wrote on Paul he claimed that "justification" does not adequately respond to the needs met by the promise contained in "repent" and "be forgiven." I shall quote a part of his argument at some length here, in justification of the somewhat unusual approach that I have taken in this chapter. He wrote that Paul had analyzed forgiveness into "justification"—a legal term, "acquitted"; and reconciliation—a personal term, restoration of community (1950, 146). Then he evaluated the effects of this:

> When Paul speaks of "justification" and "reconciliation," therefore, he is distinguishing elements which actually belong to the meaning of God's forgiveness of us; and we might argue that his neglect of the term "forgiveness" itself involves no loss—indeed, means gain, since his analysis prevents our ignoring either element in its meaning, either the justice in it or the mercy. The fact and importance of this gain should be gratefully recognized; nevertheless, it must be said that the division which Paul made in the meaning of forgiveness was one of the most tragically fateful developments in the whole history of Christian theology and therefore in the intellectual history of mankind.
>
> For although both justice and mercy are in forgiveness, they are there *together*—not simply combined and therefore separable, but united indissolubly. The justice is not mere justice, and the mercy is not mere mercy; each is modified by the other so as to make a mercy that is also just and a justice that is also merciful. When we say that God *forgives*, we are saying that *this* is the character of *his* justice and of *his* mercy. (1950, 147–48, and see 142–55)

We found that there was no separation of justice from mercy when the writers of the Old Testament spoke of forgiveness. If this was true of Paul, as Knox says, and as the unending discussions of justice and mercy in Christian theology indicate, then we may be justified in not dwelling on Paul's analysis and in moving on to the testimony of the rest of Scripture.

First John and the Rest of the New Testament

Except for 1 John, the other books of the New Testament have little to contribute to our search for the meaning of divine forgiveness, so we shall deal with them in a single chapter, concluding with 1 John, which will provide a good basis for summarizing the New Testament message. The books that call for brief mention are Ephesians and Colossians, examples of Pauline theology, although perhaps not by Paul himself, James, 2 Peter, Revelation, and the Fourth Gospel.

Ephesians and Colossians

These books will reappear in the next chapter, since they speak of human forgiveness. For now, there are three passages of interest, Eph 1:7; Col 1:14; 3:13. The first two are parallels: "In him we have redemption through his blood, the forgiveness of our trespasses, according to the riches of his grace that he lavished on us" (Eph 1:7–8a). "He has rescued us from the power of darkness and transferred us into the kingdom of his beloved Son, in whom we have redemption, the forgiveness of sins" (Col 1:13–14).

Both texts use *aphesis* of forgiveness, and equate it with redemption. Colossians emphasizes the latter meaning, describing it as rescue from the power of darkness, one way to speak of sin as a power, rather than as specific acts. This is in keeping with what we found in Paul's unquestioned letters, but unlike the other letters, here the transfer from one realm to another is explicitly said to be the result of forgiveness. Both sentences are part of the introductory material with which letters typically began. Eph 1:7 is part of the blessing and Col 1:13–14 is part of the thanksgiving, both of which tended to use formulaic expressions, so they do not add anything to the meaning of forgiveness beyond what we have found elsewhere. Colossians 2:13–14 is of greater interest because of its unusual imagery: "And when you were dead in trespasses and the uncircumcision of your flesh, God made you alive together with him, when he forgave us all our trespasses, erasing the record that stood against us with its legal demands. He set this aside, nailing it to the cross." Here, dying and rising with Christ has led to forgiveness, something Paul might have said in Romans, but did not. Forgiveness moves us from spiritual death to spiritual life, but now, instead of referring to

Christ's death with the familiar "through his blood" (Eph 1:7), his death is said to cancel a document of some kind. The extensive discussions of the passage need not be reviewed here, for recent studies explain it adequately, in spite of its unusual character (Yates 1990, 248–59; Martin 1974, 104–24). The word translated "record" appears often in commercial and legal documents, designating a statement of obligation written by a debtor with a promise to pay. This imagery thus may depict the sinner as one who is in debt to God. This is not an unfamiliar concept, and Jesus did use it in his parable of the debtors (Luke 7:41–42), but here it seems more likely to represent an indictment. The word translated "legal demands" appears in its verbal form in Col 2:20, where it refers to the ascetic regulations that some were trying to impose upon the Colossian Christians. Here, the author uses the apostolic teaching that the forgiveness of sin achieved by Christ leads to a new life in order to correct a specific error in the Colossian church. Having died to the "elemental spirits of the universe," Christians have been set free from such requirements. God erased them, canceled them in a surprising way, by nailing them to the cross. The idea seems to be that with the death of Christ the useless route to salvation advocated by some, involving "self-abasement and worship of angels" (2:18), had been put to death. Once again, forgiveness is associated with dying and rising with Christ, and it leads to a new life. "For you have died, and your life is hid with Christ in God" (3:3). This does not mean that all is really perfect, yet, for that assurance is immediately followed by a rather lengthy section of ethical instruction. What Christ has done for them, it seems they also have to do: "Put to death therefore what is earthly in you" (3:5). The next step, what to do when you fail at that, does not appear.

The Letter of James

James contains a unique passage about forgiveness and prayer, for the New Testament. The letter concludes with advice for Christians about caring for one another, with considerable emphasis on the value of intercessory prayer. Having said that those who suffer should pray for themselves, James makes illness also a concern of the church:

"Are any among you sick? They should call for the elders of the church and have them pray over them, anointing them with oil in the name of the Lord. The prayer of faith will save the sick, and the Lord will raise them up; and anyone who has committed sins will be forgiven. Therefore confess your sins to one another, and pray for one another, so that you may be healed. The prayer of the righteous is powerful and effective" (Jas 5:14–16).

Here (and in 1 John), we see evidence that tended to be missing from Hebrews and Paul's letters, that very early the church recognized the need for continuing assurances that the failures of Christians to live up to the ideal of the new birth, life in Christ, did not mean their relationship with God could not be restored. In James the Old Testament pattern of confession and prayer reappears, without any reference to a need for a human act of atonement.

The matter is complicated somewhat by the fact that sin and forgiveness are brought in as corollaries to the main subject, sickness and healing. James does not challenge the common tendency to call sickness the result of sin, although it is challenged elsewhere in Scripture (recall Job, especially). We shall see, shortly, that Jesus seemed once to make such a connection, in John 5:14, although he denied it in John 9:2–3. James at least associated the two in some way, since the clauses concerning sin and forgiveness (5:15b–16a) appear in the midst of "save," "raise him up," and "healed," all terms for healing. Prayers for healing are not our subject, nor is anointing with oil for the same purpose, so we should focus on the passage as evidence for an accepted way of dealing with sin in the early church. Later we shall want to look briefly at the post–New Testament evidence for public confession of sin as one of the ways the churches dealt with the fact that temptation was still powerful, in spite of the spiritual gifts Christians did receive.

We found that intercessory prayer for the forgiveness of others appeared with prominence in the stories of Moses and Daniel. For some reason, James cites Elijah instead, but his emphasis, that he and his readers were ordinary human beings (v. 17a), shows that he believed God would somehow use the prayers of others on behalf of the sinful (v. 16b). This led to a natural transition to a related subject, that it might be possible by one's own efforts to restore to a righteous life someone who had wandered from the truth. "My brothers and sisters, if anyone among you wanders from the truth and is brought back by another, you should know that whoever brings back a sinner from wandering will save the sinner's [Greek: his] soul from death and will cover a multitude of sins" (vv. 19–20). Sin within the Christian community is thus taken for granted ("if any one among you"), as is the possibility of restoration. Sin threatens to transfer one back into the realm of death, so James's final word reminds his readers that restoration to life is a possibility for them. The act of bringing the sinner back from wandering is said to "cover a multitude of sins." Whose sins are covered has been debated— the sinner's or the helper's? We are reminded of 1 Peter 4:8, "love covers a multitude of sins," but that does not answer the question. The two final clauses are probably intended to be understood as parallel to one another—"save his soul from death" and "cover a multitude of sins" both referring to what benefits the sinner.

Revelation and 2 Peter

These two books provide an occasion for some final comments on repentance. This theme, which plays an important role in the Synoptic Gospels and Acts, does not appear very often in the rest of the New Testament. Paul referred to one or two specific occasions for repentance in the Corinthian church (2 Cor 7:9–10; 12:21), without speaking of forgiveness. The hope that God might grant repentance to Timothy's opponents is expressed in 2 Tim 2:25. False teaching seems to be the issue here ("come to know the truth"), and repentance would enable them to escape the snares of the devil. Acts 8:22 also speaks of repentance as a gift of God. We have noted the difficult teaching of Hebrews about the impossibility of repentance. The remaining references are in Revelation and 2 Peter.

Repentance is part of the message in the letters to five of the seven churches in Revelation 2–3. Nothing is said explicitly about forgiveness as the outcome of repenting, but it seems safe to assume that this is presupposed. The author's tendency is to offer threats rather than promises. He found fault with the church at Ephesus for abandoning the love they had at first (Rev 2:5), with some of the Christians at Pergamum for succumbing to false teachings (2:16), with the church at Sardis for the inadequacy of their works (3:3), and with the Laodiceans because their Christianity had become lukewarm (3:19). At Thyatira a teacher to whom he gave the symbolic name of Jezebel had refused to repent (2:21–22) and the author uttered dire threats against her and any who continue to follow her. Much of the language in the letters is symbolic, and vague, but they do add evidence to what we found in James of the recognition that the perfect act of divine forgiveness accomplished on the cross did not mean that individual acts of forgiveness were not needed for sins that Christians continued to commit. This author's negative approach to the matter must include the belief that repentance would lead to forgiveness, although he does not state it. Later in the book, failure to repent is cited several times as the basis for the final judgment (9:20–21; 16:9–11).

Second Peter 3:9 must also take for granted that repentance would lead to divine forgiveness. Alluding to questions that had arisen about the failure of Christ to return as soon as had been expected in the early years of the church (3:3–7), Peter emphasized God's patience, concluding that the delay might provide time for "all to come to repentance." In these few passages, then, "repentance" serves as forgiveness language.

The Fourth Gospel

The Gospel according to John begins with a verse that suggests forgiveness will be a major theme, but in fact Johannine theology is more like that of Paul than of the Synoptics, in its emphasis on the new life granted to those who believe in Jesus Christ. It shows even less concern than Paul's letters for the fact that Christians continue to need forgiveness. What might have been a theme-verse, John the Baptist's announcement, "Here is the Lamb of God who takes away the sin of the world" (John 1:29), actually is, as Ernst Haenchen remarked, "not really appropriate to the Christology of the Evangelist." (1984, 153) He added, "The word *hamartia* 'sin' is likewise not a basic concept in the message of the Evangelist." Since John the Baptist plays an important role in the Gospel, it may be that this proclamation was included just because it was part of the tradition concerning the Baptist. We shall need to see what the Evangelist does say about sin, then, and to survey briefly his message concerning the saving work of Christ, largely because it will be necessary background for the study of 1 John, which has considerable to say about forgiveness.

"Sin" is normally singular, in John, and that seems significant. It is the condition from which Christ has come to save humanity. Two occurrences in the plural are no exception, for they also refer to a state rather than individual acts:

"'I told you that you would die in your sins, for you will die in your sins unless you believe that I am he" (John 8:24).

"They answered him, 'You were born entirely in sins, and are you trying to teach us?'" (John 9:34)

For John, there is essentially *a* sin, as 8:24 indicates, and that is failure to believe in Jesus (Culpepper 1998, 89–92; Ladd 1993, 264–65). Belief and unbelief are so critical for John that although he does speak at times of the last days (e.g., 5:25–29), the day when one decides for or against Jesus is judgment day. "Very truly, I tell you, anyone who hears my word and believes him who sent me has eternal life, and does not come under judgment, but has passed from death to life" (John 5:24; cf. 3:17–19). Jesus' appearance on earth defines what sin is: "If I had not come and spoken to them, they would not have sin; but now they have no excuse for their sin. Whoever hates me hates my Father also. If I had not done among them the works that no one else did, they would not have sin" (15:22–24).

John's focus on one issue—belief and unbelief—explains why he defines sin as he does and does not say much about *sins*—behavior. The few passages where behavior is in question are worth noting, but not as exceptions to his disinterest in forgiveness. The command in 5:14 is surprising. After he had healed a paralyzed man, Jesus said, "See, you have been made well! Do not sin anymore, so that nothing worse happens to you." This story (5:1–18) has much in common with Synoptic healing stories. It occurred on the Sabbath, so fits the genre of Sabbath-controversy story. But, unlike the healing of the paralytic in Mark 2:1–12, it is not told as a story of forgiveness. Perhaps we are to assume that healing involved forgiveness, but John shows no interest in that. He does have Jesus blame sickness on sin, which is the surprise, for that does not appear in the Synoptic stories, and John has Jesus contradict the idea in 9:3. The story of the man born blind, in chapter 9, could have been told in such a way that the question of sickness as the result of sin would not appear, but the introduction in which the disciples raise the question leads to Jesus' denial:

"His disciples asked him, 'Rabbi, who sinned, this man or his parents, that he was born blind?' Jesus answered, 'Neither this man nor his parents sinned; he was born blind so that God's works might be revealed in him'" (9:2–3).

Jesus thus ruled out any possibility that this could be read as a forgiveness story. There remains the story of the woman taken in adultery (John 7:53–8:11), which is a dubious testimony, for two reasons. It cannot be taken as evidence for John's theology, for there is universal agreement that it was not a part of the original Gospel. It does not appear in any important early Greek manuscript of John and is found in the standard Greek text only from about A.D. 900 on. For a long time it seems to have been a "floating" story, for in some manuscripts it appears after John 7:36 or 21:25, while other scribes thought it more appropriately belonged in Luke, after 21:38. It has been part of the New Testament tradition for a long time, however, so we shall consider it here, although not as part of John's work. The second dubious matter is the question whether it is a forgiveness story, and there is not universal agreement on that.

The story is best understood as an account of one of several attempts that were made to put Jesus into a situation where any answer he gave could be used to condemn him, like the question of paying taxes to Caesar (Matt 22:15–22; cf. vv. 23–33). There was no question about the woman's guilt, so if he opposed the death penalty he could be accused of being unfaithful to the law of Moses. On the other hand if he agreed that she should be stoned he would be counseling violation of Roman rule, for it is very unlikely that the Romans allowed Jewish courts the privilege of the death penalty (cf. John 18:31). Indeed, it is unlikely that the woman was in danger of being killed; if she had been, the guilty man should have been present also, for both were subject to death according to Deut 22:22. She was present just as a test for Jesus. As usual, he outwitted his challengers, then said to the woman, "Neither do I condemn you," adding, "do not sin again" (8:11). Some scholars take this to be a word of forgiveness, but others note that Jesus' language literally refers only to that hypothetical death penalty, so if it is a forgiveness story it is told without much emphasis on that theme (Morris 1994, 786).

To return to John's own testimony: the strongly dualistic nature of his theology did not lead him to consider the shades of gray in daily life. The contrasts were between darkness and light, death and life; and belief in Jesus Christ transfers one from one realm to another. Having quoted John 15:22, "If I had not come and spoken to them, they would not have sin; but now they have no excuse for their sin," Bultmann wrote,

"Man cannot act otherwise than as what he is, but in the Revealer's call there opens up to him the possibility of *being* otherwise than he was. He can exchange his Whence, his origin, his essence, for another; he can "be born again" (3:1ff.) and thus attain to his true being" (1955, II:25).

This so thoroughly dominated John's thought that questions of behavior have been suppressed, shifted to the sideline. The same will not be true for 1 John, however. Although the Johannine theology we have just touched on reappears, this document displays a strong concern for the daily life of the church, which inevitably involves a need for forgiveness.

I shall postpone discussion of John 20:23, the unusual verse in which Jesus gives to his disciples the power to forgive sins, until the end of this chapter, in order to comment briefly on its contribution to the development of the sacrament of Penance.

A Note about Authorship

The Fourth Gospel, 1, 2, and 3 John, and Revelation are generally referred to as Johannine literature, but from early times there have been questions about authorship. The first four documents are anonymous, but the author of Revelation does identify himself as John (Rev 1:1). He does not claim to be the apostle, and there are numerous theories concerning the identity of the author or authors of these works (Fiorenza 1985, 85–113). By the end of the second century A.D. all of them were usually attributed to the apostle John, and the possibility of apostolic authorship of one or all of them is still discussed, but fortunately that is not a question that influences our work. Under discussion are questions whether the Gospel and 1 John were written by the same person and which work may have been written first, but everyone agrees that both represent a *Johannine tradition*, no matter what hypothesis concerning the history of that tradition may be proposed. We turn to 1 John, then, expecting to find numerous parallels with the Gospel which should help us to understand the letter, but treating it as a representative of the Johannine tradition without seeing questions of priority or common authorship to be of great significance.

First John

This is a useful book for concluding this section on divine forgiveness in the New Testament, for it contains specific teachings about the continuing need for forgiveness even after one has been baptized in the name of Jesus and has received the gift of the Holy Spirit. This will lead us to consider briefly what the post–New Testament church made of the question. Although 1, 2, and 3 John have always been called letters, and 2 and 3 John clearly fit the genre, there is nothing about 1 John that resembles a letter. Commentators have classified it variously; for our purposes it will suffice just to call it a summary of the teachings of a leader in the Johannine strand of Christianity. Since he has been called John for many centuries we shall continue to call him that. The book does not have any obvious organization, for it tends to ramble from one theme to another, often returning to themes that had appeared earlier. Many passages are difficult to understand, leading Raymond Brown to comment on 3:19–21, "We have already seen that the epistolary author is singularly inept in constructing clear sentences, but in these verses he is at his worst" (1982, 453). On sin and forgiveness he even seems to contradict himself, so we face challenges, but even so, there is a good deal to be learned from the book.

A serious doctrinal controversy, including schism, led to the writing of the book. In 2:19 John speaks of those who "went out from us, but they did not belong to us; for if they had belonged to us, they would have remained with us." It is clear that the issue was of critical importance: namely, a question about who Jesus really was. At this point we learn that some of those John condemns deny that Jesus was the Messiah. "Who is the liar but the one who denies that Jesus is the Christ?" (2:22a). This issue led him to introduce the word "antichrist," which occurs only here in the New Testament. "Antichrist" in Scripture is not the great archenemy who appears in modern depictions of the Last Days, but simply someone who denies that Jesus is Christ (Rist 1962). Indeed, John says there were many antichrists in his day (2:18). It is clear that for John and his community, to believe Jesus is the Christ means to believe he is the divine Son of God the Father, for he added, "No one who denies the Son has the Father; everyone who confesses the Son has the Father also" (2:23; cf. 4:15; 5:1). Another aspect of the controversy appears in 4:1–3: "Every spirit that confesses that Jesus Christ has come in the flesh is from God." Docetism, the claim that Jesus must have been a pure spirit and only seemed to be a fleshly human being, evidently was being taught by some people John also called antichrists.

John is thus explicit in identifying a doctrinal issue that has produced schism in the church he addresses. Some commentators claim that his moral teachings also are responses to false beliefs of the schismatics (Brown 1982; Smalley 1984), but he never cites those beliefs explicitly, so others read those passages as expression of concern about the ongoing life of the faithful community (Lieu 1991; Edwards 1996). These are the texts that interest us, and fortunately we can deal with them without having to take sides in that issue.

The relationship between the thought of 1 John and the Fourth Gospel is evident from the beginning. The contrast of light and darkness appears immediately after the introduction, and John moves beyond the Gospel by using it as a way of talking about sin and forgiveness. His first proclamation, that "God is light and in him is no darkness at all" (1:5b), leads to a series of six "if"-clauses (1:6–2:2):

> If we say that we have fellowship with him while we are walking in darkness, we lie and do not do what is true; but if we walk in the light, we have fellowship with one another, and the blood of Jesus his Son cleanses us from all sin. If we say that we have no sin, we deceive ourselves, and the truth is not in us. If we confess our sins, he who is faithful and just will forgive us our sins and cleanse us from all unrighteousness. If we say that we have not sinned, we make him a liar, and his word is not in us. My little children, I am writing these things to you so that you may not sin. But if anyone does sin, we have an advocate with the Father, Jesus Christ the righteous; and he is the atoning sacrifice for our sins, and not for ours only but also for the sins of the whole world.

His first subject is thus the question that readers of Hebrews, Paul's letters, and the Fourth Gospel may ask: Does the gift of new life in Christ mean that Christians must never sin again, or even that Christians cannot sin again? John recognizes that the question has come up and answers it emphatically. We cannot claim that we have no sin (vv. 8, 10), even though that is certainly to be desired (2:1). The old message of a continuing assurance of the possibility of forgiveness—as found in the Old Testament and the Synoptics—is then emphatically reaffirmed. Note the concentration of forgiveness language. Reference to the blood of Jesus reaffirms the apostolic message: Christ died for our sins. Forgiveness is explicitly called cleansing (1:7, 9), Old Testament language that is favored by New Testament authors as well. The word "repent" does not appear, but "confess our sins" takes its place to refer to the essential human side of the reception of forgiveness (1:9; cf. Matt 3:6; Mark 1:5; Acts 19:18; Jas 5:16). A peculiarly Johannine word appears in 2:1; "we have an advocate with the Father." This is the *Paraclete*, of whom Jesus speaks in John 14:16, 26; 15:26; 16:7, identified with the Holy Spirit by Jesus in 14:26 and 15:26, but here the Paraclete is Jesus himself. Commentators note that in John 14:16 Jesus speaks of *another* Paraclete, so the Johannine authors evidently found it appropriate to use the word of both Christ and the Holy Spirit. It has been translated various ways, "advocate, intercessor, comforter." The idea of interceding on behalf of others who have sinned appears in the Old Testament, as we recall. Moses succeeded in changing God's mind about destroying the ex-slaves and starting over with him (Exod 32:7–14), and Daniel asked for forgiveness for himself and his people (Dan 9:16–19). God called upon Job to pray on behalf of his "friends," that he not deal with them according to their folly (Job 42:7–9). Christ is said to intercede for us in heaven in Rom 8:34 and Heb 7:25; 9:24. Here also, intercession seems to be involved, but of a special kind, for in the next verse Christ is called an "atoning sacrifice" *hilasterion* for sins. This much-discussed word appears only a few times in the New Testament. The debate has concerned whether it means to propitiate God's wrath or to expiate (remove) sin (Brown 1982, 217–222). The NRSV offers the non-committal "atoning sacrifice," which is just as well, as, despite the debate it is scarcely a prominent word in the thought of the New Testament authors. Relevant forms of the root appear elsewhere only in Luke 18:13; Rom 3:24–25 and Heb 2:17. The Septuagint uses it to translate *kipper*, the priest's act that God has provided in order to open the way to forgiveness. The word occurs again in 1 John 4:10: "In this is love, not that we loved God but that he loved us and sent his Son to be the atoning sacrifice for our sins." Note that once again it is God who provides, and it is an act of love. No sharp distinction should be drawn between Father and Son, then, when thinking of the Son as interceding for us with the Father or as becoming a sacrifice for sins. Brown expressed John's theology well. "It is not a case of the loving Jesus pleading with the just God, but the

just Jesus ["the righteous" 2:1] in the presence of the God who is love"
(Brown 1982, 216).

John has a clear message, then, for members of the Christian community who may have been confused by the enthusiasm of other pre-
sentations of the gospel. Christians should not sin, but they will and it is
wrong to deny it. The way to deal with sins is to confess them (perhaps
publicly, at this time) in the confidence that the forgiving power of God
will cleanse them, because Christ has died for them and continues to
be their advocate. This has always been an important passage for the
church, quoted in worship many times as the Assurance of Pardon, for
it speaks to a human need that cannot be denied. It seems unfortunate
that John returned to the subject of sin, to complicate the matter, in
chapters 3–5.

He spoke briefly of forgiveness again in ch. 2, however, in a passage that leads us to think about the role of the Old Testament in his
message. Another group of six sentences appears in 2:12–14, each one
beginning with "I am writing [or write] to you."

> I am writing to you, little children,
> because your sins are forgiven on account of his name.
> I am writing to you, fathers,
> because you know him who is from the beginning.
> I am writing to you, young people,
> because you have conquered the evil one.
> I write to you, children,
> because you know the Father.
> I write to you fathers,
> because you know him who is from the beginning.
> I write to you, young people,
> because you are strong and the word of God abides in you,
> and you have overcome the evil one.

Efforts to identify the children, fathers, and young people with
distinct groups in the church have not been very successful; especially
since elsewhere he addresses all of the believers as children (e.g., 2:1,
18, 28; 3:18). In this series it seems unlikely that he speaks of different
gifts to different groups; rather he affirms that all have received forgiveness, knowledge of God, and victory over the evil one. The third
gift associates forgiveness with redemption from the power of evil, the
theme that we have found elsewhere in the New Testament, but not in

the Old Testament. Associating forgiveness with the knowledge of God bestowed upon the children and the fathers calls to mind a specific Old Testament text, the promise of the New Covenant in Jer 31:34: "No longer shall they teach one another, or say to each other, 'Know the LORD,' for they shall all know me, from the least of them to the greatest, says the LORD; for I will forgive their iniquity, and remember their sin no more." John does not use the term "covenant" anywhere, and indeed he never quotes the Old Testament directly, but this passage and 2:20, 27 reveal that he recalls the promise of the New Covenant and affirms that it has been fulfilled in them. He used the perfect tense of "forgive" in v. 12— it has been done— with "on account of his name" referring to the power present in Christ's person. In v. 20 he returns to the subject of knowledge, "But you have been anointed by the Holy One, and all of you have knowledge," and in v. 27 it appears with another echo of Jer 31:34: "As for you, the anointing that you received from him abides in you, and so you do not need anyone to teach you. But as his anointing teaches you about all things, and is true and is not a lie, and just as it has taught you, abide in him." It matters not that John himself is acting as a teacher. He alludes to Jeremiah here as a way of dismissing the schismatics who are offering a divergent teaching: "those who would deceive you" (2:26). The knowledge of God that John's readers have received along with forgiveness will enable them to distinguish true from false teaching (4:1–6), and although he does not quote the verse, John must have gained certainty concerning this from Jer 31:34 (Brown 1982, 320; Malatesta 1978, 250–52).

Chapters 1 and 2 thus offer a very helpful message to the church. Christians are assured that "those who do the will of God live forever" (2:17), that the evil one has been overcome (2:14), and that even though they sin the one who is faithful and just will forgive them when they confess their sins (1:8). In chapters 3 and 5 we encounter John's great contradiction, however. Christians cannot sin. John does not quote Scripture, so we cannot be sure about it, but one may wonder whether the perfection of the New Covenant relationship described by Jeremiah, which had been influencing John's thought, now led him to claim, without qualification, something that 1:8 and 10 emphatically deny. At any rate, in 3:4–10 and 5:18 we encounter again the question about Christian sinlessness that appeared elsewhere.

Everyone who commits sin is guilty of lawlessness; sin is lawlessness. You know that he was revealed to take away sins, and in
him there is no sin. No one who abides in him sins; no one who
sins has either seen him or known him. Little children, let no
one deceive you. Everyone who does what is right is righteous,
just as he is righteous. Everyone who commits sin is a child of
the devil; for the devil has been sinning from the beginning. The
Son of God was revealed for this purpose, to destroy the works
of the devil. Those who have been born of God do not sin, because God's seed abides in them; they cannot sin, because they
have been born of God. The children of God and the children of
the devil are revealed in this way: all who do not do what is right
are not from God, nor are those who do not love their brothers
and sisters. (3:4–10)

We know that those who are born of God do not sin, but the one
who was born of God protects them, and the evil one does not
touch them. (5:18)

No effort to harmonize these texts with 1:8–10 has been successful. In chapters three and five one is either sinful, a child of the devil, or
righteous, a child of God, and no place for forgiveness of the children
of God is even suggested. Probably, the best we can make of this is to
look at the way the paragraph, 2:28—3:10, begins and to assume that
this is one of the several places in the book where John is by no means
as clear as he ought to have been. He has declared that they are living
in the last hour (2:18), and in 2:28 and 3:2 refers to the return of Christ
as the time when he will be revealed. What may be the key to 3:4–10
appears in 3:2: "Beloved, we are God's children now; what we will be has
not yet been revealed. What we do know is this: when he is revealed, we
will be like him, for we will see him as he is." We are not yet fully like
Christ, John admits; that still lies in the near future. Perhaps, then, it is
that near future that John describes, not at all clearly, since he uses the
present tense, as if Christians had already been perfected. "What he is
describing here therefore is the eschatological reality, the possibility that
is open to believers, which is both a fact ("he cannot sin") and a condition ("[if he] lives in him")." (Marshall 1978, 182–83) So this passage
(and 5:18) should not be taken as a denial of the need for forgiveness in
this life. This is not a satisfying explanation, for it does not correspond
with the plain meaning of those verses, but at least it follows some clues
in the context, 2:18, 28; 3:2.

Finally, John does not make things any clearer at the end of the book by speaking of two kinds of sin that Christians may commit (5:16–17) just before he wrote "We know that those who are born of God do not sin." In spite of that, he expects that one may see a "brother"—a fellow Christian—sinning. A literal translation of the Greek text of v. 16 reads, "If anyone sees his brother sinning a sin not unto death, he shall ask and he will give him life—to those sinning not unto death." Note that modern translations make the sentence clearer than it really is. Here is intercessory prayer that presumably will lead to forgiveness for the sinner, somewhat as we found it in Jas 5:14–20, but with a qualification; kinds of sins. John is not clear about who gives life; translators want us to think it must be God, but John leaves open the possibility that it might be the one who intercedes.

"There is a sin unto death." John evidently assumes that his readers know what the church of his time identified as a mortal sin—or mortal sins—but he does not offer us a clue as to what he means, except to declare that one should not try to intercede for someone guilty of such a sin. Smalley's suggestion is helpful. The concern about apostasy that runs through the book and the references to life and death elsewhere (3:14; 5:12) may indicate that sins unto death are those that deny the truth about Christ, leading to apostasy. Other sins would then be those that did not involve a deliberate turning away from God (Smalley 1984, 297–303). Readers will no doubt recognize that this passage was the starting point for the church's eventual classification of sins as venial and mortal. That takes us well beyond the bounds of this study. The next section will just touch on the beginning of the church's discussion of sin and forgiveness.

John's book, which is so helpful in chapters 1–2, with its reaffirmation of the traditional assurances concerning divine forgiveness, has now introduced two new subjects in a quite unhelpful way, for every reader needs to know more. Is it really possible that intercessory prayer, by an ordinary Christian, could lead to the forgiveness of a sinful person? What makes a sin a sin unto death? This is not a place for us to speculate, or to rehearse the speculations of the centuries. We shall not go beyond what John has written, and has not written.

Beyond the New Testament

The coming of Christianity into the world brought about dramatic changes in the lives of hundreds, soon of thousands of people. The new understanding of human sinfulness, expounded most emphatically in Paul's letters, but present also in John and Hebrews, saw it as the result of a kind of infection in the world, a disease that affected everyone and made it impossible to avoid sinning. So Paul and John wrote mostly of Sin rather than sins, a power that enslaves, and of Christ's work as the defeat of that power, the cleansing of that infection, leading to transformed lives. They and the members of their communities had experienced that transformation and they explained to their communities, as best they could, how it happened and what it meant. What the New Testament authors did not explain adequately, for future generations, was the fact (which they were well aware of) that the transformation was real but not yet complete. A major reason for that was their expectation that the consummation of all things was very near. They acknowledged the present incompleteness, but focused on the *new* so strongly that except for a few texts that we have found there is little in the New Testament about the ongoing need for forgiveness and how that is related to Christ's death and resurrection.

There was (and is) an ongoing need, however, for Christ did not return soon, and in spite of the fact that faith in him does give one the ability to resist sin and the desire to reflect his life in ours, Christians still struggle with feelings of guilt and feel the need for a better relationship with God. One of the earliest non-canonical documents, *1 Clement* (*The Epistle of the Romans to the Corinthians*, late first century AD) uses traditional language, without any suggestion that there might be a question about forgiveness. It praises the gift of repentance at some length (7:4—9:1), and although at one point it speaks of God's mercy toward "any unwilling sin" (2:3), a prayer includes "forgive us our iniquities and unrighteousness, and transgressions, and short-comings" (60:1–2), which seems quite comprehensive (see also 50:5; 51:1). Most of the works that can be dated during the first half of the second century show no indication that Christians were troubled by anxiety over whether sins committed after baptism could be forgiven. The *Didache*, or *Teaching of the Twelve Apostles*, (early second century) advises Christians, "In the congregation thou shalt confess thy transgressions, and thou shalt not betake thyself to prayer with an evil conscience. This is the Way of Life" (4:14; cf. *Epistle of Barnabas* 19:12; also early second century). Public confession in worship was the practice in the early years, evidently in the belief that repentance and prayer were all that God required for forgiveness. When instructions for the observance of the Lord's Supper are provided in the *Didache*, worshippers are advised, "On the Lord's Day of the Lord [*sic*] come together, break bread and hold Eucharist, after confessing your transgressions that your offering may be pure" (14:1).

Around the middle of the second century Polycarp's *Letter to the Philippians* reminded readers of the Lord's Prayer, saying, "If then we pray the Lord to forgive us, we ought to forgive for we stand before the eyes of the Lord and of God" (6:2), having said just before, "knowing that we all owe the debt of sin" (6:1). At about that same time, *2 Clement* (not by the author of *1 Clement*) also called for repentance so that one might "share in the mercy of Jesus" (16:1–2; cf. 17:1). This author adds something we did not find in the New Testament, an idea that will profoundly affect the church's future teaching about forgiveness. "Almsgiving is therefore good even as penitence for sin; fasting is better than prayer, but the giving of alms is better than both" (16:4). To God's free gift of forgiveness, guaranteed by the blood of Christ, are now added things people can do in order to contribute to or assure it. Fasting, depriving oneself, is presumably self-punishment, in addition to an outward sign of mourning over one's sinfulness. Almsgiving is a good work, which evidently is believed to cancel out an evil deed. These ideas introduce a whole new story, which we cannot pursue, but it is not hard to understand why they appeared. People oppressed by guilt feel as though they need to *do* something, and as the church developed the sacrament of Penance it provided for that need.

The documents mentioned thus far show no evidence of distress over the passages in Hebrews and 1 John that suggest repentance and forgiveness after baptism is impossible, but this did become a major issue in the late second century and for several centuries thereafter. The question first appears in an early second century work, *The Shepherd of Hermas*. The "Shepherd" is an angel who appears to Hermas, offering instruction and interpreting the author's visions. The focus of the book is ethical, and the Shepherd calls himself "the angel of repentance" (Mandate 12.6; Parable 9.33). Repentance is in fact the major theme (e.g., Vision 2.2–3; Mandate 12.6; Parable 6.1; 7; 8.11). The passage that has interested historians most is Mandate 4, in which the hypothetical case of an adulterous wife is taken up. The Shepherd teaches that if she repents her husband must take her back, for "there is One who is able to give healing." He adds, however, "one who hath sinned and repented must be received, yet not often; for there is but one repentance for the servants of God" (Mandate 4.1). Hermas tells the Shepherd that he has heard even the possibility of one repentance challenged, by teachers who claimed there is no other repentance but that associated with baptism. The Shepherd insists there is one more opportunity after baptism, but only one, for "if he sin off-hand and repent, repentance is unprofitable for such a man" (Mandate 4.3; also Vision 2.2). This early work thus takes up a problem that Christians have struggled with over the centuries. The idea that one could sin and repent, sin and repent, sin and repent indefinitely would make nonsense of the high ethical demands the New Testament placed upon believers.

The question whether forgiveness was available for sins committed after baptism was not settled quickly, however, and readers who are interested must turn to the histories of Penance for that complex story (Watkins 1920; Haslehurst 1921; Rahner 1982). The helpful article on the early history of penance by T. Worden begins with a comment that leads us to consider a text that I omitted when discussing forgiveness in the Fourth Gospel (1957, 65–79, 115–27). He finds it remarkable that although forgiveness of sins for the baptized was a crucial question for the church during its first three centuries, no writer appealed to John 20:23 in order to claim that Christ had given that power to his disciples, thus to the church. The early Fathers understood the text to refer only to the church's power to forgive sins through baptism, but by the fifth century Cyril of Alexandria clearly stated the interpretation that has been held by the Roman Catholic Church to this day: "They who have the Spirit of God remit or retain sins in two ways," that is, by baptism and penance (Haslehurst 1921, 67).

The passage in John 20 is tantalizingly brief and without much context. "Jesus said to them again, 'Peace be with you. As the Father has sent me, so I send you.' When he had said this, he breathed on them and said to them, 'Receive the Holy Spirit. If you forgive the sins of any, they are forgiven them; if you retain the sins of any, they are retained'" (vv. 21–23). A Protestant might be inclined to understand Jesus' words as saying that when those who have received the Holy Spirit forgive people who have sinned against them, God ratifies that forgiveness, and so the text would belong in our next chapter, "We Forgive One Another." In Roman Catholicism, however, it is understood to have conferred the power to forgive all sins (on earth) to the Apostles and thus to the church. The sacrament of Penance, based on this interpretation, became one of the major issues that has divided Protestant movements from Catholicism (Brown 1970, 1041–45). Calvin, for example, devoted considerable space in his *Institutes of the Christian Religion* to his demonstration of the non-scriptural status of Penance as a sacrament (Book III, ch. IV; Book IV, ch. XIX.14), and in his commentary on the Gospel according to John he interpreted 20:23 as commissioning the Apostles only to proclaim the forgiveness of sins, since Christ alone can forgive.

It was by combining John 20:23 with Matt 16:19 and 18:15–18 that the conclusion about the church's power to forgive sins was reached. Here is another place where we cannot profitably devote space to an endless discussion. Briefly, note that Matt 16:19 says nothing about sin or forgiveness: "I will give you the keys of the kingdom of heaven, and whatever you bind on earth will be bound in heaven, and whatever you loose on earth will be loosed in heaven." Jesus seems to have chosen the terms "bind" and "loose" from the Jewish tradition of his time, in which authorities taught that the law "bound" one to certain obligations or "loosed" one from others. The Matt 16:19 passage would thus seem to refer to ethical teaching, but the same expression reappears in 18:18, after Jesus has prescribed a procedure by which a believer should deal with a person who has sinned against one (to be discussed in the next chapter). Without mentioning repentance or forgiveness it presumably offers a way by which personal reconciliation might be achieved, but if not, when the matter is taken to the church, we see that it becomes a matter of ecclesiastical discipline. In spite of almost universal agreement that the three passages should be read together, there may be grounds for questioning how useful the texts in Matthew are for the interpretation of John 20:23.

4

We Forgive One Another

HUMAN FORGIVENESS MUST BE AN IMPORTANT SUBJECT FOR THE NEW Testament, for it appears in the Lord's Prayer, the only human activity that Jesus included in the Prayer. Because of that, one would think that such an important subject would have been mentioned more often than it is, but it appears in only a few places outside of the Synoptics. Jesus was emphatic about the need for human forgiveness. The writers of the other New Testament books seem to have seen no need to add to the tradition of his teachings that they must have known. Paul wrote about one actual case, in 2 Cor 2:5–11. Someone had deeply offended both Paul and the congregation at Corinth, but that person had repented. It is thought that this may have been the man who had married his stepmother (1 Cor 5:1–13), and this may be so, but it may be more likely that it was an offense committed against Paul himself. At any rate, the offender had been disciplined, so Paul wrote, "This punishment by the majority is enough for such a person; so now instead you should forgive and console him, so that he may not be overcome by excessive sorrow" (2 Cor 2:6–7). Then he added, "Anyone whom you forgive, I also forgive" (v. 10). Although he avoided the word "forgive" when he wrote of our relationship with God, as we have seen, he used it as others did of human relationships. Elsewhere, in his defense of his apostleship he wrote, sarcastically, "How have you been worse off than the other churches, except that I myself did not burden you? Forgive me this wrong!" (2 Cor 12:13). It seems remarkable that no other examples of human forgiveness or instructions concerning it appear in the New Testament letters except for the significant echoes of the Lord's Prayer in Eph 4:32 and Col 3:13, which we shall consider in connection with the Prayer. Even the beautiful description of the Christian life in Rom 12:9–21, which reads like a reflection on the Sermon on the Mount, saying "Bless those who persecute you," "do not repay anyone evil for evil," and "never avenge yourselves," does not counsel Christians to forgive one another.

Human Forgiveness in Jesus' Teaching

We turn to the Synoptic Gospels, then, and essentially to Matthew, since Mark and Luke record only brief parallels to the teachings of Jesus found in the first Gospel. Earlier, we considered Jesus' instruction to pray for divine forgiveness, in the Lord's Prayer, and the unusual word for sin, "debt," that appears in the prayer. Now, the time has come to consider the correspondence between divine and human forgiveness, and we shall see that this is in fact the major point that Jesus made about the latter act. It will help us to compare at once the relevant texts:

- "And forgive us our debts, as we also have forgiven our debtors (Matt 6:12).

- "For if you forgive others their trespasses, your heavenly Father will also forgive you; but if you do not forgive others, neither will your Father forgive your trespasses" (Matt 6:14–15).

- "Whenever you stand praying, forgive, if you have anything against anyone; so that your Father in heaven may also forgive you your trespasses" (Mark 11:25).

- "Forgive, and you will be forgiven; give and it will be given to you" (Luke 6:37b–38a).

- "And forgive us our sins, for we ourselves forgive everyone indebted to us" (Luke 11:4).

- The Parable of the Unforgiving Debtor is an elaboration of this point (Matt 18:23–35).

We may as well cite the related passages in the epistles here, before noting two other texts in the Gospels:

- . . . and be kind to one another, tenderhearted, forgiving one another, as God in Christ has forgiven you" (Eph 4:32).

- "Bear with one another and, if anyone has a complaint against another, forgive each other; just as the Lord has forgiven you, so you also must forgive" (Col 3:13).

The other two texts appear in Matthew 18, preceding the Parable of the Unforgiving Debtor. After Jesus' instructions on ways for his disciples to deal with others who have sinned against them (Matt 18:15–20), a passage referred to briefly in the earlier discussion of John 20:23 and to which we shall return eventually, Peter asked the Lord how many times one should forgive such a person—as many as seven? Once we have come to understand the primary concern Jesus expressed in the first group of passages we shall have a sound basis for understanding Matt 18:21–22 and its parallel in Luke 17:3–4.

What do we make of the way Jesus worded the parallel between divine and human forgiveness in every one of the texts quoted above? We are more comfortable with the order in Eph 4:32 and Col 3:13. Paul, or his disciple, seems to have it right; human forgiveness is dependent on and a reflection of prior divine forgiveness. If we had only Matt 6:14–15 it might be difficult not to claim that Jesus said we must show ourselves to deserve God's forgiveness before he will grant it, but that is contrary to everything else we find in Scripture. The context of the saying, in the Sermon on the Mount, teaches us what he did mean by it. It is a part of his definition of the character of his followers. Throughout the Sermon Jesus seems to make impossible demands of his disciples; for example, "For I tell you, unless your righteousness exceeds that of the scribes and Pharisees, you will never enter the kingdom of heaven" (Matt 5:20). This and numerous other verses seem to be saying that we must be saved by our own good works. Unless Paul and John and the author of Hebrews got it all wrong, though, it seems that we must understand Jesus' true intent by his life, by his gracious treatment of those who had no special righteousness to commend them. We have read some of the Gospels' examples of that, and now remind ourselves of Jesus' summary of his mission: "I came not to call the righteous, but sinners to repentance" (Matt 9:13; Mark 2:17; Luke 5:32).

The key to understanding the hard sayings of the Sermon, as interpreters have shown us, is the recognition of its eschatological nature. Matthew summarized Jesus' early preaching as "Repent, for the kingdom of heaven has come near [or "is at hand"]" (Matt 4:17). At another time he proclaimed, "the kingdom of God is among [or "within"] you" (Luke 17:21). The Sermon is addressed to his followers who by faith in him have already experienced God's gracious work within them and thus must begin to demonstrate in their lives the truth that the transformation of human lives promised by Jeremiah (not quoted by Jesus except at the key moment—the Last Supper) had begun to appear.

Jesus' clearest statement that this is what he meant appears beside what many see as the hardest of his sayings, "Love your enemies and pray for those who persecute you" (Matt 5:44). Why try to do something so contrary to human instincts? Answer: "so that you may be children of your Father in heaven; for he makes his sun rise on the evil and on the good, and sends rain on the righteous and on the unrighteous" (Matt 5:45). And the paragraph concludes, "Be perfect, therefore, as your heavenly Father is perfect" (v. 48).

That daunting sentence reminds us of Lev 19:2, "You shall be holy, for I the LORD your God am holy," a verse that Jesus certainly was echoing. The author of an article on the duty to forgive in Judaism reminds us of Lev 19:2 and other Old Testament texts that led the rabbis to make the duty to reflect God's attributes in the life of the Jew a central element in their teaching (Newman 1987, 155–72; esp. 164–68). Having praised the God of Israel "who executes justice for the orphan and the widow, and who loves the strangers, providing them with food and clothing," Deuteronomy continues, "You shall also love the stranger, for you were strangers in the land of Egypt" (Deut 10:18–19; cf. Lev 19:34). As God behaves, so his people must behave. Newman emphasized that "God's most essential traits are compassion and willingness to forgive," citing Exod 34:6–7. So, "To the extent that Israel is to pattern its own moral life on God's example, the obligation to forgive must become one of its central moral duties." (Newman 1987, 166) There is a significant parallel between this Jewish interpretation of the Old Testament and Jesus' emphasis on human forgiveness. He does not cite Exod 34:6–7, but shortly after saying that "children of your Father in heaven" are marked by love for their enemies, the prayer he teaches focuses on another way that we must reflect God's character—forgiveness. It seems to be absolutely essential, for Jesus spoke of no other quality in this way: that if we will not forgive we cannot be forgiven.

It should be emphasized again that this is directed to Jesus' followers, to those who have responded to the grace of God that they found to be immediately present in Jesus' presence. The Parable of the Unforgiving Debtor makes it explicit that the hard saying about God's unwillingness to forgive those who will not forgive is addressed to those who have already received divine forgiveness. The parable appears only in Matthew's Gospel, just after Peter's question about how many times one must forgive an offender, a passage we shall turn to shortly. The parable does not allude to that question, so Matthew may have placed it here only because both paragraphs dealt with forgiveness. It puts into dramatic form the teaching expressed elsewhere, about the essential correspondence between divine and human forgiveness.

> For this reason the kingdom of heaven may be compared to a king who wished to settle accounts with his slaves. When he began the reckoning, one who owed him ten thousand talents was brought to him; and, as he could not pay, his lord ordered him to be sold, together with his wife and children and all his possessions, and payment to be made. So the slave fell on his knees before him, saying, "Have patience with me, and I will pay you everything." And out of pity for him, the lord of that slave released him and forgave him the debt. But that same slave, as he went out, came upon one of his fellow slaves who owed him a hundred denarii; and seizing him by the throat, he said, "Pay what you owe." Then his fellow slave fell down and pleaded with him, "Have patience with me, and I will pay you." But he refused; then he went and threw him into prison until he would pay the debt. When his fellow slaves saw what had happened, they were greatly distressed, and they went and reported to their lord all that had taken place. Then his lord summoned him and said to him, "You wicked slave! I forgave you all that debt because you pleaded with me. Should you not have had mercy on your fellow slave, as I had mercy on you?" And in anger his lord handed him over to be tortured until he would pay his entire debt. So my heavenly Father will also do to every one of you, if you do not forgive your brother or sister from your heart.

The king's "slave" was obviously a high official. In Hebrew any royal official might be called *'eved melek*, servant/slave of the king (e.g., 1 Kgs 11:26; 16:9; 2 Kgs 6:8; Jer 25:19). Jesus chose a fantastically large figure to represent the amount he had presumably embezzled—equal to the wages of ten thousand day laborers for fifteen years. It needs to be an immense number, for the king's amazing graciousness in forgiving such a large debt represents what it means for God to forgive. Then, Jesus depicted the unforgiving human spirit in an appropriately extreme way, by having the official who had just been forgiven an enormous debt demand immediate payment of a mere one hundred denarii—one hundred days' wages—from one who owed him. As a result he lost his forgiven state, and was held responsible for his original debt, to be tortured until he could pay it, which was probably never.

This is a remarkably harsh parable. The king even orders torture. It is harsh because forgiveness is that crucial. Although the parable concludes, "So my heavenly Father will also do to every one of you, if you do not forgive your brother or sister from your heart," surely the torture in the story is an element taken from the way kings did act, and not from Jesus' understanding of what God is like. The conclusion to be drawn from the parable for real life is quite terrible, though. If you do not forgive those who have sinned against you, you have broken the gracious relationship God has established with you in spite of your sins, and the sins you commit now will remain unforgiven.

The story adds an essential element that is not explicit in the Sermon on the Mount. The one who needs to forgive has already been forgiven. He has done nothing to qualify himself for the king's gracious action, but if he had really understood what the king had done for him, it ought to have changed him, made him willing also to forgive. This is the basis for the correspondence that Jesus made between human and divine forgiveness. He addressed his followers, who had been forgiven, had begun to participate in the new life as children of their heavenly Father. The children's character must reflect their Father's character, or how can they claim to be his children? Their lives from then on must reflect God's forgiving nature, for Jesus, the most important aspect of God's character, but not as if they had to *earn* God's continuing forgiveness. C. F. D. Moule expressed the Christian's position clearly with two words, desert and capacity. Jesus did not teach that our willingness to forgive earns or merits God's forgiveness, makes us *deserve* it; rather it creates within us the capacity to receive it (1982, 278–86).

In a very helpful study of Jesus' demand for the forgiving spirit, Peter Brunner emphasized the transformation of the human spirit that one's full acceptance of God's forgiveness must bring about. He does not cite the Psalmist's plea in Psalm 51, or the promises of Jeremiah 31 and Ezekiel 36, or the claims of fulfillment in Paul, John, and Hebrews, but we have done that and recognize that they lie behind his interpretation. He wrote, with reference to Matt 18:21–35:

> We see in this parable a central feature of New Testament proclamation, made crystal clear in the fifth petition of the Lord's Prayer, "Forgive us our debts, as we forgive our debtors."

The Lord's Prayer is the prayer of the Christian congregation, those who have received the comprehensive, unconditional forgiveness of God that has become flesh in Jesus Christ. But Christians know that they need God's forgiveness new each day, for daily they fall short of God's will for them, daily they incur new guilt. So they need forgiveness daily, and thus we pray in every worship service, "Forgive us our debts." But the Lord's Prayer teaches us that the forgiveness we now invoke is no longer given by God without condition. The petition continues, ". . . as we forgive our debtors."

Every breath we breathe is a gift because of God's forgiveness in Jesus. God's incarnate forgiveness in Jesus is the foundation of our existence, that which determines everything else. And that forgiveness must now have its effect in everything we think and say and do. Especially our relation to our fellow humans must be permeated by the fact that we live only in the forgiveness of God . . . Those who are unable to forgive others, who cannot let go of their anger over an injustice done to them, make known that they have not really received the great, comprehensive, unconditional forgiveness of God. Only those have truly received the incarnate forgiveness of God whose hearts are thereby transformed and recast by God's forgiving love. Only those have truly received God's forgiveness in Christ who have—if I may put it this way—received it in the flesh, who have received it so that it permeates and saturates their whole way of life as the power that makes all things new. (2001, 285)

The question about whether sins committed after baptism could be forgiven, which we have seen troubled some in the early church, perhaps need not have arisen if they had simply focused on the prayer they used regularly in worship, "Forgive us our debts as we forgive our debtors."

Another large number appears in the paragraph just preceding the parable we have been considering: "Then Peter came and said to him, 'Lord, if another member of the church sins against me, how often should I forgive? As many as seven times?' Jesus said to him, 'Not seven times, but, I tell you, seventy-seven times'" (Matt 18:21–22). Luke 17:3–4 contains a partial parallel: "Be on your guard! If another disciple sins, you must rebuke the offender, and if there is repentance, you must forgive. And if the same person sins against you seven times a day, and turns back to you seven times and says, 'I repent,' you must forgive."

In both cases the text is not explicit about whether it refers to the same sin, repeated many times, or to various sins. The point clearly is not to establish rules about when and how to forgive, but to express in a different way the need for Jesus' followers to reflect in their behavior the unlimited graciousness of God. These are not numbers to calculate with. Seven was a symbolic number, representing perfection; Peter would not have chosen five or nine. Jesus' extravagance, seventy-seven, or seven times a day, is thus another way of pointing toward God's forgiving nature, which is beyond calculation, but which must be our model.

Divine forgiveness is thus far more than "remission of sins," as some authors have claimed. It has the transforming power that is not subsequent to forgiveness but an essential part of it. The Ephesians text mentioned earlier, emphasizes this: "Be kind to one another, tenderhearted, forgiving one another, as God in Christ has forgiven you. Therefore be imitators of God, as beloved children, and live in love, as Christ loved us and gave himself up for us, a fragrant offering and sacrifice to God" (Eph 4:32—5:2). In two ways, especially, the children of God are to imitate their Father, by forgiving and by loving; forgiving as God forgives and loving as Christ loves, he who said, "Love your enemies" and who, "while we were enemies," died for us (Rom 5:6, 10).

This in no way advocates indulgence, ignoring or condoning sin, as it might be misunderstood to do. As John Knox has emphasized, for forgiveness to take place sin must be identified, challenged, and acknowledged as wrong and as requiring correction.

> Forgiveness is the restoration of a personal relationship, whether between men or between men and God (and these two are truly one); but this personal relationship—this community—cannot be restored or sustained through the ignoring or the mere forgetting of the wrong which destroyed it. The wrong must be acknowledged and in some way dealt with . . . When two persons, the wronged and the wrongdoer, can remember the wrong together in the same way and as a shared experience, then, and only then, is it truly forgiven. The wrong thing must be completely accepted for what it is and must be appropriately handled. (1950, 146–47)

These comments will serve as an introduction to the final group of passages that we need to consider. I include them because interpreters always discuss them together and because one of them, John 20:23, speaks of the disciples' power to forgive sins. The earlier discussion of that text in this book suggested that by itself it might well be taken to mean no more than this: that when those who have received the Holy Spirit forgive ones who have sinned against them, God confirms that forgiveness. The parallels with Matt 16:19 and 18:15–20 are few, but each text has regularly been taken to shed light on the others. In chapter 18 Matthew brought together three paragraphs concerning sin. The two we have considered focus on forgiveness (Peter's question, and the parable); in the first one (vv. 15–20) the possibility of forgiveness seems to be implicit, but the focus is on what to do about an unrepentant sinner.

> If another member of the church sins against you, go and point out the fault when the two of you are alone. If the member listens to you, you have regained that one. But if you are not listened to, take one or two others along with you, so that every word may be confirmed by the evidence of two or three witnesses. If the member refuses to listen to them, tell it to the church; and if the offender refuses to listen even to the church, let such a one be to you as a Gentile and a tax collector. Truly I tell you, whatever you bind on earth will be bound in heaven, and whatever you loose on earth will be loosed in heaven. Again, truly I tell you, if two of you agree on earth about anything you ask, it will be done for you by my Father in heaven. For where two or three are gathered in my name, I am there among them.

Here, Jesus offers a procedure. When a sin has been committed, the victim should confront the offender privately, evidently to gain an admission that wrong had been done so that forgiveness would be possible. "If the member listens to you, you have regained that one" (v. 15b). If there is no confession and repentance, two more steps are possible, admonitions from one or two others, then a public accusation before the congregation. If that fails to bring about a change, "let such a one be to you as a Gentile and a tax collector" (v. 17b), no longer a member of the community. Gentiles and tax collectors were people for whom Jesus showed great compassion, but without repentance, sincere response to an offer of forgiveness, it could be no more than an offer. The passage thus presupposes that there will be tensions among Jesus' followers and describes one of the functions of the new community as that of seeking to bring about reconciliation when one member has sinned against another. It also shows concern for the integrity of the community, prescribing disciplinary measures when sinful behavior threatens not only one member but the whole congregation. The binding and loosing mentioned in v. 18 and also in Matt 16:9 probably refer to decisions about church discipline, rather than formal declarations concerning the forgiveness of sins.

Questions Jesus Did Not Answer

In the introduction to this book I pointed out that the contemporary literature focuses heavily on interpersonal forgiveness, while the biblical authors have much more to say about the forgiving God than human forgiveness. We have now seen that Jesus had one primary concern about the latter subject, and this may frustrate one who is searching for answers to a good many contemporary questions. The reason for Jesus' apparent disinterest in rules about if and when and how is not hard to find. Earlier I alluded in passing to the emphasis many scholars make on the eschatological tone of the Sermon on the Mount. When Jesus said, "Blessed are the meek, for they shall inherit the earth" (Matt 5:5), he was not referring to anything that was likely to happen before the consummation of the work that he had begun, with the inbreaking of the kingdom of God. He described ways the lives of the citizens of that kingdom would reflect the character of God himself, lives that his disciples were then commanded to strive toward—even now. So he focused on the kind of person they needed to try to be rather than on rules.

He did not talk about forgiving oneself, a subject of considerable interest to authors today.

He did not discuss the temptation to use forgiveness as a sort of coercive measure, to advance one's own self-interest.

He made no comment on another much-discussed question—whether there are cases when it is wrong to forgive.

His own behavior, with respect to the paralyzed man and the sinful woman, raises a question that he did not discuss, although Scripture as a whole suggests the way to approach it. Is forgiveness without repentance meaningful or justifiable? We have found this: Because forgiveness in Scripture is never said to be meaningful without reconciliation, then it might be offered before the offender repents—as God in fact does—but it will not happen, will not be real unless the offender finds it possible to accept it. Forgiveness is often spoken of now with reference only to the one who has the forgiving spirit, and psychologists discuss the value of that with interest, but it has not happened, in the biblical sense, unless it is received.

Is it then not possible to forgive the dead? This is another question that interests counselors, but seems not to have interested Jesus. Here, as above, a distinction must be made between the forgiving spirit and the completion of an act of forgiveness.

"Forgive" is used in international relations today, in discussions of whether wealthy nations should cancel enormous debts owed by impoverished nations. Although "enormous debts" may remind us of the unforgiving debtor, the subject is different, and it would be surprising if Jesus had offered advice on that.

One more: This is a section that should not be extended, for these are questions that a book on forgiveness in the Bible should not try to discuss, but here is another one that appears in the literature. Is anyone competent to forgive a sin committed against someone else? That would seem to change the meaning of the word as it is used in Scripture. Exactly what it would mean when used that way is another matter for discussion elsewhere. But didn't Jesus do that? Consider what he could have meant by "Your sins are forgiven." We assume that the paralyzed man had sinned against someone. He needed forgiveness from that person, and Jesus could not offer that. That is not all there is to any sin, in Scripture, however. Any sin is also a personal offense against God, and with the passive formulation, "your sins are forgiven," Jesus assured him that God had just then made his move toward the man to begin to heal the break his sins had caused.

In my little commentary on Ezekiel I entitled the section on Ezekiel 18 "The Past is Not Irrevocable," and I have preached a sermon called "Erasing the Past." Those expressions are exaggerations, of course; we cannot touch the past; it has happened and cannot be changed. I used them because the effects of the past on the future *can* be changed, by forgiveness. Forgiveness means that the past does not matter anymore, for the one who has done wrong and for the one who has been wronged. That can be hard to believe, for a person oppressed by guilt and for one suffering the pain of being sinned against. It has to be experienced to be believed, so one does well to wonder what a book can do to contribute toward the overcoming of something that is not intellectual, but affects the deepest levels of the human spirit. The excuse for this book is that it reminds readers of a very long series of people who did experience the forgiveness of God, and found their lives changed by it, including the ability to become forgiving people. It does happen.

Bibliography

Attridge, Harold. 1989. *The Epistle to the Hebrews: A Commentary on the Epistle to the Hebrews.* Hermeneia. Philadelphia: Fortress.

Auerbach, Eric. 1953. *Mimesis: The Representation of Reality in Western Literature.* New York: Doubleday.

Aulén, Gustaf. 1951. *Christus Victor: An Historical Study of the Three Main Types of the Idea of the Atonement.* Reprint, 2003. Eugene, OR: Wipf & Stock.

Bailey, Kenneth E. 1983. *"Poet and Peasant"; and "Through Peasant Eyes": A Literary-Cultural Approach to the Parables of Luke.* Grand Rapids: Eerdmans.

Barrett, C. K. 1959. "The Background of Mark 10:45." In *New Testament Essays: Studies in Memory of Thomas Walter Manson, 1893–1958,* edited by A. J. B. Higgins, 1–18. Manchester: University of Manchester Press.

Barth, Karl. 1952. *Prayer according to the Catechisms of the Reformation.* Translated by Sara F. Terrien. Philadelphia: Westminster.

———. 1960. *The Faith of the Church: A Commentary on the Apostles' Creed according to Calvin's Catechism.* Edited by Jean-Louis Leuba. Translated by Gabriel Vahanian. Living Age Books. New York: Meridian.

Bateman, Herbert W., IV, editor. 2007. *Four Views on the Warning Passages in Hebrews.* Grand Rapids: Kregel.

Beilby, James, and Paul R. Eddy, editors. 2006. *The Nature of Atonement: Four Views,* with contributions by Gregory A. Boyd, Joel B. Green, Bruce R. Reichenbach, and Thomas R. Schreiner. Downers Grove, IL: IVP Academic.

Betz, Hans Dieter. 1995. *The Sermon on the Mount: A Commentary on the Sermon on the Mount, including the Sermon on the Plain.* Hermeneia. Minneapolis: Fortress.

Bird, Michael F. 2007. *The Saving Righteousness of God: Studies on Paul, Justification and the New Perspective.* Paternoster Biblical Monographs. Milton Keynes, UK: Paternoster.

Block, Daniel I. 1997. *The Book of Ezekiel Chapters 1–24.* New International Commentary on the Old Testament. Grand Rapids: Eerdmans.

———. 1998. *The Book of Ezekiel Chapters 25–48.* New International Commentary on the Old Testament. Grand Rapids: Eerdmans.

Bock, Darrell L. 1994. *Luke 1:1—9:50.* Baker Exegetical Commentary on the New Testament 3. Grand Rapids: Baker.

Bornkamm, Günther. 1971. *Paul.* Translated by D. M. G. Stalker. New York: Harper & Row.

Bovon, François. 2002. *Luke 1: A Commentary on the Gospel of Luke 1:1—9:50.* Translated by Christine M. Thomas. Hermeneia. Minneapolis: Fortress.

Bråkenhielm, Carl Reinhold. 1993. *Forgiveness.* Translated by Thor Hall. Minneapolis: Fortress.

Branscom, Harvie. 1934. "Mark 2:5, 'Son, Thy Sins Are Forgiven.'" *Journal of Biblical Literature* 53:53–60.

Brown, Raymond E. 1970. *The Gospel according to John (XIII–XXI)*. Anchor Bible 29A. Garden City, NY: Doubleday.

———. 1982. *The Epistles of John*. Anchor Bible 30. Garden City, NY: Doubleday.

———. 1994. *The Death of the Messiah: A Commentary on the Passion Narratives in the Four Gospels*. Anchor Bible Reference Library. New York: Doubleday.

Brueggemann, Walter. 1994. "Exodus." In *New Interpreter's Bible*, edited by Leander E. Keck, 1:685–982. Nashville: Abingdon.

———. 1997. *Theology of the Old Testament: Testimony, Dispute, Advocacy*. Minneapolis: Fortress.

Brunner, Peter. 2001. "The Forgiveness of God and the Judgment of God." *Word & World* 21:279–88

Büchler, A. 1922/23 and 1923/24. Ben Sira's Conception of Sin and Atonement. *Jewish Quarterly Review* 13:303–35; 14: 52–83.

Bultmann, Rudolf. 1951–1955. *Theology of the New Testament*. 2 vols. Translated by Kendrick Grobel. New York: Charles Scribner's Sons. Reprint, Waco, TX: Baylor University Press, 2007.

Caird, G. B. 1994. *New Testament Theology*. Completed and edited by L. D. Hurst. Oxford: Clarendon.

Calvin, John. 1850. *Commentaries on the First Twenty Chapters of the Book of the Prophet Ezekiel*. Edinburgh: Calvin Translation Society.

Carley, Keith W. 1975. *Ezekiel among the Prophets*. Studies in Biblical Theology 2/31. London: SCM.

Carson, D. A., et al, ed. 2001. *Justification and Variegated Nomism*, Vol. 1, *The Complexities of Second Temple Judaism*. Grand Rapids: Baker Academic.

Cerfaux, Lucien. 1967. *The Christian in the Theology of St Paul*. London: Chapman.

Craigie, Peter C., et al. 1991. *Jeremiah 1–25*. Word Biblical Commentary 26. Dallas: Word.

Culpepper, R. Alan. 1998. *The Gospel and Letters of John*. Interpreting Biblical Texts. Nashville: Abingdon.

Daly, Robert. 1978. *The Origins of the Christian Doctrine of Sacrifice*. Philadelphia: Fortress.

Davies, W. D. 1955. *Paul and Rabbinic Judaism: Some Rabbinic Elements in Pauline Theology*. Rev. ed. New York: Harper & Row.

DeSilva, David. 2000. *Perseverance in Gratitude: A Socio-Rhetorical Commentary on the Epistle "to the Hebrews."* Grand Rapids: Eerdmans.

Dodd, C. H. 1936. *The Apostolic Preaching and Its Developments*. London: Hodder & Stoughton.

Dunn, James D. G. 1983. "The New Perspective on Paul." *Bulletin of the John Rylands Library* 65:95–122.

———. 1988. *Romans*. Vol. 1, *Romans 1–8*. Word Biblical Commentary 38A. Dallas: Word.

———. 1998. *The Theology of Paul the Apostle*. Grand Rapids: Eerdmans.

Edwards, Ruth B. 1996. *The Johannine Epistles*. New Testament Guides. Sheffield: Sheffield Academic.

Eichrodt, Walther. 1970. *Ezekiel: A Commentary*. Translated by J. A. Baker. Old Testament Library. Philadelphia: Westminster Press.

Enright, Robert D., and Joanna North, editor. 1998. *Exploring Forgiveness*. Madison: University of Wisconsin Press.

Fitzmyer, Joseph A. 1970. *The Gospel according to Luke (I–IX)*. Anchor Bible 28. New York: Doubleday.

———. 1985. *The Gospel according to Luke (X–XXIV)*. Anchor Bible 28A. New York: Doubleday.

Fiorenza, Elizabeth Schüssler. 1985. "The Quest for the Johannine School: The Book of Revelation and the Fourth Gospel." In *The Book of Revelation: Justice and Judgment*, 85–113. Philadelphia: Fortress.

Freedman, David Noel. 1955. "God Compassionate and Gracious." *Western Watch* 6:6–24.

———. 1964. "Divine Commitment and Human Obligation: The Covenant Theme." *Interpretation* 18:419–31.

Fretheim, Terence E. 1994. "Genesis." In *New Interpreter's Bible*, edited by Leander Keck, 1:319–674. Nashville: Abingdon.

———. 2002. *Jeremiah*. Smyth & Helwys Bible Commentary 15. Macon, GA: Smyth & Helwys.

Garnet, Paul. 1977. *Salvation and Atonement in the Qumran Scrolls*. Wissenschaftliche Untersuchungen zum Neuen Testament 3. Tübingen: Mohr/Siebeck.

Glueck, Nelson. 1967. Ḥesed *in the Bible*. Cincinnati: Hebrew Union College Press.

Gorman, Frank H., Jr. 1990. *The Ideology of Ritual: Space, Time and Status in the Priestly Theology*. Journal for the Study of the Old Testament Supplement Series 91. Sheffield: JSOT Press.

Gowan, Donald E. 1986. *Eschatology in the Old Testament*. Philadelphia: Fortress.

———. 1996. "Amos." In *New Interpreter's Bible*, edited by Leander Keck, 7: 337–432. Nashville: Abingdon.

———. 1998. *Theology of the Prophetic Books: The Death and Resurrection of Israel*. Louisville: Westminster John Knox.

———. 2000. *Eschatology in the Old Testament*. 2nd ed. Edinburgh: T. & T. Clark.

———. 2001. *Daniel*. Abingdon Old Testament Commentaries. Nashville: Abingdon.

Greenberg, Moshe. 1983. *Ezekiel 1–20*. Anchor Bible 22. Garden City, NY: Doubleday.

———. 1997. *Ezekiel 21–37*. Anchor Bible 22A. New York: Doubleday.

Haber, Joram Graf. 1991. *Forgiveness*. Savage, MD: Rowman & Littlefield.

Haenchen, Ernst. 1984. *John*. Vol. 1, *Chapters 1–6*. Translated by Robert W. Funk. Hermeneia. Philadelphia: Fortress.

Hanson, Paul D. 1995. *Isaiah 40–66*. Interpretation. Louisville: Westminster John Knox.

Hare, Douglas R. A. 1990. *The Son of Man Tradition*. Philadelphia: Fortress.

Haselhurst, R. S. T. 1921. *Some Account of the Penitential Discipline of the Early Church in the First Four Centuries*. London: SPCK.

Heen, Erik M., and Philip D. W. Krey, editors. 2005. *Hebrews*. Ancient Christian Commentary on Scripture 10. Downers Grove, IL: InterVarsity.

Hengel, Martin. 1981. *The Atonement: The Origins of the Doctrine in the New Testament*. Translated by John Bowden. Philadelphia: Fortress.

Hill, David. 1967. *Greek Words and Hebrew Meanings: Studies in the Semantics of Soteriological Terms.* Society for New Testament Studies Monograph Series 5. Cambridge: Cambridge University Press.

Hoffman, Yair. 1995. "The Deuteronomist and the Exile." In *Pomegranates and Golden Bells: Studies in Biblical, Jewish, and Near Eastern Ritual, Law, and Literature in Honor of Jacob Milgrom*, edited by David P. Wright et al, 659–75. Winona Lake, IN: Eisenbrauns.

Hooker, Morna D. 1959. *Jesus and the Servant: The Influence of the Servant Concept of Deutero-Isaiah in the New Testament.* London: SPCK.

Hunter, A. Vanlier. 1982. *Seek The Lord! A Study of the Meaning and Function of the Exhortations in Amos, Hosea, Isaiah, Micah, and Zephaniah.* Baltimore: St. Mary's Seminary & University.

Jewett, Robert. 2006. *Romans: A Commentary.* Hermeneia. Minneapolis: Fortress.

Jones, L. Gregory. 1995. *Embodying Forgiveness: A Theological Analysis.* Grand Rapids: Eerdmans.

Klawans, Joseph. 2000. *Impurity and Sin in Ancient Judaism.* Oxford: Oxford University Press.

Knight, George A. F. 1959. *A Christian Theology of the Old Testament.* Richmond, VA: John Knox.

Knox, John. 1950. *Chapters in a Life of Paul.* New York: Abingdon-Cokesbury.

————. 1961. *The Ethic of Jesus in the Teaching of the Church: Its Authority and Its Relevance.* New York: Abingdon.

Koester, Craig. 2001. *Hebrews.* Anchor Bible 36. New York: Doubleday.

Ladd, George Eldon. 1993. *A Theology of the New Testament.* Rev. ed. Edited by Donald A. Hagner. Grand Rapids: Eerdmans.

Lane, William. 1991. *Hebrews 1–8.* Word Bible Commentary 47A. Dallas: Word.

Lapsley, Jacqueline. 2000. "Shame and Self-Knowledge: The Positive Role of Shame in Ezekiel's View of the Moral Self." In *The Book of Ezekiel: Theological and Anthropological Perspectives*, edited by Margaret S. Odell and John T. Strong, 150–52. SBL Symposium Series 9. Atlanta: Society of Biblical Literature.

Levine, Baruch A. 1974. *In the Presence of the Lord: A Study of Cult and Some Cultic Terms in Ancient Israel.* Studies in Judaism in Late Antiquity 5. Leiden: Brill.

Lichtenberger, Hermann. 1980. "Atonement and Sacrifice in the Qumran Community." In *Approaches to Ancient Judaism*, vol. 2, edited by William Green, 159–71. Brown Judaic Studies 9. Chico: Scholars.

Lieu, Judith M. 1991. *The Theology of the Johannine Epistles.* New Testament Theology. Cambridge: Cambridge University Press.

Lindars, Barnabas. 1991. *The Theology of the Letter to the Hebrews.* New Testament Theology. Cambridge: Cambridge University Press.

Lindström, Fredrik. 1994. *Suffering and Sin: Interpretations of Illness in the Individual Complaint Psalms.* Coniectanea Biblica: Old Testament Series 37. Stockholm: Almqvist & Wiksell.

Lyonnet, Stanislas, and Leopold Sabourin. 1970. *Sin, Redemption, and Sacrifice: A Biblical and Patristic Study.* Analecta Biblica 48. Rome: Biblical Institute Press.

Mackintosh, H. R. 1934. *The Christian Experience of Forgiveness.* Rev. ed. Library of Constructive Theology. London: Nisbet.

Malatesta, Edward. 1978. *Interiority and Covenant: A Study of* einai en *and* menein en *in the First Letter of John.* Analecta Biblica 69. Rome: Biblical Institute Press.

Marshall, I. Howard. 1978 *The Epistles of John*. New International Commentary on the New Testament. Grand Rapids: Eerdmans.

―――. 1978a. *The Gospel of Luke: A Commentary on the Greek Text*. New International Greek Testament Commentary 3. Grand Rapids: Eerdmans.

Martin, Ralph P. 1974. "Reconciliation and Forgiveness in the Letter to the Colossians." In *Reconciliation and Hope: New Testament Essays on Atonement and Eschatology presented to L. L. Morris on his 60th Birthday*, edited by Robert Banks, 104–24. Grand Rapids: Eerdmans.

Maurer, Christian. 1971. "*Sunoida, Suneidesis*." In *Theological Dictionary of the New Testament*, edited by Gerhard Kittel and Gerhard Friedrich, 7:898–919. Translated by Geoffrey W. Bromiley. Grand Rapids: Eerdmans.

McKane, William. 1970. *Proverbs: A New Approach*. Old Testament Library. Philadelphia: Westminster.

―――. 1986 *A Critical and Exegetical Commentary on Jeremiah*. Vol. 1. International Critical Commentary. Edinburgh: T. & T. Clark.

Milgrom, Jacob. 1990. *Numbers: The Traditional Hebrew Text with the New JPS Translation*. Philadelphia: JPS Publishing Society.

―――. 1991 *Leviticus 1–16: A New Translation with Introduction and Commentary*. Anchor Bible 3. New York: Doubleday.

―――. 2000. *Leviticus 17–22: A New Translation with Introduction and Commentary*. Anchor Bible 3A. New York: Doubleday.

Moo, Douglas. 1996. *The Epistle to the Romans*. New International Commentary on the New Testament. Grand Rapids: Eerdmans.

Moore, George Foot. 1971. *Judaism in the First Centuries of the Christian Era*. New York: Schocken.

Morris, Leon. 1995. *The Gospel according to John*. New International Commentary on the New Testament. Grand Rapids: Eerdmans.

Moulder, W. J. 1978. "The Old Testament Background and the Interpretation of Mark X.45." *New Testament Studies* 24:120–27.

Moule, C. F. D. 1982. "'. . . As we forgive . . .': A Note on the Distinction between Deserts and Capacity in the Understanding of Forgiveness." In *Essays in New Testament Interpretation*, 278–86. Cambridge: Cambridge University Press.

Murphy, Jeffrie G. 2003. *Getting Even: Forgiveness and Its Limits*. Oxford: Oxford University Press.

Newman, Louis E. 1987. "The Quality of Mercy: On the Duty to Forgive in the Judaic Tradition." *Journal of Religious Ethics* 15:155–72.

Nygren, Anders. 1952. *Commentary on Romans*. London: SCM.

Pedersen, Johannes. 1940. *Israel: Its Life and Culture*. 4 vols. Translated by A. Møller and A. I. Fausbøll. London: Oxford University Press.

Perrin, Norman. 1967. *Rediscovering the Teaching of Jesus*. New York: Harper & Row.

Peterson, David. 1982. *Hebrews and Perfection: An Examination of the Concept of Perfection in the "Epistle to the Hebrews."* Society for New Testament Studies Monograph Series 47. Cambridge: Cambridge University Press.

Pierce, C. A. 1955. *Conscience in the New Testament*. Studies in Biblical Theology 1/15. Chicago: Allenson.

Plummer, Alfred. 1910. *An Exegetical Commentary on the Gospel according to Matthew*. London: Elliot Stock.

Rahner, Karl. 1982. "The Penitential Teachings of the Shepherd of Hermas." In *Penance in the Early Church*, 114–21. Theological Investigations 15. New York: Crossroad.

Ringgren, Helmer. 1995. *The Faith of Qumran: Theology of the Dead Sea Scrolls.* Expanded ed. Translated by Emilie T. Sander. Edited with a new introduction by James H. Charlesworth. Christian Origins Library. New York: Crossroad.

Rist, Martin. 1962. "Antichrist." In *Interpreter's Dictionary of the Bible*, edited by George Buttrick, 1:140–43. New York: Abingdon.

Sakenfeld, Katharine D. 1975. "The Problem of Divine Forgiveness in Numbers 14." *Catholic Biblical Quarterly* 37:317–30.

———. 1978 *The Meaning of Ḥesed in the Hebrew Bible: A New Inquiry.* Harvard Semitic Monographs 17. Missoula, MT: Scholars.

Salom, A. P. 1966–1967. "Was Zacchaeus Really Reforming?" *Expository Times* 78:87.

Sanders, E. P. 1977. *Paul and Palestinian Judaism: A Comparison of Patterns of Religion.* Philadelphia: Fortress.

———. 1985. *Jesus and Judaism.* Philadelphia: Fortress.

Schechter, Solomon. 1961. *Aspects of Rabbinic Theology: Major Concepts of the Talmud.* New York: Schocken.

Schimmel, Solomon. 2002. *Wounds not Healed by Time: The Power of Repentance and Forgiveness.* Oxford: Oxford University Press.

Scholer, John. 1991. *Proleptic Priests: Priesthood in the Epistle to the Hebrews.* Journal for the Study of the New Testament Supplement Series 49. Sheffield: JSNT Press.

Simian-Yofre, H. 2004. "*rḥm.*" In *Theological Dictionary of the Old Testament*, edited by G. Johannes Botterweck et al., 13:437–52. Translated by Geoffrey W. Bromiley. Grand Rapids: Eerdmans.

Smalley, Steven S. 1984. *1, 2, 3 John.* Word Biblical Commentary 51. Waco: Word.

Stamm, Johann Jacob. 1940. *Erlösen und Vergeben im Alten Testament: Eine begriffsgeschichtliche Untersuchung.* Bern: Francke.

Stendahl, Krister. 1976. *Paul among Jews and Gentiles, and Other Essays.* Philadelphia: Fortress.

Swete, Henry Barclay. 1909. *The Gospel according to St Mark: The Greek Text with Introduction, Notes, and Indices.* 3rd ed. London: Macmillan.

Tannehill, Robert C. 1996. *Luke.* Abingdon New Testament Commentaries. Nashville: Abingdon.

Taylor, Joan E. 1997. *The Immerser: John the Baptist within Second Temple Judaism.* Studying the Historical Jesus. Grand Rapids: Eerdmans.

Taylor, Vincent. 1952. *Forgiveness and Reconciliation: A Study in New Testament Theology.* 2nd ed. London: Macmillan.

Todd, James Cameron. 1904. *Politics and Religion in Ancient Israel: An Introduction to the Study of the Old Testament.* New York: Macmillan.

Watkins, Oscar D. 1920. *A History of Penance.* 2 vols. London: Longmans, Green.

Watts, John D. 1987. *Isaiah 34–66.* Word Biblical Commentary 25. Waco, TX: Word.

Weiss, Johannes. 1959. *Earliest Christianity: A History of the Period A.D. 30–150.* 2 vols. Translated by F. C. Grant et al. Harper Torchbooks. New York: Harper.

Westermann, Claus. 1969. *Isaiah 40–66.* Translated by David M. G. Stalker. Old Testament Library. Philadelphia: Westminster.

————. 1985 *Genesis 12–36: A Commentary.* Translated by John J. Scullion. Continental Commentaries. Minneapolis: Augsburg.

Whybray, R. N. 1978. *Thanksgiving for a Liberated Prophet: An Interpretation of Isaiah Chapter 53.* Journal for the Study of the Old Testament Supplement Series 4. Sheffield: University of Sheffield Department of Biblical Studies.

Wicks, Henry J. 1915. *The Doctrine of God in the Jewish Apocryphal and Apocalyptic Literature.* London: Hunter & Longhurst.

Widmer, Michael. 2004. *Moses, God, and the Dynamics of Intercessory Prayer: A Study of Exodus 32–34 and Numbers 13–14.* Forschungen zum Alten Testament 2/8. Tübingen: Mohr/Siebeck.

Wilson, N. M. 1965–1966. "Was Zacchaeus Really Reforming?" *Expository Times* 77:282–85.

Worden, T. 1957. "The Remission of Sins." *Scripture* 9:65–79, 115–27.

Worthington, Everett L., Jr., editor. 1998. *Dimensions of Forgiveness: Psychological Research & Theological Perspectives.* Laws of Life Symposia Series 1. Philadelphia: Templeton Foundation Press.

Wrider, Anne Johnson. 1985. "Water, Fire, and Blood: Defilement and Purification from Ricoeurian Perspectives." *Anglican Theological Review* 67:137–48.

Yates, Roy. 1990. "Colossians 2,14: Metaphor of Forgiveness." *Biblica* 71:248–59.